That's
CATS!

That's CATS!

A COMPENDIUM OF FELINE FACTS

Grace Mc Hattie

David & Charles

Contents

Preface

The Harvard Law states: 'Under laboratory conditions, cats will do what they damn well like.' I agree, so this isn't a book about laboratory cats; it's a book about cats which have been loved, observed and studied under the conditions in which most of us keep our cats — as pets.

The hope is that *That's Cats!* will not only inform but entertain. It has been written with the benefit of many years' personal experience of cats and cat behaviour learned at first hand. I have kept large numbers of cats all my adult life and can sympathise with those experiencing problems because at one time or another I have shared them. *That's Cats!* aims to help keep cats fit, healthy and happy by guiding their owners to a greater understanding of their needs and explaining their behaviour in the home and garden. The factual sections are enlivened with real cat stories of past and present; the Casebook sections attempt to give an answer to your problems in understandable language, without pseudo-science or psychobabble.

The book is based on the thousands of questions I have been asked by cat-lovers during the last two decades. Sometimes cat-lovers are initially shy about asking for advice — after all, the general consensus of opinion is that cats are 'easy' pets to keep. But any creature as intelligent and complex as the average feline has very definite needs, and owners must have a considerable knowledge and understanding of these in order for both to live in harmony.

I hope this book will help towards that ideal.

Grace Mc Hattie

INTRODUCTION

Why do we keep cats?

People choose pets which reflect facets of their own personalities

Opposite:
The Titch pair – feline Yuppies and a surrogate family

What attracts us to cats as pets? Evidently people choose pets which they believe reflect facets of their own personalities; psychoanalyst Carl Jung (1959) said that animals often represent 'the expressions of the unconscious components of self'. Cat owners have been said to be independent go-getters, those who don't automatically join the herd; they can be complex people with hidden depths of character, people who are less concerned than, say, dog owners about the opinion and goodwill of others.

Cats have also been said to have feminine qualities, they are crafty, cunning, untrustworthy and devious (if you don't like them — or women), and companionable, highly intelligent and loyal (if you do). There appear to be more female cat owners than male, although the evidence is conflicting; a 1986 Mintel survey reported that men are slightly more likely to own a cat than women. One thing is certain: there are a lot of cat owners. In the USA there are now 57,900,000 cats and they have overtaken dogs as the most popular pet; in the UK the situation is similar — the Pet Food Manufacturers' Association (PFMA) estimated that in 1989 there were nearly 7 million cats in more than 4½ million homes, *ie* that cats were owned by one-quarter of the population. Other statistics suggest that the true numbers may be 25 per cent higher. These are cats kept in households, and the figures do not include feral cats or those in rescue shelters.

Southern England has the highest proportion of cats in the United Kingdom; and in any small animal veterinary practice in that part of the country, approximately 70 per cent of the patients are cats. Either this reflects the increasing numbers of cats in the area, or owners are becoming more perceptive about their cats' illnesses — or cats aren't as healthy as they used to be.

There are no UK statistics to determine why we keep cats. In a survey in the USA, 10 per cent of Americans kept cats as a status

> **Can cats be 'owned'? I've always thought they were too independent to have owners.**
>
> I believe cats can be 'owned' in that they are their owner's responsibility. Every cat group or household will have a dominant cat — a top cat — who will lay down the rules for the other cats. In a household of humans and felines, the owner is (or should be) the top cat; owners who allow their cats to be boss usually end up with a neurotic feline on their hands.
>
> With the title of top cat goes the responsibility for your cats' welfare, and the role of food, shelter and companionship provider. In return, you lay down the rules of the household, and if you are sufficiently dominant in your role as top cat, your cat obeys them. It will continue to live with you of its own free choice as most cats have the opportunity to leave if they wish. Given all that, I think that makes you your cat's owner.

symbol, 30 per cent kept them for companionship, and 60 per cent said that although they owned a cat, they ignored it most of the time!

A survey in a cat magazine in 1988 asked readers to pick out words used to describe cats: 95 per cent chose 'affectionate'; 91 per cent 'good-tempered'; 82 per cent 'loving', 'playful' and 'irreplaceable'; 76 per cent 'intelligent' and 'friendly'; and others used words such as talkative, home-loving, cheeky, determined, sensitive and caring. Only 4 per cent thought that 'solitary' or 'sly' were appropriate.

In her psychology report for Hilife Gourmet cat food, leading psychologist Jane Firbank identified four groups of cat owner, including a new type of couple which she called the 'Titch' pair — the Two Income Two Cat Household. Such people are high achievers who see their cats as part of their lifestyle, and Jane says:

There is a growing trend towards the cat-owning no child family, where typically both partners are in full-time jobs. They do not intend to have children yet. Indeed, they may still be testing out their relationship before making a final commitment.

Cats, relatively undemanding, needing little exercise, able to live in a town flat, make a good surrogate family, and are company for each other while the owners are at work. Their behaviour provides a continuing source of interest, and they enable a couple to test each other's suitability for real parenthood, to practise the attitudes and discipline they will need. If a partner consistently ducks out of food shopping, visits to the vet and cleaning up messes, it can be taken as a bad omen.

Responsible people, they are eager to achieve independence. They will often have strong cultural interests, but are not primarily 'people' people: they choose friends carefully and prefer to socialise in style rather than indiscriminately. Their cats are often pedigree; all part of creating personal style.

Longhaired cats, on the other hand, tend to be owned by more people-orientated people; often those whose livelihood depends on their own appearance, according to Jane. She says:

More than any other type of cat, these are baby symbols. Their flat faces and bulging foreheads, short muzzles and long, strokable hair are features which make them less animal-like; even their body proportions are more childlike than those of other cats, relatively short and thick and with short legs. They need more grooming ('mothering') than other cats.

People who choose a fluffy, pedigree cat are image conscious, as careful about their own grooming as about their cat's. Fluffies such as Chinchillas are the favourite choice of celebrities and media people who depend a great deal upon their own appearance for their livelihood.

They tend to be sophisticated, and demand high standards — but those who meet their standards will find they are approachable and friendly, and usually enjoy entertaining and being entertained. They're conventional, though, and will not choose a 'bohemian' lifestyle; they are nervous of uncharted situations and fear being out of control. In love, they prefer romance and caring to raw passion.

They are not usually loners or leaders, and excel in a career which involves social skills — the ability to get on with people. They are happiest within a solid support network, and there is often some other person or group masterminding their career. Longhaired cats are a popular choice for the wives of successful men.

The above description could well describe the Royal dress designers,

Longhaired pedigree cats require more care – just like children

Moggies don't have to be put on a pedestal – they put themselves there

the Emmanuels, who owned a fluffy Chinchilla. As a complete contrast however, Her Royal Highness Princess Michael of Kent owns a number of Siamese; according to Jane, the sort of person who prefers these sleek, foreign-type cats is quite different:

Just as the fluffy cat has been bred to look like a soft, harmless child or cuddly toy, the exotic shorthaired cats look wild and predatory, and their breeding tends to emphasise their sleekness, agility and wildness.

Their owners can also be exotic — often rebellious and unconventional, sometimes innovative, probably right up-to-date with fashion in both their clothes and their house décor. They are often not highly sociable, preferring to spend time with close friends, though when they do entertain they do it with style. They are often adventurous, willing to take risks and seek challenge, and dislike being confined and constrained by ordinary life. Even if they appear to be stuck in a conventional rut, their choice of such a pet reflects an inner wildness, a hidden impulse to break out and let loose . . .

However, the vast majority of cat owners (approximately 93 per cent in the UK and at least 60 per cent in the USA) have non-pedigree cats — the good old moggy. Of these, Jane says:

The moggy owner is usually less demanding of his or her cat, and the moggy is more likely to be one of a number of pets.

Moggy owners are less concerned about their image than the other types, and are usually practical, down-to-earth people, sociable but with a strong independent streak. They have a strong sense of responsibility and like to be in control of their lives. They are tolerant, however, and usually do not extend this control to family and friends.

In love, moggy owners can show an earthy directness, but do not welcome clinging relationships; they value their privacy. They are warm and caring, but will probably see their cat as a friend rather than a child substitute.

Jane Firbanks' analysis is fascinating and, I believe, spot on in most cases. However, her analysis doesn't allow for the fact that when the vast majority of cat owners buy a cat, they have no idea what they are letting themselves in for, let alone any informed opinion as to what sort of cat would suit them and their lifestyle.

Most people acquire their first cat by accident. A friend's cat has kittens, and it is decided than a pet will teach the children responsibility and caring skills. Or a cat turns up on the doorstep and out-acts Meryl Streep in its impersonation of a poor, un-

Opposite:
A cat turns up on the doorstep and uses all its powers of persuasion

Do cats understand what we are saying?

Much of their understanding is taken from our tone of voice, attitude, stance, body language. I know when I'm in a bad mood I don't have to say a word — my cats scatter at my approach.

Yet I have personal experience of a cat seeming to understand a long and complicated conversation, of a subject she could not have been expected to understand. I once gave a home to a moggy who was pregnant with her first litter. She was an excellent mother and doted on her kittens, but was so protective of them that I was sure she would be upset when the time came to part. I found a home for one of them with a friend of mine, but before he came to collect it, I took the mother cat aside and explained what was to happen — I told her which kitten, and said that this friend, whom she knew and liked, would look after it very well and take good care of it. Then I left her. She immediately went over to her kittens and, from the three of them, rounded up the one which was to leave. She took him behind the settee on his own, where she proceeded to give him a last wash and brush-up. She then walked away without a backward glance and disappeared until after my friend had collected the kitten and left. She then returned, and never looked for that kitten again.

wanted, starving creature which would be oh, so grateful for a little taste of that delicious chicken it can smell cooking and a warm bed for the night. The one night becomes five thousand, and another cat has found a home.

Others feel that perhaps a pet will add something to their lives — and isn't a cat an 'easy' one, particularly for today's busy, working owner? It would seem to be the perfect choice — a cat doesn't need to be taken for walks, and can 'look after itself'. Nevertheless, it requires companionship and time, and its physical and psychological needs are much more complex than most new owners realise; if these are not taken care of, it will become a stressed, unhappy and possibly even destructive animal which creates tension in the household instead of easing it.

These are the first-stage cat owners: if they manage to survive they will discover that life is not complete without a bundle of purring fluff on their laps and a welcoming miaow on their return home. This is probably a non-pedigree cat; when it dies, they will progress to the second stage — usually still without knowing what they are doing — and decide that this time, something a little more upmarket would be in order: a pedigree cat. Most people, however, have still only heard of two breeds of pedigree cat, the

The Siamese is the most popular shorthaired pedigree breed, but they're not the right cat for everyone

Siamese and the Persian — both of which, although delightful, are probably most unsuitable for the vast majority of people, one because it is so noisy and demanding and the other because it requires without-fail thorough daily grooming.

The problem is that a cat, especially a pedigree cat, is a low-profile pet. Dog lovers can see a wide variety of dogs being walked in the park, can chat to their owners and learn about new breeds; but pedigree cats are usually kept indoors, so cat lovers rarely see the less-common breeds.

Cat shows provide a good opportunity to familiarise oneself with different breeds of cats, but here again there is a snag as it isn't easy to find out when they are being held. Cat shows are held by cat clubs or by charities, both of which have limited funds. A cat club will appoint one of its members as show manager, an unpaid and extremely busy position; he or she may already have a full-time job but is a cat fan — often a cat breeder — who displays some organising ability and is willing to take on the year's work required to produce a one-day cat show. However competent they are, they are not skilled in promotion, public relations or advertising. Their small budget doesn't allow for much paid-for publicity — so cat lovers who don't read cat magazines simply don't hear that a show is being held. Most shows attract only a few hundred spectators, and even the largest shows in Britain would probably not have more than 10,000, a tiny percentage of the 4, 500,000 cat owners in the UK.

Ragdoll kittens – a breed which has suffered from ignorance

Do cats feel jealousy?

Without doubt. It's quite common to see a cat being made a fuss of by an owner, and a companion cat immediately joining in with little cries for attention. So cats can certainly be jealous if they feel another is getting more attention then they are.

They can also feel jealous of another person — a new boyfriend or husband, for example — if that person receives the attention they once enjoyed. However, it's easy enough to prevent cats from becoming jealous by remembering to pay them at least as much attention as they are used to. And as cats sleep for approximately sixteen hours a day anyway, it need not be particularly time-consuming!

Modern legends

Legends are not just things of the past. Around us, new legends are springing up all the time; those who make a study of the subject refer to them as urban legends. What makes them legends instead of fact is that they can never be proven; typically, they are things which happen to a friend of a friend and the source of the story can never be tracked down. They appear time and again in different parts of the country and at different times, but the basic facts remain the same. The cat, of course, is not to be left out of the urban legend, so here are a few stories I've collected about the cat which appear with surprising regularity.

An elderly lady, her only companion her beloved cat, calls out the fire brigade to rescue her feline from a tree. Despite the fact that the fire brigade in the United Kingdom doesn't actually rescue cats from trees, in the legend an entire team turns out. They rescue the cat and the old lady, overcome with gratitude, offers them refreshments. However, as they drive off after having tea with the old lady, the fire engine runs over and kills the rescued cat. The first time I heard this story was during the firemens' strike in the 1970s and the rescuers were army volunteers; in more modern versions they are always regular firemen.

A woman looks out of her window and sees her Alsatian with her neighbour's cat in its mouth. It appears to be trying to dig a hole to bury it. Horrified, she rushes out to rescue the cat and

continued opposite

Nor does the media help increase knowledge of the feline species. For example, if a woman's magazine wants an article on gardening or cookery, it will be commissioned from a specialist; however, an article about cats is usually delegated to a staff writer, someone who may have no interest in cats at all, or who last owned a moggy when she was four years old. I have often been phoned by writers wanting to pick my brains because what they thought was an easy assignment has turned out to be anything but. One journalist said, 'I'm writing an article about cats, but I don't actually know much about them — will you tell me everything you know?' Since a large book isn't nearly enough to cover everything there is to know about cats, that was impossible; and as I'm sure there are more cat lovers in Britain than there are dedicated gardeners or cooks, the media should perhaps rethink its treatment of felines.

Even those magazines which have a 'specialist' writer often get it all wrong. Their columnist is usually a vet, and while vets are obviously experts on animal illness, they should not be employed to write about animal breeds, or their detailed care, or particularly about cats (other than their illnesses) — many media vets are not even sympathetic towards cats. For some reason they all seem to be 'dog' men, so to ask them to write about the characteristics of, say, different breeds would be like asking a doctor who doesn't like children to write about kiddies' fashion or hairstyles.

One such vet managed to make eighteen errors of fact in one article, and offended certain breeders so badly that the magazine had to devote a further article to that breed to put the facts straight. The many who complained were told, 'But our vet is an expert!' But again, it had not been appreciated that most vets can only be considered 'experts' on animal illness.

The same problem is encountered in book publishing. A vet may have made a television programme about Mongolian gerbils, so he is then asked by a publisher to write a book about cats for no better reason that they feel they should have a cat book on their lists and the vet is a 'name'. The fact that it is in entirely the wrong field doesn't appear to worry them.

Such a policy by book publishers can have the most surprising results. For example, in 1981 an American breed of cat called the Ragdoll was imported into the UK; most of the British cat books which were written from that time onwards stated with great authority that the Ragdoll was unable to feel pain, and this fallacy kept appearing because many of them were written by people who had never even seen a Ragdoll. The British Ragdoll Club had to take the unprecedented step of taking two Ragdolls to the highly respected Glasgow University Veterinary College where they were thoroughly examined and pronounced completely normal in every way. This is not the only error which occurs in cat books, but it may be the most spectacular.

So it is hardly surprising that prospective owners are unable to garner sufficient accurate knowledge of cats to make an informed choice. Even television doesn't help — yet everyone who works in it seems to own a cat, and the profile of the average cat owner is perfectly described in the producers, directors and researchers who make our television programmes. Every time I go to the studios I spend hours behind the scenes, trapped by the team who always have hundreds of questions about their cats' behaviour and care; yet the same people hesitate to produce cat programmes more than once a year because they maintain 'there just isn't any interest in cats'!

Their thinking is understandable, even though it is wrong. To a cat owner, a cat is a special animal, so by association that makes the owner special. What these people are unwittingly saying is, 'Well, I'm interested in cats — but I'm special. Our viewers aren't as interested in cats as I am — because they're not.' They are wrong, because they believe they are *untypical* cat owners. But what is a typical cat owner? The profile comes as a big surprise to most people.

The 'average' cat owner is *not* the Little Old Lady of popular legend, who in fact accounts for only 6 per cent. No, the 'average' cat owner is an important consumer, the very person that all product advertisers want to target. According to the PFMA, he is younger than the average dog owner (35–44), and lives in owner-occupied accommodation in the wealthiest parts of the UK (the South, East Anglia and Wales) where the head of the household is in full-time employment. 19 per cent of cat owners are in the AB socio-economic groups *ie* professional people, as compared to 15 per cent of dog owners; and there is a lower cat ownership among DEs *ie* manual and unskilled workers (25 per cent) than there is dog ownership (32 per cent). So the cat is a posh pet, with wealthy owners.

They need to be — a survey commissioned by a cat magazine at the beginning of 1988 showed that 6 per cent of their readers spent up to £500 a year on their cat; more than 30 per cent spent £300, and 47 per cent spent £200. 80 per cent bought their cats Christmas presents, and 65 per cent purchased edible treats each week.

Cat owners are big spenders on their cats and on everything to do with cats, much more likely than other pet owners to collect ornaments, cards and so on, depicting them. Greetings card manufacturers have realised this and know that any card featuring a cat will be a top seller. Also, cat owners are much more likely to buy books about their pets than other pet owners — these are

continued

discovers it is not moving. She takes a taxi to the veterinary surgery where the vet pronounces it dead on arrival. Having paid a lot of money for a taxi and the veterinary examination, she now has to pluck up courage to break the news to her neighbour. When she finally does, her neighbour says matter-of-factly: 'Yes — the cat died yesterday and we buried it in the garden. Your dog must have dug it up again.' Although this story appears all over the country with minor variations, the dog involved is always an Alsatian and the vet is always incompetent — any first-year veterinary student would be able to recognise that a cat had been dead for twenty-four hours, particularly if its fur is full of soil!

A man who has been shopping for his Sunday lunch starts talking to an old lady on a bus. She is carrying a plastic bag and reveals that it contains the body of her beloved cat. She is taking it for burial in the country. When he gets home, he opens the bag containing his leg of lamb and finds, instead, the body of the cat. Should this story be true, there must be a surprising number of legs of lamb buried throughout the English countryside.

The last story is more of a journalist's urban legend — a sure-fire space filler on a slow news day. An owner takes off her very valuable diamond ring. . . and her cat swallows it. This gives the newspaper the opportunity to say that the owner is awaiting developments.

hardly ever remaindered, and book publishers are almost guaranteed a good return on any cat book. One author brought out a cat and a dog book simultaneously; the cat book sold so many more copies that he very quickly wrote another one, which was published the following year!

However, one point seems to have escaped publishers' attention. Just as cats hate to be laughed at, so cat people hate seeing

CAT SUPERSTITIONS

There are more superstitions connected with black cats than cats of any other colour, despite the fact that some of the superstitions contradict one another.

Black cats are considered very lucky in the UK but unlucky in the USA where white cats are the luck-bringers. In Russia, blue is the favoured colour. In other parts of the world, particularly in Japan, the tortoiseshell cat is considered very lucky.

Nineteenth-century Yorkshire sailors always kept black cats because they believed it meant they would never drown. The cats had to be closely watched, or they would be stolen by other sailors equally unwilling to drown. A black cat aboard ship

was considered particularly lucky, especially if it had no white hairs. But the word 'cat' was never spoken on board ship for fear of conjuring up storms.

It is not surprising, given the danger of their occupation, that early sailors were particularly superstitious. One type of cat was even referred to as 'ships' cats: polydactyl cats (*ie* those with more than the usual eighteen toes) were considered very lucky by sailors and were carried aboard many ships. Consequently, the offspring of those many-toed cats taken on English ships to the New World now predominate in the east coast of the USA, although they are uncommon elsewhere.

Several centuries ago, English maidens kept black cats because it would ensure they would never be short of boyfriends. And if they were afflicted with a stye on the eyelid, rubbing it with a black cat's tail would make it disappear.

In Ireland, it was believed black cats could absorb their owners' pain, and they were kept in sickrooms for that purpose.

Even today in the UK we believe we will have good luck if a black cat crosses our path. In some areas of the country, it is necessary to stroke the cat three times for luck. However, it is an omen of ill-luck if a black cat runs away from us. Good fortune is certain if a black cat enters a house uninvited; but if it is chased away, it will take all the luck of the household with it.

It was once believed that if a sick person was washed and the washing-water thrown over the household cat, the illness would be transferred to the animal. If a cat left a household where there was illness, the sick person would die. And it was an omen of worse health to come if a sick person saw two cats fighting or dreamt of a cat.

Black is lucky in Britain, white in the USA, blue in Russia – but the Japanese believe that the luckiest cats are tortoiseshell

a cat made into a figure of fun, and a book which appears to do this will send them into paroxysms of rage; unfortunately they have often bought it before they realise the content. Non-cat people don't understand this, and this could account for the popularity of the 'humorous' anti-cat books; I believe these are bought as mistaken and as unwelcome presents for cat-lovers who may be too polite to point out what they really think of them. Fun-poking isn't appreciated in other areas, either — when a breakfast television station held a 'Fattest Cat' contest, its mailbags bulged with letters of complaint. Only when a pet is identified with by its owners as closely as is the cat, can such disrespectful treatment generate so much avid complaint.

Vets find cat owners particularly generous when it comes to paying for treatment for their pets, and it makes no difference whether their cats are expensive pedigrees or were 'free-to-a-

One of forty reasons to keep a cat – a warm welcome at the door

What's the best cat to buy if you've never had one before?

A forgiving one! Possibly the best type of cat for you is the non-pedigree. They're pretty hardy, and can forgive a minor mistake or two. If buying a kitten from a litter, ask whoever has raised them about their personalities. You should try to choose a cat which isn't too athletic, demanding or faddy about its food. Learn as much as you can about cats before you bring it home, make friends with a good vet, hide all your best ornaments and lay in a supply of feline necessities.

Then be prepared to tear your hair out and wonder why you have ever bothered — kittens are energy machines, and it will exhaust you just watching them. You'll have to keep them safe, however, and train them in the rules of your household. But they're great fun, too, and when you've got used to one another and become fond of each other, you'll wonder how you ever lived without a cat.

---

good-home' moggies. In fact, some vets say that cat owners feel they acquire kudos by the amount of money they are willing to spend on their cats; they also seem more willing than dog owners to take out pet health insurance, to help pay those veterinary bills.

So why do cat people keep cats? Research into the subject has been carried out by the insurance company Pet Plan, who discovered forty reasons why the cat is such a popular pet:

Habit: as a child there was always a family pet.
Someone to come home to: a warm welcome at the front door.
An excuse: We can't stay— must get home to feed the cat.
Entertainment: a kitten's antics are amusing.
Social reasons: a pet can help overcome shyness by breaking the ice and stimulating conversation.
Pest control: cats are still the best mouse catchers!
Tactile: affection.
Fashion: to fit in with the latest style.
As a living creature which relies and depends on the owner.
Provides a sense of being needed, particularly for the elderly and those living alone.
Therapy: for those suffering from stress — stroking is said to calm and soothe.
Affection: offered when no-one else will — important for the elderly, disabled and ill.
As a pet to help fill the gap left by *bereavement.*
Provides a *framework or routine* to a day.
Teaches children *responsibility,* kindness and consideration.
Teaches children to *relate* to others.
Company for parents once children have left home.
As a substitute brother or sister for an only or lonely child.
Company for a single person.
Creates a *shared interest* for the whole family.
As a chosen member of the family: pets can be chosen while family can't!
Company and *new interest* for women staying at home for the first time.
Teaching children about *essential experiences* and situations.
A *family friend* — on your side.
Someone to *love.*
Someone to *rely on.* A pet will always be there for you in return for little more than love and food.
Buying a pet often goes hand-in-hand with setting up a *new home* or getting married.
Cats don't talk back and they *listen* when no-one else does.

Good companions for children.
Company for an ageing pet or to replace a pet which has died.
Re-homing or rescuing an unwanted animal.
Adoption by a stray.
A chance to *show off* and have pride in your pet.
A way of *meeting people.*
A hobby or *interest* for anyone who is socially isolated.
Showing: an inexpensive hobby which gets people out of the
    house.
A pet may be *bequeathed* in a will.
Company for an existing pet which may be left alone while the
    owner is at work.
Love of animals.
Beauty: your cat is always more beautiful than anyone else's!

So why do we keep cats? I believe that we love cats because cats are a challenge. A dog will love and respect anyone who doesn't mistreat it — and sometimes those who do, but a cat will make you work for its love and respect. A cat will *not* automatically love or obey its food-provider and authority figure: it has sufficient independence and free spirit subtly to suggest that we need cats more than cats need us. Yet the cat is a loving and responsive animal, and when it does respond to us we feel an enormous sense of achievement.

Cats *are* special creatures — and that makes cat people special, too.

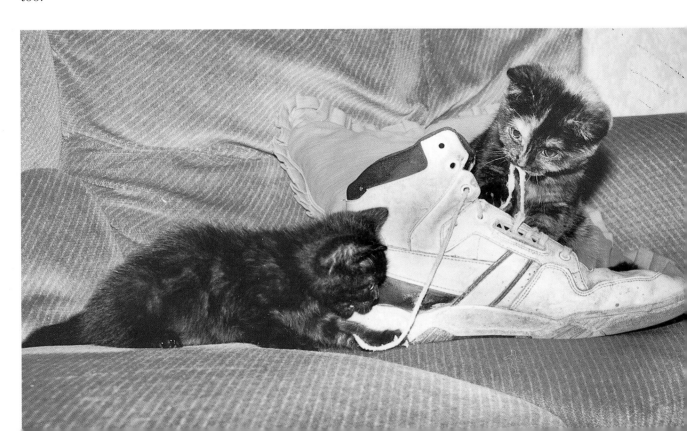

THE CONTENTED CAT

The feline's special needs

Surely a kitten only needs four square meals a day and something to play with to be happy?

We'd all like to believe that our cat is contented. And the easiest way to have a contented cat is to start off with a contented kitten. But this isn't always easy if owners have acquired their cat as an adult for they don't know how it has been raised or what traumas it has suffered in its early life. Cats, fortunately, are adaptable. Although a cat which has had a poor upbringing may take many years to overcome its reservations about people, others soon recognise that they have found a friend and begin to settle down within a few weeks or even days.

For those who take on a kitten, there is a special responsibility to make its kittenhood a time of growing joy, to ensure it grows into a well balanced, healthy and contented cat.

THE CONTENTED KITTEN

Do kittens need to be kept contented? Surely they are happy little souls who need nothing more than three or four square meals a day and a table-tennis ball to play with? In truth, kittens need the following:

- consideration and understanding
- companionship, kindness and patience
- a safe environment
- a regular routine
- good veterinary care
- some basic equipment
- a proper introduction to family members and pets
- some guidance as to what is expected of them

From this it is immediately apparent that the kitten's new owner is the most important person in its life; how that owner reacts to it and smoothes its path in its new home is vitally important to its happiness and well-being. A kitten shouldn't be brought into a home and left to its own devices. It will cope — kittens are born survivors — but not as well as one with a supportive and understanding owner. It won't know the house rules with no-one to lay them down and it will become unruly. Many such kittens are rehomed each year because they haven't been taught how to behave or how to relate to their people.

Breeders of pedigree cats quite unselfconsciously — and in a way which makes many people smile — call themselves their kittens' 'mums'. But this is a totally appropriate description of the role they play — and the role which new kitten-owners should play — in the lives of their cats.

For the first months of its life a kitten's real, furry mum is not only the supplier of nourishment, warmth and comfort; she is also the kitten's supreme authority and teaches it how to behave. She will allow a little naughtiness, but when it oversteps the mark she will clout its ear with a none-too-gentle paw, or grip its neck between her teeth until it goes still. If there are other cats in the household, they will quickly teach the kitten their dominance in much the same way, and it will learn not to steal food, not to play too roughly and, basically, not to make a nuisance of itself.

The new owner takes over these roles when the kitten leaves

Feline mothers are the supreme authority – they stand no nonsense from their kittens when it's wash-time

Treat a new kitten like a toddler and keep it out of danger

Properly-raised kittens will be used to people, cats and maybe dogs too

its mother, providing food and comfort but also making clear to it what is, and what is not, allowed. Every social group has rules and laws, whether that group be human, feline or a mixture of both, and a new kitten has to learn those of its new home — furthermore it will expect rules to be laid down, as it has been used to for the first few months of its life. Without guidance, the kitten becomes bewildered; and later it may take advantage of the situation with behaviour which the owner feels to be inappropriate.

The new owner must understand what experience of life their kitten has had. If bought from a reputable source, it will have been raised with people and cats and will know how to react to both; but its total life experience is somewhat limited, nevertheless. It will have spent its first month in its kittening box, knowing nothing but its mother's care, the warmth of her body and the gentle handling of humans. For the following month (or two, in the case of pedigree kittens) it will have led an indoor life, becoming completely familiar with its home which will smell comfortingly of itself, its litter mates and its mother. It will know all the nooks and crannies, the warmest places to nap, when to expect a meal and which other household cats can be relied on for a game and which will cuff it around the ear. It has spent its entire life sleeping in a warm, living ball of brothers and sisters.

Then it goes to a new home.

It doesn't understand why its entire world, all it has ever experienced, has changed. Why are the rooms all different? Why do they smell so strange? Where is its mother, and the human who has looked after it?

Opposite:
For two or three months, a kitten will have had littermates to play with

This is where the new owner's consideration is vital: if you try to understand how that bewildered kitten is feeling, you won't expect it to become a member of the household overnight. Everything is strange to it, and that *has* to be allowed for.

Unfortunately, this is where so many new owners go astray. In a consumer society we are used to going to a shop, making our purchase, taking it home and plugging it in — and it works. Perhaps the fact that money usually changes hands when we buy a pet leads us to have unrealistic expectations of them. But animals aren't like that, and we need to understand that they have their own needs and problems — very much like a human baby, in fact.

We wouldn't expect to bring home a new baby from the hospital and by the end of the first day have it toilet-trained, sleeping through the night and eating only at times convenient to us. In many ways, a kitten is like a baby and we must adapt ourselves in some ways to suit it — though fortunately, the adaptation

PRUDENCE KITTEN

Anyone who remembers children's television in Britain in the 1950s will remember Prudence Kitten. She was a black-and-white cat — at least, we assumed she was; television in those days was also black and white. She was a favourite with children, with her inexhaustible good sense and fund of good advice in those years of austere programmes and presenters in dinner jackets.

It was about this time that we acquired a kitten of our own — also black with a little patch of white — so it seemed obvious that she too should be called Prudence. We weren't to realise that this bundle of black-and-white fur was to remain part of our lives for more than twenty years; long after her namesake was lost to memory.

In those days, I and my parents lived in a London flat. Pru lived a sheltered existence and probably wouldn't have known what fresh air was. Her favourite occupation was to sit in the window of the sitting room, looking out over the vestigial balcony, which was draped with untidy foliage from the plane tree outside. As a child, I imagined she was planning all sorts of painful deaths for the sparrows and pigeons to which it provided a home.

Strangely enough, for a town cat, Pru's only other window entertainments came from horses. In those days, the milk was delivered by horse and cart from the Express Dairy nearby. Our milkman's nag was called Duffle, and it was a special treat for me to be allowed to feed him with a lump of sugar. And I could be sure that, if I looked up to our window, Pru would be there, attracted by the sound of hooves and the jingling of harness. Better still was the altogether more impressive twice-daily clatter of the King's Troop of the Royal Artillery, which used our road on its way to and from morning exercises in the park. Here the sound of the harness and chains was mixed with and almost drowned by the clatter of horses and the grinding of metalled gun-carriage wheels on tarmac. Pru heard them long before we did and

That comforting feeling of a kitten relaxing on your back

required is much less and takes a very much shorter time!

So if you are buying a kitten, be prepared to rearrange your life a little, for a short time, to fit around it. If you have a job, take a few days' holiday so you can give it the companionship it will miss and the regular mealtimes it has been used to. Treat it like a cross between a baby and a toddler; it is still a baby in experience but it is as mobile as a toddler - and just as curious. If you are a working owner who is out of the home all day, consider whether you should buy a second kitten for company. Eight or ten hours is a very long time for it to be left on its own each day, and kittens do become bored.

Look around your home with a kitten's eyes and see the dangers. A kitten can squeeze through a gap of less than 5cm (2in): can it get behind the kitchen cabinets? Can it climb into the back of the refrigerator? Can it climb up the chimney? Can it get through that open window? If it can, it will. More than one new owner has been faced with an enormous plumber's bill for

---

Matchstick cats and cats

The famous artist, L.S. Lowry, said that he couldn't paint dogs. So when he had to paint a dog, he painted a cat instead — then painted the tail out.

---

would immediately arch her back in expectation, hissing in annoyance as they went by.

When I was eleven and Pru was seven, we moved to the country. Pru disdained to take advantage of the increased freedom to explore the world outside the family home. We lived in a pretty village near Canterbury, much frequented by tourists, who'd pass close to our front window on their way to the neighbouring lych-gate of the picturesque and ancient parish church. Pru would doze on the sill, waking only to hiss and spit at the gongoozlers who would often forget their manners and stare through our curtains. This reaction was no more than they deserved; I would have done the same if I had been able to match the dignified fury of a little black-and-white cat.

I think Pru did try to become a country cat but simply found it a bore. On a couple of occasions, we found presents of mangled sparrow or vole on the back doorstep. But her heart wasn't in it. She much preferred to sit on my back, as I lay full-length on a carpet reading a book or watching television, sometimes for hours at a time. I was considered by the rest of the family to be Pru's favourite, but the relationship became an intermittent one over the next few years as I went away for long periods, first to boarding school and then to university.

Whenever I returned, it wouldn't take long before we re-established our routine. I — an almost-adult sixties' undergraduate, determined to be cool — would obligingly lie full length on the rug for Pru to cuddle on my back, just as if I had never been away. My family found this surprising, as Pru in the interim had become a very tetchy cat indeed. Visitors would be flattered on arrival, as she would sit on their laps and curl up, making them feel instantly accepted.

But then, inexplicably, she would suddenly and with some venom dig in her claws and skitter off. Later we discovered she'd developed a skin disease which made stroking her a painful business.

Towards the end of her life, her condition deteriorated to the point where lumps of fur would fall out. Nevertheless, whenever I returned home on my increasingly infrequent visits, she still expected to lie on my back in quiet communion, as she had done for so many years. More than once, we wondered if it might not be kinder to have her put to sleep. But, although her tetchiness continued to grow, she'd always been a self-contained cat; she seemed to have all her faculties about her.

Eventually, at the age of twenty-one, it was obvious that she had reached the end of the road. She could no longer jump down from a chair because of the pain in her paws, so my mother took her to the vet for the last time. I was away when the end came. I was twenty-five years old, but I cried when I was told what had happened.

Pru was a difficult cat to get to know, and most people decided not to bother. But even now — fifteen years later — I miss her dreadfully.   P C

I've just moved into a one-bedroomed apartment. Is it fair to keep a cat in such a small home?

That depends on a lot of things. If the cat has to share a one-bedroomed apartment with two adults, several children and a Doberman Pinscher, the answer is no. But one adult and one cat can share a one-bedroomed apartment if it is spacious enough for them to get away from one another when they want, and if there are enough places for the cat to hide and play. Ideally, a cat in a small apartment should have access to the outside and should not be kept indoors all the time.

extricating a kitten from the innards of an electrical appliance, or has had to dismantle the kitchen units to rescue their pet.

Look around and see the temptations: do you have a treasured indoor plant? Your kitten will eat it, so move it to a locked room for the time being. Do you own a fabulous collection of porcelain figurines? Your kitten will knock them over, so put them in a display cabinet for a while and when you do bring them out, Blu-Tack them to the table. Is your three-piece suite new and pristine? Cover the arms and back with plastic sheeting so that it isn't scratched, and train your kitten to use a scratching post.

Above all, don't expect your kitten to act 'normally' for at least a week or ten days, the usual length of time needed for a kitten to *begin* to settle down. However sweet and quiet it is at its breeder's home, when you take it away it may become a creature which could outwhirl the whirling Dervishes and out-volume the Mormon Tabernacle Choir. I, too, have telephoned a breeder and asked 'Are you sure you gave me the right kitten?' And now that I breed kittens, *I* have had the same plaintive enquiry from perplexed owners.

I once sold a kitten to a friend who fortunately understood cats well. Yet even she was somewhat taken aback when this kitten (who in his first three months with me was so relaxed and self-contained that he hardly ever lay on my lap, and never miaowed except at mealtimes) howled like a Banshee for his first week unless she took him on her lap and comforted him constantly. 'Are you sure you gave me the right kitten?' she asked, for his brother was a noisy, self-opinionated little devil, and she thought she'd got him by mistake.

Yet that noisy little brother settled into *his* new home without a miaow, and surprised his new owner with his excellent manners: 'Are you sure you gave me the right kitten?' she asked.

I'm absolutely sure I gave each owner the right kitten — I just know not to expect a kitten to behave 'normally' for at least that week or ten days after going to its new home. Few new owners are prepared for this, and how could they be? How many kittens do you buy in a lifetime? For most people it is only ever two or three, and memory (thankfully) fades. I, however, go through this annually, for I can't resist cats; and to have a cat, you usually have to go through the kitten phase — and I buy a new one every spring.

A shy kitten may act assertively, a quiet kitten may be boisterous, a noisy kitten may be quiet and withdrawn; but if you can bear with this settling-down phase in the knowledge that it will not last, you are well on the way to settling down with your kitten. It is obviously not a good idea to name your kitten during this period, unless this is after its physical characteristics, because by the time it has settled down, the name will probably be totally inappropriate!

Introducing your kitten

First impressions are vital. When *we* meet someone new, we form an almost unshakeable impression of them within the first five minutes, and a kitten, too, will react for months — even years — on the first impression it receives of its new family. Children must be made to understand that felines are often wary of young people at first, and that this wariness will be reinforced if the child handles them roughly or frightens them. Tell children they must not rush to pick up the kitten when it first arrives — difficult as it is to hold back when everyone wants to fuss over the new arrival, it should be allowed to approach members in its own time and in its own way. It may climb on a lap when it feels sleepy, or it may brush against legs, or climb on the desk when homework is being done. These actions can be taken as an invitation to stroke it.

Of course, many kittens are very friendly and approach immediately to be fussed over; but whatever the kitten's temperament, *it* should be allowed to make the first move. It may misunderstand if someone rushes towards it with arms outstretched, and the resulting fright may take some time to subside enough for it to trust that person completely.

When a kitten is being introduced to an existing family pet, especially another feline, careful introductions are especially important. There is one basic rule which should never be forgotten: *do not make friends with your kitten until your cat has made friends with it.*

This is a vitally important rule because you don't want your cat to view your kitten as a usurper of your affection or as a threat in any way. Cats do feel jealous, and jealousy causes stress; and stress can cause other problems such as indiscriminate soiling — it can even cause a cat to leave home. Many have left when a kitten has been introduced tactlessly, some to move just a few doors away.

The best way to introduce the two is to have a friend bring the new kitten into the home in its carrier. In this way your cat associates the kitten with the friend, not with you. You should be relaxed and, if possible, stroking your cat on your lap. The friend should bring in the carrier, open it — and then you must leave the felines to it. You'll find that your cat will jump down to investigate and will first approach the kitten to sniff it; as soon as it realises the kitten has a 'foreign' smell, it will hiss at it — or the kitten may hiss at the cat.

What will follow, is a display of territorial behaviour. Most likely your cat will demonstrate that the kitten is an interloper on its territory — there will probably be a long and noisy confrontation, with hissing, spitting, slashing and maybe even biting, all designed to demonstrate who is the dominant feline.

I've got a fourteen-year-old cat and recently bought a kitten. Since I brought the new kitten home, my old cat goes out and stays away for weeks at a time. What can I do?

At the age of fourteen, your cat is quite elderly and possibly set in her ways. Kittens can be too active and playful to make good companions for some old cats. A human equivalent would be a person of seventy suddenly being expected to share his or her home with a demanding toddler. Some cats don't want their lifestyles disrupted to such an extent, and may move in with a neighbour or simply disappear for days on end.

Obviously, elderly cats shouldn't be left to roam the streets, so try to bring her back home. Make sure that introductions between cats and new kittens are carried out correctly; there is then less likelihood of a sour relationship. Give your old cat some space of her own — a room of her own to sleep in, for example.

Not all old cats reject kitten companions. Many take on a new lease of life and begin acting years younger when they are given a playful companion.

Although the noises may be bloodcurdling, *do not interfere:* it has to be gone through some time, and if you split the two up it will happen again. And for a kitten which has been raised with other felines, it is not as fearsome as you might think; it will know the language of body postures from its littermates and other household cats, and so knows very well how to make itself look small and unthreatening. It has been used to being bottom of the heap, all its life, due to its small size, so it is no great shock to it. Just ensure that there are some hiding places in the room for the kitten if it feels too threatened; if there are none, place a few empty cardboard boxes around in which it can hide.

Claws can be trimmed slightly to blunt them before the introduction is carried out, so that there are no accidental injuries. Any fighting is not usually intended to cause injury; it is largely ritualistic, to demonstrate the pecking order. I have never heard of any cat injuring a two- or three-month old kitten, apart from the occasional accidental scratch.

Remember not to side with the kitten during the introduction, and not to intervene. If you do, your cat will become bewildered; after all, there is an interloper in the house, so you would expect your cat to see it off. Your cat must believe that he or she remains *your* cat and hasn't been replaced in your affections.

Some owners give up too easily when the hissing and spitting starts. They immediately separate the two, locking one away; but when they try again the following day, they have the same result. After a few days they convince themselves that their cat doesn't like the kitten and they rehome the kitten. In fact they haven't given the two a proper chance to get to know one another, and have put the poor kitten (and their cat) through a lot of unnecessary stress. So don't give up. The noisy and unpleasant ritual is much more difficult for you than for the kitten — or your cat.

A kitten will have settled down and sorted out its place in the hierarchy (on the bottom) usually within a week or two. Some even manage to make friends with their feline house-mate within a couple of hours — it just depends on the temperament of both, and how well suited they are to each other.

Introductions between two adult cats should be carried out in exactly the same way, although adults may take much longer to settle down together. It may take three months or more, or just a few days; again, it depends how well the cats suit each other.

Part of the problem when two felines meet for the first time is that they smell foreign to one another. If at the first attempt you feel you must separate them (and this is very rare), you can re-introduce them the following day after making them smell more alike. This can be done by sprinkling talcum powder over both cats and brushing it out, or by wiping over their coats with a

The cat who talked

Amazing tales of cats' almost magical abilities still abound. None is more amazing than the story of Whitey, a starving stray kitten taken in by a Mr and Mrs James Deem of Florida.

In their fascinating book *Living Wonders* (Thames and Hudson) John Michell and Robert J.M. Rickard report that when Whitey was about six months old he jumped onto the Deems' bed and said, 'Mama, I'm hungry'. Ruth Deem, undoubtedly somewhat surprised, asked 'What did you say?' and Whitey repeated, 'I'm hungry'. Mrs Deem didn't mention this remarkable feat to her husband, but several days later he was stroking Whitey and told him

continued opposite

Introducing a new kitten into a household where there is already a cat can be worrying for the owner. The cat must show the kitten that it is an interloper. Vicious-looking fighting may ensue but kittens are rarely, if ever, hurt by cats. The kitten has its ears laid back flat against its head to protect them from the cat's claws

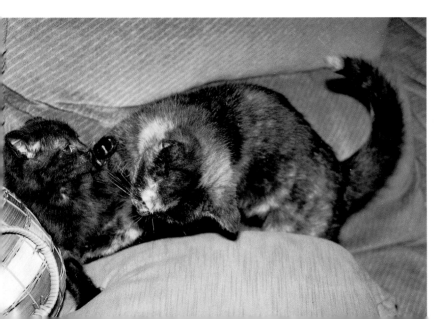

continued

jokingly that he was a bad cat. 'I am *not* a bad cat,' Whitey replied.

Whitey spoke frequently to the Deems after that, and was also heard to talk by the Deems' neighbours. One neighbour who looked after Whitey while the Deems were away, smacked him one day with a newspaper because he was fighting the other family cat. When the Deems returned, Whitey told tales. 'Mama, he hit me!' he said. When asked what he had been hit with, he replied, 'Newspaper'. Another neighbour, trying to pick Whitey up, heard him say, 'You can't catch me'. He tried — and he couldn't.

Whitey talked at least once a day, often in a complaining manner. There were many phrases he could say, including 'Why no-one love me?'; 'I want to go home'; 'I want out'; and 'I love Mama'.

Whitey was 'interviewed' by more than one journalist, including Suzy Smith of *Fate* magazine. Unfortunately Whitey had been ill from poisoning just prior to her visit, and refused to say a word.

Ancient beliefs

'The wisdom of our fore-
fathers teaches us, that if a
cat be carried in a bag from
its old home to a new house,
let the distance be several
miles, it will be certain to
return again; but if it be
carried backward into the
new house this will not be
the case.'

'The horse ridden by a man
who has got any cat's hair
on his clothing will perspire
violently and soon become
exhausted. If the wind blows
over a cat riding in a
vehicle, upon the horse
drawing it, it will weary the
horse very much.'

'If any shall dream he fought
with a cat that scratched
him sorely, that denotes
some sickness or affliction.'

solution of cider vinegar in water (one tablespoon cider vinegar to a litre of water) — don't get any of it in eyes, nose or mouth.

For really difficult introductions, the newcomer can be placed in a large cat pen with water, a bed and a litter tray in full view of the other cat, so that both can become used to the other's sight and smell without being able to cause harm. After a day or so, let the kitten out of the pen at feeding time when the two will have food on their minds rather than fighting. However, it is very rarely necessary to go to these lengths and I would hesitate to place a kitten in a position in which it felt so vulnerable.

Your kitten must have its own feeding bowl and this should be placed at least a couple of metres away from your cat's bowl. Strange felines don't like eating close together at first, although when they become used to one another, their bowls can be moved closer.

Only introduce two felines if both are in good health. Illness increases the stress level anyway, and an introduction to a strange feline is an additional stress they may be unable to cope with. It's particularly important to ensure that your new kitten is healthy before introducing it to your cat; any infection it may be harbouring can be passed on, so if you are not 100 per cent sure, keep it in 'quarantine' for the first week.

The new kitten will have to be kept in a room of its own which contains all its needs; water, food and a litter tray. It would be extremely lonely if left completely on its own, so family members should take it in turns to spend as much time as possible with it. A pedigree kitten should have had two inoculations against feline respiratory disease and enteritis (illnesses which can be fatal), at nine weeks and twelve weeks; and it will take at least another week after the second inoculation before the kitten is completely covered against these illnesses. When the vet inoculates, he or she will also check the kitten's general health and notify the breeder of any problems. So if you already have a cat, a thirteen-week-old inoculated kitten is your best insurance policy against bringing at least two illnesses into the home — though there are many other infections which cannot be inoculated against, so take no chances with your cat's health.

If you are placing your kitten in 'quarantine,' you should wash your hands thoroughly after touching it; ideally, you should wear different clothes and shoes in the quarantine room. It isn't often necessary to go to such lengths, but if your kitten seems off-colour, or is off its food, has diarrhoea (which may, however, just be a sign of over-eating), is sneezing with a discharge from eyes or nose, or has any other symptom you are unsure of, quarantine it before visiting your vet as soon as possible.

If your kitten is not a pedigree, it will almost certainly not have been inoculated and may never have been checked over by a vet. In this case you should take any new kitten straight from the place of purchase to a vet for a check-up before taking it home. Infection spreads so easily between felines, and many kittens are bred and kept in incorrect conditions without proper hygiene precautions. Just ask any vet how many new owners have brought in a kitten which became ill within a week or two of purchase and subsequently died.

You may find that your kitten begins to sneeze even if it is healthy and has been inoculated. Many cats and kittens react to stress by sneezing, and the stress of settling into a new home is often enough to start the sneezing. It may be nothing to worry about if the kitten is bright, eats well and has no discharge from nose or eyes: but if in the slightest doubt, contact your vet.

What else does a kitten need?

I've already recommended that your kitten should have a health check-up from a vet as soon as, or even before it is purchased; it is important therefore to find a good vet before you buy your kitten. Most owners simply visit the nearest or the cheapest, but this isn't the way to choose. Ask around so as to discover the best *cat* vet in the neighbourhood — some vets are best with farm animals, some are best with dogs, but you want to find one that is best with cats. If he or she owns a cat (or several cats) this is a good sign, as a surprising number of vets are dog people.

Having chosen your vet, build up a relationship: visit your vet at least annually, for your cat's booster inoculations and its checkup. Steer clear of those vets who just give the yearly boosters and forget the checkup; my vet told me recently that when he gave his automatic checkup to an animal presented to him for booster inoculations, the owners virtually went into hysterics. Their previous vets had only given boosters, so when his stethoscope was taken out they immediately panicked, thinking something was seriously wrong! However, your cat should and must be checked over thoroughly every year — after all, if it is feeling a little off-colour, it can't very well tell you about it. Ask your vet's advice on worming preparations and flea preparations; most vets nowadays sell these, and a wide variety of necessary equipment including cat litter and cat food.

If your kitten is under nine weeks, make an appointment for its first inoculation against feline respiratory disease and enteritis, to be given at nine weeks; there is a second inoculation at twelve weeks and thereafter a yearly booster.

When visiting your vet for the inoculations, discuss the neutering of your kitten and take his advice as to the age this should be carried out: this is usually between four to nine months for a male,

---

Tiger tail

According to Burmese legend, the cat came first in the order of creation of felines, and the tiger a long time afterwards. The tiger was a helpless sort of creature, so asked the cat to teach it some of its skills, promising obedience in return. The cat took pity on the tiger and taught it to purr, to climb and to hunt; but one thing the cat did not teach the tiger — how to thrash its tail from side to side. According to Burmese legend, the tiger cannot do this; it can only move its tail up and down, and for this it has never forgiven the cat.

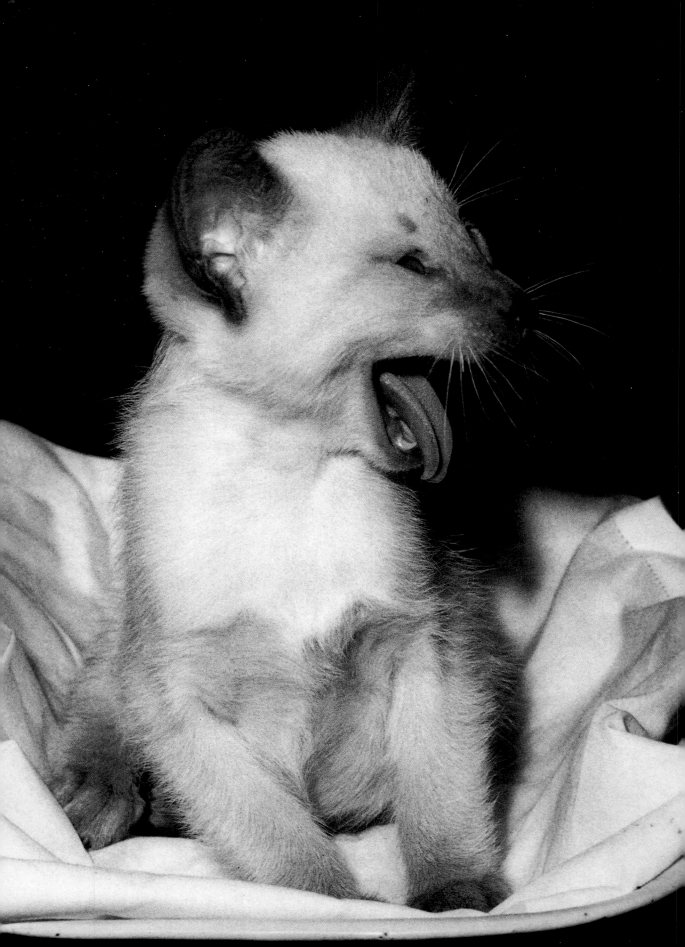

and four to six months for a female, though it can sometimes be as early as three months. Kittens mature rapidly, especially the Siamese types, so neutering must be considered at an early stage — some Siamese are sexually mature at four months, and most kittens will be able to mate at the end of the first winter after they attain the age of six months. So it doesn't give you much time to make the appointment! There is no benefit in allowing a cat to have even one litter before being spayed. One litter is often recommended for a bitch, but this is because bitches may suffer from urine scald if their bodies are not fully mature before spaying. However, urine scald is not a problem with cats.

But why should kittens be neutered? All welfare organisations agree on one thing: there are many more cats than there are homes available. My own estimate is that every year in the UK alone, over a quarter of a million cats find their way into rescue shelters because they are unwanted; furthermore a large proportion of them are pregnant, thrown out when nature took its course. However, these are luckier than the countless thousands of others who are left to roam the streets or join feral colonies, where their life expectancy is reduced to a mere six years.

So be a responsible owner — your cat will thank you for it.

Opposite:
Siamese kittens mature very early – as early as four or five months – so neutering should be discussed with your vet at an early stage

All cats and kittens love to strop. It exercises their muscles, sharpens their claws and leaves their scent behind. The laid-back ears of this cat demonstrate how enjoyable stropping is

What else does a kitten need to keep it happy?

Besides companionship, understanding and a good vet, your kitten has a number of physical needs, too. You must decide where it is going to sleep (its own choice might not be the best for either of you). It will need certain equipment to keep it comfortable and it will require a routine, and above all, it will need regular mealtimes.

A kitten cannot eat very much at a time, so its ration of about 200g of good quality food per day should be divided into four meals; this will satisfy most three- to four-month-old kittens, but if yours seems genuinely hungry, increase the amounts as necessary, and increase amounts as it gets older. If the kitten's sides are bulging after its meals, or it has diarrhoea, or it passes faeces more than a couple of times a day, you may be overfeeding it. Food specially formulated for kittens can usually be bought nowadays from pet stores; also from vets, sole suppliers of particular high quality foods. Because kittens have higher requirements for protein and other nutrients than the average adult cat, their food must be good quality.

Three meals a day can be given from around four months, and this can decrease to two as the cat reaches adulthood. However, a young growing cat of eight to twelve months old will require more food than an adult cat of the same weight; as cats' metabolisms vary, you can judge this best by observing your individual kitten.

Meals should be given at around the same time each day, if possible. Cats and kittens have a remarkably accurate internal

A SAM BY ANY OTHER NAME

Our ginger cat, Sam, went missing when he was a year old. As we lived on a main road, we thought the worst. We asked everywhere, but no-one had seen him, and we walked around the roads calling him. We never found him.

He had an endearing habit of running up my back and sitting on my shoulders, especially if I was doing some washing at the sink. We missed him dreadfully.

Two years later, I went to work in a flower shop in the next village. A woman who worked there was always running to the fish shop to buy best fish for her cat. She talked about him constantly and told me his name was Blue. She and her husband had just returned from Australia and Blue, she said, means ginger out there! They weren't able to have children, so Blue was their child. She told me

Blue had a silly trick of running up her back . . . and the penny dropped.

I asked her where she had got him and she said he was found outside a shop in the village. No-one knew where he had come from, so they had kept him.

She was worried about letting me see him, saying he could not be Sam. I reassured her that we would not take him back but would like to satisfy ourselves that it was him.

We met him. He had put on a lot of weight, but he had the same little brown spots inside his mouth that Sam had had. We were happy. Sam — or Blue — had not come to a horrible end as we had imagined, but had two new owners who adored him.

Clare Tester

clock and they can become quite stressed by late or missing meals. Don't leave food out all day if you have more than one cat as you will be unable to monitor how much food each is getting.

You should provide your kitten with its own feeding-bowl, and it will also need a litter tray and litter until it is able to go out-of-doors (approximately a week to ten days after its second inoculation); the litter tray should also be available for use beyond that age, especially at night.

A scratching post should be provided as all cats and kittens love to strop, and it is important that they can — stropping provides aerobic muscle-stretching exercise, marks the post with their scent, and allows them to keep their claws in shape. Buy one which is big enough to allow your kitten to stretch out fully (a kitten-sized one will soon be outgrown) — ideally it should be at least 75cm (30in) high.

The kitten should have its own bed, although it will not necessarily use it. Although attractive and cosy catbeds are available, a clean cardboard carton with a soft liner is often enjoyed just as much, and in the interests of hygiene boxes have the advantage that they can be burned after a few weeks, and the liner washed or replaced.

Decide in the early days where your kitten will sleep at night — for example, if it is allowed to sleep on your bed, it will complain loudly if, later on, you decide it should sleep somewhere else. So start off with all routines as you mean to go on; let your kitten know where it should sleep, and if you would like it to sleep in its own bed, place a warm (not hot) water bottle there to encourage it. Pet bed heaters — like electric underblankets — can be a boon to a new kitten (but *don't* use an electric underblanket designed for humans!).

Let your kitten know what it can, and cannot do. If it strops on the furniture, for example, remove it with a loud, firm 'NO' and place it by its scratching post, praising it when it uses it. In the same way, teach it not to jump on kitchen work surfaces, or anywhere else you would prefer it not to go. Don't ever shout at it or smack it, as cats and kittens don't respond well to this sort of treatment — it makes them nervous and frightened, and causes stress which can lead to behavioural problems.

Your kitten must learn the other household rules, too; for example, if it persists in pestering you for food from your plate, put it outside the room while you are eating. And don't let it become a fussy eater; accustom it to a variety of food from an early age, and in particular to the food which you want to give it.

If you follow these guidelines, you'll know you have done everything possible to keep your kitten contented, and this should allow you both to share a happy life together.

Show people

Cat shows are held all over the country on almost every weekend of the year. What makes people show their cats?

For cat breeders, showing is important to make others aware that they are breeding good stock. A kitten from champion parentage will sell more easily, and for more money, than a kitten without eminent parents. Not everyone who shows cats is a cat breeder; many people treat their visits to shows as social events, where they meet their friends. Yet showing is such hard work, these cannot be the only reasons.

Shows are often hundreds of miles away from owners' homes, which necessitates setting out at 2am or 3am every other Saturday morning. There are no financial inducements (other than the subsequent sale of kittens), because prizes are usually inexpensive rosettes or small trophies; yet entry fees are high — much higher than at dog shows. Owners have to pay their own travelling expenses and meals, and have to spend weeks or months before the show preparing their cats.

The reason most people show their cats is because, literally, they enjoy 'showing off'. Because cats aren't taken for walks to the extent which dogs are, it is the only opportunity most owners have to let everyone see what a beautiful cat they have. And because cat owners identify so closely with their pets, they share the reflected glory; an admired cat is an admired owner. The same reasoning

continued overleaf

continued

can be seen at work when owners enter cat competitions in magazines or on television; the prizes are often negligible, but the competition gives the owner the opportunity to let others realise what a wonderful pet he/she owns.

Some owners get the showing 'bug'. Showing is hard work, and also stressful to the owner — besides the preparation and travelling, there is always the fear that they will be turned back on arrival by the duty vet for some unnoticed ailment; because of this, winning a rosette at the end of a long and tiring day becomes a euphoric experience. So they want to win more. And to become a champion, a cat must win three times at three shows within a specified period. So after a first win, an owner has an incentive to keep showing, and may even have become hooked on the experience.

As in all specialist interest groups, a very few people become so caught up in cat showing that they lose all sense of proportion. There have been many reported cases of cats being harmed by people jealous of their success. Cats at shows have had their drinking water poisoned, or hatpins stuck into them. Some have had talcum powder

continued opposite

THE CONTENTED CAT

There is every chance the contented kitten will grow into a contented cat if you continue to provide for all its needs, but owners must be prepared for changes in a cat's behaviour as it grows. Obviously a kitten should be lively and playful and a bit of a handful, but few owners are prepared for its behaviour as a teenager, or can recognise when their cat is middle-aged.

It might be helpful to give a short table of human equivalents of cat ages because, if you can recognise where your cat is in its life, you will have a fuller understanding of its behaviour at any time.

Treat this as a rough guide because, like humans, cats age at different rates: where one sixty-year-old person is old and inactive, another may be running marathon races; where one fifteen-year-old cat does nothing but sleep, another acts like a three-month-old kitten.

HOW OLD IS YOUR CAT?

CAT'S AGE	HUMAN EQUIVALENT
0 – 4 weeks	(baby) 0 – 1 years
5 – 8 weeks	(toddler) 1 – 3 years
2 – 9 months	(child) 3 – 14 years
9 – 15 months	(teenager) 14 – 20 years
15 months – 7/8 years	(young adult) 20 – 40 years
7/8 years – 10/12 years	(mature adult) 40 – 60 years
10/12 years onwards	(older adult) 60 onwards

The average life expectancy of a cat is around fifteen years, but many lead active and happy lives into their twenties and a few even manage the early thirties. The oldest cat known was thirty-four years five months old when she died.

So what can you expect from your kitten as it grows up? As a baby (under four weeks of age) everything has to be done for it; as a toddler (at five to eight weeks) it has to be carefully supervised; as a child of two to nine months, it is active, playful

The golden years – and this elderly cat is enjoying life as much as he ever did

Cats knead with their paws when happy, just as they kneaded when feeding from their mothers as kittens. This cat is kneading the ground

and adventurous. All these stages are expected, but the teenage phase can take many owners by surprise.

Just like human teenagers, many cats seem to have a super-abundance of energy — if they have a feline friend they can use up some of it in play, but if they don't they may start playing boisterously with their owners, jumping out and ambushing them and giving them painful nips. Like human teenagers, they should be kept fully occupied or they can get into mischief. Regular play sessions, where the play is of the owner's choosing, will help ward off boredom, and plenty of company is important — as is understanding if the cat becomes hyperactive. Plenty of high quality, varied food should be given, as cats at this age will eat a lot — probably a quarter as much again as an adult cat. One word of warning: if you are feeding a prepared cat food, hyperactivity can be *caused* by the food you are giving, as some cats react to certain brands by becoming 'hyper' — their behaviour returns to normal when their food is changed; this is another good reason for feeding a wide variety of food and not just one brand of canned food ('a wide variety' does *not* mean different flavours of the same brand).

However boisterous and time-consuming your teenage cat turns out to be, remember it is just a phase, and one you will probably miss once it is past. Your cat's middle years, however, are often the best: if it was a contented kitten, it is now truly a contented cat — it has a good relationship with its owner, is well adjusted to family life, it returns affection with affection, and is at the peak of its physical powers. For the owner, it is less demanding, and it should be enjoying excellent physical health. Keep up the yearly booster injections for enteritis and cat 'flu, and the

continued

sprinkled on their coats, which although it doesn't harm them, automatically leads to disqualification. For this reason, many owners sit by their cats' pens all day.

There is also a thriving poison pen industry in the cat world. Anonymous letters making various claims against cat owners and breeders arrive regularly at the offices of the registration organisations and cat magazines. And it is common for certain rumours to be deliberately started, for example that a particular breeder has an infectious disease in her household; the person so libelled often has to resort to publishing a vet's report in order to refute it.

Dressage for felines

In 1952, a novel test was introduced to the Kensington Kitten and Neuter Cat Club Festival: cats were tested on their deportment! The idea originated from the custom perpetuated by many London flat-dwellers of taking their cats for walks in the park on leads. It was judged by Lady Aberconway, who said that the main point she would look for was 'if the cat looked happy and is collaborating; if it likes being taken on a lead and is not being bullied'.

The winners were Russian Blues, a Siamese and, in a class for pairs, two Manx. One Blue Persian refused to budge and was sold to a USA visitor at the show — although the two events were probably not connected.

complete health check at the same time.

Don't leave good health to your vet alone, however. Cats are stoic creatures and often display few symptoms of illness until it is well advanced; so be alert for any change in behaviour which may indicate that your cat is feeling unwell. If your cat is not as friendly as it once was, this may the reason. Some urological problems will cause your cat discomfort which changes its behaviour, but it may display no other signs until the illness reaches a critical stage. Don't let it get to that point — take it to the vet as soon as you notice *any* change, even if you think you are being over-anxious.

Continue to groom your cat, worm it and treat it for fleas as necessary. Clean its ears regularly if they are waxy, and check its teeth for tartar. If you see a red line along the gums, if it has difficulty in eating or its breath smells, it may have to have its teeth cleaned by a vet before gingivitis sets in and it loses some teeth. Always check the contents of litter trays — this can tell you more about your cat than anything else. if your cat appears constipated, add a little bran to its food; if it has diarrhoea, withhold all food for twenty-four hours; and if the problem doesn't clear up very quickly, see your vet. If you see your cat straining to pass urine or faeces, or see blood in the litter tray, *contact your vet immediately:* the problem may be critical and could lead to death within a few hours if left untreated.

With luck and good health care you'll both sail through your pets' middle years with few or no problems; but always be alert. A veterinary bill is always preferable to the heartache of a lost pet.

The golden years should be just that. Your cat will slow down and may become more dependent upon you; it will appreciate your warm and comforting lap to sleep upon, and it may become less tolerant of change, noise and children. It may have a few 'accidents' outside its litter tray. But the problems of looking after an older cat are few compared to the many good times you have spent together, and the friendship you have shared and will continue to share.

It is a good practice to groom an old cat more frequently — it is stiff, and unable to reach the parts it reached before, and less able to expel hairballs if it swallows fur as its muscles will have lost tone. It may become constipated for the same reason, so you could add a little bran to its food (start with a quarter teaspoon per day and build up until you achieve the desired effect).

Rethink your cat's diet. An older cat requires less protein but of a higher quality — an excess makes the kidneys work too hard in converting it, and kidney failure can affect three-quarters of all cats over ten years old. Any prepared foods should be from quality protein sources, then add your own refinements. Carbohydrates should be increased, so add cooked pasta, rice, cooked peeled potato and bread (or toast) to your cat's food in the ratio of one-quarter to one-third carbohydrate. Increased vitamins are also necessary — the B group and in particular B_{12}, and C and E. Yeast tablets will supply B vitamins, and are also excellent for reducing stress (and old age may be a constant stress); vitamin C can be purchased in tablets and mixed into food. There is no need to worry about an overdose of vitamin C or the B vitamins because they are water soluble, so any excess will be excreted. Vitamin E — which many consider helps prolong youth — can be purchased in capsules, the end snipped off and a little added to food (take the rest yourself — it's said to be excellent in helping relieve the pain of varicose veins, amongst other things). Your cat may get fatter as it ages, or it may get thinner. If either tendency becomes excessive, make sure your cat has a veterinary checkup as soon as possible. There are now foods specially formulated for older cats, and available from vets, which should provide the nutrients your cat requires whilst maintaining its body shape.

An elderly cat may also tend to incontinence, so give it a clean litter tray on every floor if you live in a two- or three-storey house. Old, stiff leg muscles slow down a cat and it may not be able to negotiate stairs to get to a tray in time. And if accidents do happen, don't scold; your cat will already be devastated at soiling outside its tray. Speak soothingly and don't make a fuss — your annoyance will only increase your cat's stress levels, which will make another accident more likely.

Continue to check your cat's teeth regularly for tartar, and gums for gingivitis; and keep up the yearly booster inoculations and health checkups — although some older cats have built up a tolerance to enteritis and cat 'flu, others have lowered resistance. If your cat begins to eat, or drink, or urinate more or less than it should, arrange for a health check-up; and it is much less stressful for your cat if you can arrange for this to be done in your own home, although there is an additional charge for a housecall.

Try to keep stress to a minimum. A cat sitter while you are on holiday is less stressful to your cat than sending it to a cattery. If your cat is reluctant to go out of doors, respect it and provide a litter tray (or several) and let it stay indoors. Give it a warm and comfortable place to sleep. If you turn off the heating at night, provide your cat with a pet-bed heater — they don't cost much to buy or to run.

Now and again, put yourself in your cat's place: what would make *you* feel secure and comfortable if you were the human equivalent of your cat's age? Think about this regularly and you will have a contented and happy companion for many years to come.

Do cats grieve after a death in the family? My husband died recently, and my cat won't eat and is very moody. If it is grieving, is there a cure?

Only the same 'cure' as for the rest of us — time.

Yes, cats do grieve if a person they love dies — or if a loved feline companion dies. And just as with humans, the depth and duration of their grief varies. It can take six months to a year for a cat to come out of this grieving period and begin to eat and act as it did before, and this should be accepted as a natural reaction to the loss of a loved one. *Your* cat is fortunate in that he still has you, and still has your home to live in. Some cats living with one owner have to cope with the loss of the person, *and* with transplantation to another home or a rescue shelter as well.

At this time, your cat will benefit a great deal from your company, from conversation and from gentle stroking. And, I'm sure, so will you. Perhaps you can help one another through a very difficult period.

A cat can be contented with a completely indoor life – and can remain much safer – as long as all its needs are taken care of

An indoor cat should have other feline company, especially if it is a friendly Siamese

THE INDOOR CAT

Can cats be contented if kept entirely indoors? Yes, and a survey has shown that they are likely to live twice as long — they cannot be stolen or run over (and half of *all* cats are killed in road accidents), or pick up disease from another cat; and if your home has been made safe for your cat, it cannot get into danger — be locked accidentally into a shed or vehicle, fall off a roof, get into fights, be chased by a dog.

So many owners, when their cat no longer wants to go out of doors, ask how can they persuade it to do so. The short answer is — don't. Your cat may have a very good reason for no longer wanting to go outside; perhaps a feline bruiser is making its life miserable — perhaps there is a cat-chasing dog running loose — perhaps a neighbour is continually frightening it — or perhaps the cat is just old, and prefers the comforts of indoors.

Many cats don't get the choice, because more and more owners are keeping their cats indoors from kittenhood. This isn't just pedigree animals (and many pedigree cats come from long lines of cats which have always been kept indoors) — the non-pedigree cat is also being kept inside, for safety. And they *can* lead happy and contented lives *as long as everything they require is provided for them.*

You can easily tell how successfully you are providing for their needs if you have a mixture of indoor/outdoor and indoor cats, as I have. My pedigree cats have always been kept indoors, but my non-pedigree cats, acquired earlier, have always had the choice of going outside on demand. However, life is obviously so comfortable *indoors* that they ask to go out at the most only three times a day, spend about two minutes outside each time, and then miaow desperately to come in again. Everything they need is indoors; they just like to have a quick check over their outside territory, then come inside to be comfortable.

So what does an indoor cat need to keep it contented, fit and healthy? First of all, it needs space. You cannot keep a cat happy in one room — it must have places to play and hide, and halls or rooms large enough to run about in. It must also have things it can climb, whether this is a dresser or a cat climber; it must be able to get high off the floor and away from other cats if it feels like some peace and quiet.

An indoor cat should have other feline company, to play with, to help exercise it and to keep it alert. It needs human companionship too, which is why the most contented indoor cats have a non-working owner, or an owner who works at home. And it needs somewhere to go when it wants to be alone, so a number of rooms which are not out-of-bounds is essential.

Regular exercise is just as important for an indoor cat. We — us humans — are all now convinced that we need daily exercise to counteract the sedentary life which most of us lead; we no longer need to hunt for our food or till the fields, so we simply don't

When I'm ill my cat always seems to know. She always comes up to my bedroom and lies on the bed. How does she know?

Cynics may say that a cat will always enjoy lying on a bed warmed by a human body — cats also like to be undisturbed, so if an owner is ill he or she is less likely to move about or get up.

I prefer to believe that cats are very sensitive to our moods and become attuned to sympathetic owners. If a cat loves its owner, it will want to be with that person, whether in the living-room or the bedroom. Cats have been known to curl themselves around an injured feline companion, sharing their body warmth, and they may wish to do so with an ill owner.

I know one elderly man who became hypothermic during bitter winter weather and was unable to move. His cat lay on top of him all night and kept him warm. He insists his cat not only saved his life, but knew that if she left him he would die.

Cats need sunshine, which manufactures vitamin D on their coats

Q. Are not the skins of cats a very considerable branch of commerce in some countries?
A. Yes; as furs, they are valued for some purposes, but those of the Spanish cats are most esteemed.

Q. What people export a great many of them?
A. The Russians; they even send them into China.

Q. Is not the hair of the wild grey cat very long, and of a fine white grey?
A. Yes; it is a savage formidable animal found wild in the woods of Europe, Asia and America.

Q. Were not cats considered as sacred objects by the Egyptians?
A. Yes; and whoever accidentally killed one was liable to severe punishment.

Q. What story does Herodotus, the Greek historian, tell us about this?
A. That whenever a cat died a natural death, the inhabitants of the house used to shave their eyebrows in token of sorrow.

Q. What was done with the animal?
A. It was embalmed and nobly interred.

Q. What story does Southey relate about cats, in his history of the Brazils?
A. That the first couple of cats which were carried to Cuyuba sold for a pound weight of gold.

get the exercise which our forefathers did. It is the same with the average domestic cat. Well fed, they no longer need to hunt, nor do they have to fight other cats for territory, food, or a female; so they get little natural exercise, and an 'only' cat may get virtually none at all. Two play sessions per day of around ten minutes each will therefore keep your cat fit and healthy, and strengthen its cardio-vascular system.

A high quality, varied diet is vital because indoor cats have no way of supplementing any deficiencies by catching and eating prey. A constant supply of growing greenstuff must be provided, because normally a cat would seek out and eat herbs and swallow grass to help with digestion and expelling hairballs. So grow some greenery specially for your cat to nibble; using flower pots or small tubs, sow a selection from the following every ten days to two weeks: grass, wheat, oats, catnip, chives, parsley — even budgie seed.

Grass is most commonly used by cats, and they will shear off long blades and swallow them. Buy grass seed which has not been treated with any chemical (fertiliser or weedkiller) as cats will sometimes uproot the seeds when eating the grass; untreated seed from any garden centre or hardware store can be used. Cocksfoot grass is a type often used specifically for cat-nibbling, but is more difficult to find — and more expensive. It can be found on sale at some cat shows and from specialist cat equipment suppliers.

Catnip *(Nepeta cataria)* is a herb which most cats adore. It has a relaxing effect on them, though it makes them playful, too. Catnip grown indoors will probably be eaten before it is more than a few centimetres tall; but if you do have some left, it can be dried by hanging it in loose bunches in a cool, dry place until it is brittle. Store it in a lidded container and stuff toy mice with it, rub it on a scratching post to persuade your cat to use it, or just sprinkle it on the floor when you want your cat to relax. Catnip seed is available from specialist nurserymen.

Experiment a little to find out what other greenery your cat likes — when buying herb seeds for the garden, plant a few in indoor pots, too. If they are suitable for human consumption and if your cat enjoys them, it will do it no harm and may even have some unlooked-for beneficial effects. Many cats enjoy chives, a member of the onion family of which many wonderful things are claimed; also parsley, which is a good source of iron (it also helps keep the breath fresh!).

If you don't provide greenery for your cat to nibble, it will eat your potted plants instead — and some of those *are* poisonous, including daffodils, crocuses, hyacinths and iris. So are azaleas and chrysanthemums, and dieffenbachias and poinsettias are extremely toxic — even the humble spider plant can cause upsets. Although not toxic itself, the spider plant absorbs toxins, such as carbon monoxide, from the atmosphere; a spider plant kept in a smoker's household could therefore be very dangerous to a cat, if eaten.

The owner of an indoor cat should think twice before buying a home which doesn't get much sunshine. Cats love to lie in the sun, and it is believed that the sun's rays manufacture vitamin D on the cat's coat, which it then absorbs while grooming. Ultra-violet rays don't pass through glass, so an indoor cat won't get the full benefit of sunshine unless the owner builds a wire screen to fit the open window. This will keep the cat safe indoors whilst allowing the sun's rays to fall unobstructed on the cat. However, owners of white cats should be careful that their cats don't become sunburnt; white ears have pink, easily burnt skin, and a sparse fur covering which is often not enough to protect it.

The equipment already discussed for an indoor/outdoor cat is essential for an indoor cat: a litter tray, situated in an acceptable position, which is kept clean, disinfected (with diluted household bleach) and free from smell; a comfortable bed which the cat can call its own; and a scratching post. Cats must, and will, strop — if you don't give them a post, they will strop on the furniture. Sometimes they will strop on the furniture anyway, but that is a question of training. If your cat has decimated a wicker basket or chair, it is obviously because it is an excellent stropping facility: so think twice before throwing it out. Is there an out-of-the-way corner in which you could place it, where you wouldn't see it but your cat could reach it? If so, try to keep it, however tatty it looks, because your cat will thank you.

These are essential requirements for the indoor cat; and if your cat goes out-of-doors too, it will still enjoy all these indoor facilities. Provide everything your cat needs, including the most important component — your company — and you will have a truly contented cat.

All Creatures. . .

James Herriot is not the only vet who found that moving from one end of the United Kingdom to the other caused language difficulties. One vet moved from the south to Suffolk and had a phone-call from a client. 'I'm bringing in my Betty,' said the caller.

'That's fine,' the new vet replied, assuming that Betty was the name of the sick animal. 'What *is* your Betty?'

There was a long silence. 'It's a Betty', was the puzzled reply. The vet subsequently found out that 'Betty' was the Suffolk slang term for a cat.

Outdoor cats get a lot of exercise. Indoor cats should have their own aerobics classes

Symptoms of discontent

My cat has just started to grab his tail in his mouth and walk about everywhere like this — why?

I can only assume he is playing. Having caught his tail, he must be proudly showing off his trophy. Make sure he has enough toys to chase and carry and he may stop carrying his tail.

Sometimes we can provide everything — and more — that our cats could possibly need, and they're still not happy. Why should this be? Many of the cases that I have come across fall into two categories: fearful felines and unfriendly felines.

Friendliness is something we tend to expect from our pets as our natural right: we feed them, take them to the vet when necessary and put a roof over their heads — the least they could do is show some gratitude.

Of course, it doesn't work like that — especially with cats. Computer buffs have an expression 'garbage in, garbage out', meaning if you programme a computer with rubbish, that's what you'll get out of it. In a way, cats are very similar in that you will only get out of your relationship what you are prepared to put into it.

So those owners who simply put food in front of their cats once or twice a day and otherwise ignore them, won't have the same relationship as the owners who try to understand their cats better, who try to make their life more comfortable, and who spend more time with them.

Of course, some cats are much harder to get to know than others; their experiences in early life can colour their relationship with humans for a long time afterwards. But even feral cats — those born and raised wild, with no human contact for months — can become friendly to those willing to take the time to get to know them, and some will do so remarkably quickly.

Fearful cats are fearful either as a result of previous experiences, or through an instinct for self-preservation which may not be immediately apparent to the owner. Most cats demonstrate a healthy wariness of the unknown; a cat entering an unknown room for the first time will check it out thoroughly for dangers, even ignoring any strange cats that might be present while it is doing so. Such wariness is natural and could save a cat's life.

Whatever a cat may fear, the owner should respect that fear, whether he understands the reason for it or not, and if possible should endeavour to keep the feared object away from the cat. For example, many cats are afraid of strange children, although they will accept and love the children in their own household. Perhaps children have frightened or hurt them in the past and the memory and fear remains. Keep such a cat away from strange youngsters, and make sure that any visiting children respect its feelings by leaving it alone.

In the same way, fears of household objects or certain people need not become disabling for, with a little forethought, your cat need not confront them.

There are cat owners who insist that felines are unfriendly, ungrateful, unloving creatures. The following casebook section will reveal that such remarks tell us much more about the owners than the cats!

I have a six-year-old cat who is very nervous. She won't be stroked or touched at all. What can I do?

Many cats are nervous of humans if they haven't been able to 'bond' with people during the first few important weeks of life. If a kitten sees no-one but its mother or other cats during the first month or so, it will only feel comfortable in the company of felines. Some kittens born in the wild may be distrustful of humans all their lives, even if given a home by a caring owner; others will slowly come round to accepting human company, but should be allowed to do so at their own pace. If they are some months old before being homed, they may never be as friendly as kittens reared in a home environment.

I owned the mother of this cat and I bred her, so she should be used to me. When she was a kitten, I decided I wasn't going to keep her. I left her in her pen and I never touched her because I didn't want to become attached to her. Then I changed my mind and kept her. So how can I make her more friendly?

Anyone who breeds kittens should handle them once or twice a day from birth for the first few weeks. This enables the breeder to check that they are healthy and are not harbouring any infections — for example, in the umbilical cord area. They should also be weighed daily to check that they are receiving enough food. At three weeks or so, kittens become aware of their surroundings and can become very bored in a kittening box or pen; like babies, they are naturally curious and need mental stimulation. At this stage therefore they will enjoy sitting on an owner's lap where they can look around and begin to learn about the world outside. At four weeks, they will be able to climb out of their kittening box and will want to explore. Kittens which are brought up as part of a caring

household, free to come and go from box or pen, don't grow up to be nervous of humans.

If you had sold your kitten, she would have been just as nervous in her new household, and this would have reflected very badly on your expertise as a cat breeder. All you can do now is be very patient with her, and *don't* try to *force* her to be friendly. It can take ten years to undo the harm done in the first ten weeks, and sometimes it can never be undone.

TRY Patience and yet more patience. Don't try to stroke an unwilling cat. Provide all its requirements, but if it prefers to spend all the daylight hours hiding under a bed, allow it to do so. Once it understands you are no threat to it, it may come around — but only in its own time. Always let a nervous cat make the first friendly move, and don't be too quick to try and pick it up. Cats must be allowed to set their own pace when they are approaching people offering friendship.

COMMENT A person with so little knowledge of the feline species should not breed cats until she has learned more about them. Cat clubs are an excellent place to learn more about cats of all types. However, cat breeders should try to ensure this situation doesn't arise by refusing to sell kittens for breeding to those who have neither experience, knowledge, or even common sense.

Unfriendly intentions. The cat sees a dog and its back paws edge closer to its front paws, causing the back to arch, while the cat watches the dog all the way out of sight

Cat 'flu and enteritis

Cat 'flu is the name commonly used among owners to describe the very serious illness, feline respiratory disease (FRD). It is caused by a number of different viruses, but the most common are feline viral rhinotracheitis, and the less severe feline calicivirus.

The viruses are most often transmitted when an infected cat sneezes over another cat, which is why cats must be inoculated against these viruses before they can be shown at a cat show or before they book into a holiday cattery.

The symptoms include sneezing, runny eyes and/or nose, lack of appetite, breathing difficulties and ulcers in the mouth. FRD can be fatal for many cats, especially young kittens and elderly cats. Treatment will include antibiotics for secondary bacterial infections, eye ointments or drops, vitamins and possibly treatment for dehydration. Many cats suffering from FRD lose their will to live, and an

continued opposite

When I moved house, I left my cat for some months at my old address, with a male friend, until I was settled. Now my cat is with me again but is not very friendly, and prefers my new boyfriend to me. Has she just become more used to men than women?

Your cat may be sulking; she may see your disappearance as a rejection of her. If so, it will take time and patience to build up your relationship with her again. Let her take it at her own speed; once she understands that you won't be leaving her again she may be as friendly as before. Many cats can be left for long periods by their owners without being any less friendly, but some take separation badly; we all react differently to what we see as rejection.

You may be right in surmising that she has simply become more used to men than women — some cats are 'men' cats and some are 'women' cats. A timid cat may well prefer women with their quieter voices and gentler movements; but a cat with a strong personality may respond better to the rougher handling and play typical of a male owner.

The third alternative is that your new boyfriend may be an exceptionally nice person! Cats are expert judges of character and your cat may be simply approving your choice.

TRY Taking things slowly. Don't push your friendliness on your cat; she won't respond except at her own pace. Be patient, and show her you would still like to build up the relationship you had before.

If she really is a 'man' cat and you notice that your boyfriend is rougher in play than you are, start emulating him. Many of us are very gentle with our cats, but most enjoy a good 'roughing up' from time to time, having their ribs and behind their ears scratched vigorously, rather than a gentle stroke along the back. Some cats even enjoy being slapped on the flanks,

(but not too hard)!

OUTCOME This owner realised she was treating her cat too much like fragile porcelain, and that her boyfriend was providing a rough-and-tumble playtime which it thoroughly enjoyed. Now she doesn't treat her cat with such delicacy and it is settling down with her again — but still prefers her boyfriend.

COMMENT They say that elephants never forget, but cats have longer memories.

I have three pedigree cats. The female is younger than one of the males and older than the other. The problem is that they don't like her and either ignore her most of the time or fight with her. I was told she was the last of her litter to sell, so was in a pen on her own when I bought her.

So much of the information we need about the kittens we buy is not usually forthcoming, and anyway, many of us don't think to ask. Really we need to know how kittens are raised from day one to week twelve before we buy them; the way they have been treated in this vital time will affect how they relate both to us and to other felines.

We don't know how long this kitten was living in a pen on her own. It may have been for just a few days after her littermates were sold, but she may have been without kitten company for all her short life. If so, she would simply not have learned how to relate and react to other cats — her body language will be all wrong.

When kittens begin to play at around four weeks, their play is a learning process. They are learning to stand up for themselves and to hunt but — and this is more important for a domestic cat — they are also learning the social skills they need for life with other felines. If a child was brought up in a remote home and isolated from other children, we wouldn't be surprised if, later in life, that child found it difficult to relate to others and make friends. It is in childhood that we learn the lessons which help us through our lives. A lonely child becomes a lonely adult, not realising that those subtle nuances of speech and body language which indicate a friendly personality are missing from his repertoire.

So it is with a kitten. A kitten raised with other felines soon learns not to approach a more dominant cat directly, not to stare at it (because a stare is a threat), not to steal its food, or its bed. A kitten raised alone, without this experience, will commit many social gaffes without realising it is doing so. This may be the problem with your cat.

However, there are other considerations, such as the sexual state of the cats concerned.

The males are both neutered. The female has been spayed recently. Is this a factor?

It may be. Generally, a household of cats living together will live more peaceably if all are neutered. Dominance and pecking order is related to the sexual state, with entire males often the most dominant in the group. Entire females, especially if they have had kittens, can be dominant in a household of neuters, but the pecking order can change as females kitten or as cats of either sex are neutered. If all cats in a household are neutered, the pecking order will change very little, once they are all adult. This in itself provides a form of stability in a cat's life — and cats are creatures of habit.

The fact that you have now had the female spayed may help her settle down with the neutered males, and they may accept her more happily.

It's possible that your female simply has a personality which clashes with the other cats — many cats living together barely tolerate each other. Often, when a disliked cat leaves the household, the re-maining cats undergo a personality change and become happier, friendlier and calmer.

YOU SHOULD choose the home from which you buy a kitten carefully. A home where the furniture is scratched and a variety of kittens and cats live in a tumble of confusion but look clean and healthy, is always preferable to a breeding establishment with rows of clinical pens if the kittens have spent all, or most, of their day there.

Always ask how the kittens are raised. If you've chosen the breeder carefully, you should be told the truth.

Don't keep a mixture of neutered and entire cats, unless the entire cats are to be used for breeding. Most neuters are happiest living with neuters.

Try to choose a kitten whose personality will fit in with other cats in the household.

OUTCOME After the female was spayed she became more acceptable to the males, but they remained friendlier towards one another than to her.

Our two cats are very unfriendly towards one another. We allowed our cat to have a litter so that we could keep one of the kittens as company for her, but now that he is an adult she hates him. He suckled from her for ten months — could this be the reason?

It could be part of the reason. Kittens should be completely weaned by eight weeks because it is tiring for a mother cat to keep producing milk for her offspring, and kittens are well able to thrive on solid food from four weeks onwards. As well as this, it is painful for the mother to be suckled by large kittens with strong teeth and claws.

It is surprising that your cat allowed her kitten to suckle for so long. Many non-pedigree cats will allow their kittens to suckle for several months, but some pedigree cats will begin to run away

continued

owner's careful nursing can sometimes be the difference between life and death.

Feline infectious enteritis (FIE) or *panleucopaenia* is almost always fatal; it is transmitted by a virus shed in urine, faeces, saliva and vomit. The symptoms include a high temperature, sunken eyes, painful abdomen, vomiting of a greenish liquid, and dehydration. Treatment will include blood transfusion in severe cases, antibiotics and intravenous fluids.

Both illnesses can be *prevented,* and prevention is much easier than cure. Cats can be given a yearly combined vaccination against both diseases (this also gives a vet an opportunity to give a cat a yearly health check-up); kittens can be vaccinated against both diseases at nine weeks and again at twelve weeks. They should be kept entirely indoors until a week or ten days after the second vaccination. Thereafter just one annual booster injection will keep cats free from these two killer diseases.

Neuter or Not?

As there are so many unwanted felines, pet cats should be neutered while still kittens. So why do a few owners resist neutering? These are some of the reasons they give.

'I want my cat to have kittens so I can keep one as company for her.' Cats don't enjoy sharing their homes with grown-up offspring, and most fight like cat-and-dog. If you want company for your cat, find an unrelated cat or kitten at a rescue shelter. That way, you're helping the over-population problem, not adding to it.

'I let my cat have kittens and I always find good homes for them.' Even if you do — and really good homes aren't that easy to find — those kittens are depriving *other* kittens of homes. I know one otherwise intelligent person who proudly told me that his cat had been allowed to have kittens all her adult life. She'd had 140 of them and he'd found homes for them all. But if all those homes had had the same attitude to neutering as he did, his cat could have been responsible for 50,000 offspring in a period of ten years!

'Neutering is cruel.' It isn't. The operation is carried out under general anaesthetic and the cat doesn't feel a thing. Male cats are usually running around demanding their breakfasts half-an-hour after coming round from the anaesthetic, and female cats don't take much longer to recover. After the operation their hormone levels alter naturally, so they have no maternal or sexual feelings. They don't feel they are missing anything.

continued opposite

He's a beautiful, healthy kitten — but he's living in a rescue shelter. He's one of the 250,000 who find their way to a shelter each year

from their kittens when they are as young as four weeks old.

Most kittens will suckle as long as they are allowed to — not only is their mother's milk much more delicious than anything that comes out of a can, but suckling is a very comforting activity, too. Kittens must be gradually weaned from their mother's milk over a period of several weeks.

An additional complication in this case is that in my experience, closely related cats often *don't* get on very well once they are both adults, So these two cats may not have become friends even if the younger one hadn't been dependent on his mother for such a long time.

YOU SHOULD provide an unrelated kitten for company for your cat. There are hundreds of thousands of cats and kittens in rescue shelters, any one of which could be ideal company for your cat — and the volunteers are very helpful in finding one with a suitable temperament.

Don't allow your cat to become pregnant just so that one of her kittens will provide company for her. Cats can have five or six kittens at a time, and even if you are lucky enough to find good homes for them, they're depriving *other* kittens of a home.

COMMENT My advice wasn't particularly helpful in this case because I didn't think the two cats would ever really be friendly, though they may mellow a little over the years. If the cat-fighting becomes impossible to live with, the only alternative (and it is a last resort) is to rehome one of the cats. This, you will find, is easier said than done, unless the cat in question is a particularly rare and beautiful breed of pedigree cat. Even Siamese and Persians, once they are adults, have difficulty finding new homes — there aren't enough for the cute little unwanted kittens born every year, let alone for adult cats. Cat shelters often

Not all cats are friendly with each other, especially if closely related

can't take them in, either — they're full to overflowing.

However, if the cats aren't doing any actual damage to one another, this owner may be worrying needlessly. Very often, cats won't 'get on' when the owner is around, but *do* provide excellent company for one another when the owner is at work, cuddling up to sleep together. Cats can be very self-serving.

I bought a kitten for my daughter and the kitten is lovely — except she bites my daughter when she's being stroked on the stomach. Is there something wrong with the kitten?

Your kitten is behaving in a completely natural way. When two kittens play, one will roll onto its back and the other will bite it around the head, trying to hold it down with its front paws and scrabbling away at its stomach with its back claws. This type of play helps kittens learn how to defend themselves, when, as adults, they may have to fight for real.

What is happening here is that stroking the kitten's stomach is triggering its 'fight mode', and it is instinctively biting back at the attacker — your daughter's hand. As long as your kitten doesn't bite your daughter in any other circumstances, you can rest assured

Many cats will attack if their stomachs are stroked – it triggers fight mode

that it is perfectly normal behaviour — and usually, this sort of bite isn't meant to hurt, but to restrain.

YOU SHOULD stop tickling your cat's tummy if it reacts by biting.

OUTCOME The biting ceased as soon as the tickling did.

I'm retired and living on my own. Some months ago I bought a kitten for company and he is now ten months old. The problem is that he bites me. He chases my feet and nips my ankles, which is very painful. He also leaps at my hands when I'm knitting and chews the edge of the carpet. Why does he behave like this when I love him so much?

The short answer is that your cat is a teenager — and like all teenagers has a lot of energy. He's playing with you, using up some of his excess energy, though he doesn't realise, of course, that his play is too rough for a retired owner to appreciate.

Young kittens will chase anything which moves — including hands and feet — but should be discouraged from biting or hanging on. Quite apart from the pain of even a playful nip, such antics can easily lead to an elderly owner having a fall. The fact that yours also chews the carpet leads me to assume that he is bored.

Provide plenty of toys for him to play with. These need not be ex-

continued

'I want my cat to have one litter of kittens for her health.' Any woman who has ever had a baby will tell you that her health has not been improved by the experience — quite the opposite, in some cases. Kittening is not always an easy experience; cats can and do die in the process. Sometimes a Caesarian section is necessary, or other veterinary assistance during or after the birth for cat or kittens, and this can also be very expensive.

'Neutering makes cats fat and lazy.' It doesn't. Cats only get fat if they eat too much. Once they are fat they become lazy because even walking is an effort. I've owned many neutered cats over the years and not one has ever been fat *or* lazy. If a neutered cat starts to put on weight, cut down slightly on its food.

'I can't afford to have my cat neutered.' The operation isn't expensive, and it can save you a lot of money in the long run. Entire toms get into fights over females and may need frequent veterinary attention for their injuries — that can cost a great deal more than the operation. Entire toms also spray their pungent urine everywhere, and new furniture is expensive. Females may need veterinary attention before, during or after giving birth, and their kittens may become ill — it all costs money. If you really can't find the money for neutering, contact your local animal or cat charity who may be able to help.

pensive — for example, table tennis balls can be chased for hours. Even better are plastic golf practice balls which have holes in them and can be hooked in the air. Anything which rolls erratically is a source of amusement: wine corks, empty sewing thread spools, plastic eggs from amusement arcades and those plastic lemons which have held lemon juice.

Cardboard boxes are great fun too, especially if a ball is placed inside one. Make a mouse — it can be any shape — from offcuts of strong fabric, and stuff it with catnip. An enormous amount of fun can be had by 'going fishing': attach strong twine to a rod and tie a catnip mouse to the other end of the twine — hold the rod and dangle the mouse in front of your cat, and watch him chase it. He'll be tired out in ten minutes!

All cats need exercise and play, and the kitten and teenage cat in particular. Given enough to occupy their bright minds and use up their energy, cats won't chase and bite their owners. Yours will quieten down as he gets older, but it may take some time.

YOU SHOULD play with your cat twice a day for ten minutes at a time — this is the average attention span, then he will probably settle down for a nap.

Discourage him from biting your ankles or getting under your feet. Lift him away each time he does it, saying 'NO' in a loud, firm voice.

Make sure he has feline company. If you cannot have another cat, allow him out to play several times a day with the neighbouring cats.

Carry a few small toys around in your pocket; then if he leaps out, ambushing you and biting your feet or ankles, throw one down to redirect his attention.

COMMENT The ideal companion for an older person is an older cat; kittens are much too lively, and need a great deal of attention. There are adult cats which for various good reasons have been placed in shelters all over the country and which need homes. These cats don't necessarily want to go to places where there are children or a lot of noise — many would love just to curl up peacefully on a pensioner's lap.

Because they are older, they are usually quieter and slower in their movements, and of course are completely house-trained. Some shelters have special homing arrangements for the older cat, and will guarantee veterinary bills so that a retired owner has no additional money worries.

My cat has developed a very nasty habit — she bites me, and it is not a friendly bite. If I put my hand towards her to stroke her, her ears go back and she bites. Sometimes she will sit and stare at me, and then she jumps up and wraps her arms round my arm and sinks her teeth in. I've tried your suggested training, but to no avail; my vet says there is nothing physically wrong with her.

When a cat changes its behaviour in any way, and particularly if it has been friendly and then becomes aggressive, it should always be taken for a veterinary checkup — it may be because it is feeling unwell.

As this cat has been cleared by a vet, other causes for its biting should be considered. Make sure *you* are not behaving in a way which would make a cat attack you; if, however, you sit quietly, not staring at your cat, and it reacts with a threatening stare and an attack, then it is acting in a genuinely aggressive way. In fact it is unnatural for a cat to be aggressive towards people, unless it was mistreated in early life (although this is more likely to make it timid). As your cat was normally friendly, at one time, this can be ruled out.

Your cat could be suffering an allergic reaction to something in its environment. First check her food — some children can become aggressive and hyperactive when they have eaten something containing certain food colourings and flavourings, and in the same way, some cats react badly to those used in cat food. This reaction can be diarrhoea, sickness or hyperactivity, and some become aggressive and may bite their owners.

Try feeding a completely different brand of food, made by a different manufacturer. Change gradually, first mixing a little of the new brand with a lot of the old, then gradually decreasing the amount of the old brand and increasing the new over a period of a week or so. If it is the food brand your cat is reacting to, she should start to improve quite quickly, certainly within a couple of weeks of the changeover.

If there is no improvement, investigate your surroundings for any chemicals which may be affecting your cat, especially those which she may come into contact with frequently, such as products used on floors and soft furnishings. For example, if your settee or carpet is treated with a stain-resisting chemical, bar your cat from that room for at least a week, to see if her behaviour improves.

TRY changing the brand of food you feed — and don't give up if your cat shows a reluctance to change foods; cats do *not* know what is best for them!

Check your surroundings for any products which may be causing a reaction in your cat. Although allergies often take the form of rashes, breathing difficulties or running eyes, they can appear as aggression, too.

COMMENT Although a cat food may cause no problems in 99.9 per cent of cats, yours may be in the remaining 0.1 per cent. We are all now aware of the importance of healthy diets and of the dangers of additives, yet we feed our cats on products which contain colours to make them appear more attractive to *us,* and additives which make the food more appealing to our cats but which have no nutritional value at all. Always remember, just because a cat prefers a particular brand of food, it doesn't mean it is the best food for that cat — it may be the tastiest, but this may mean it is the one with the most additives.

OUTCOME The owner suspected that food might be the problem here; her cat's mother had been sick every time she ate a particular brand of canned food, and the same food was being given to this cat. Once it was given more home-cooked food and a different brand of cat food, within two weeks it had stopped biting.

I can't pick my cat up. She hates it and runs away as soon as she possibly can. Apart from that, she purrs and is friendly.

If a cat which normally enjoys being picked up starts to complain, do check that there is nothing physically wrong with her — an ill cat may feel pain when picked up and naturally will object. However, if this cat has never allowed you to pick her up, it may be that her early upbringing is affecting how she reacts to you.

I bought her from a pet shop, where she was displayed in a pen. Could this be the reason?

She may not have been handled enough in kittenhood — or she may have been handled too much. If she was taken out of her pen frequently and handled roughly by potential customers, she may not wish to repeat the experience.

Fortunately, she is otherwise friendly towards you. Allow her to come around to being handled in her own time; she probably will, if treated gently.

YOU SHOULD never initiate touch between you. Allow your cat to come to you — let her rub against your legs or sit near you, but without

touching her first. Speak to her warmly and quietly so that she knows you enjoy her touch. After some weeks of this you could try a very gentle stroke, but if she shrinks away, respect her feelings and don't try to touch her again for several weeks.

COMMENT It often happens that an 'untouchable' cat decides one day — quite literally one day — that her people are all right, and settles down on their laps as if she had always had a place there. I have heard of many a stray which lived in the garden, fed by the homeowners for several years but growling and strongly resisting any sort of human contact. Then one day it has scratched at the house door, walked in, and settled in front of the fire, and in a single day has turned into a friendly, possessive lapcat.

I've had a cat for several years, and I bought a kitten for company for her some months ago. She liked him at first but now she beats him up, although they do cuddle up to sleep together. What can I do?

Some garden-living strays suddenly lose their fear of people and move indoors after years outside

Your male kitten is growing up and like most boys everywhere, wants to try to show his supremacy over your female. If both are neutered, this shouldn't lead to any real problems and what owners often see as a beating-up, the cats see as no more than a way of finding out who will be boss cat. Until now, your female has been boss because she was the adult, but as your male matures the pecking order may change.

This is a natural process which your cats will go through, and although there may be a few bloodcurdling fights, the problem should cease once supremacy has been established. If your female doesn't think much of your male and insists on being top cat, the arguments will go on a while longer until one concedes.

The beating-up is not anything to worry about in this case; the cats settle down to sleep together so they can't be too violently opposed to living with each other. If they were, separate sleeping rooms would give them a little territory of their own, at least at night.

YOU SHOULD let them sort it out for themselves. After all, cats have been living together peaceably for thousands of years without human help or intervention.

My cat was a stray I rescued three years ago, but she shows no affection. She only comes near me when I feed her, then she turns her back on me. Does this mean she doesn't like me?

Your cat may be a little afraid of you. By turning her back on you, she is not demonstrating dislike, but that she is no threat to you — she is recognising that you are the

Back-turning isn't a sign of dislike in the cat world but it may mean that the cat is nervous or afraid

dominant 'cat' in the household. Submissive cats will turn their backs on more dominant cats to show they have no wish to fight, and most cats will not attack a cat with its back turned.

If your cat was a stray, she will have learned the basics of body language thoroughly in order to stay out of trouble; she would have been meeting cats of all descriptions, and would have had to battle for her food and a place to sleep. Old habits die hard, and even though your cat now has a caring home, she is still exhibiting the language she learned as a stray. You've been very patient with her, and it is galling when such care and love is rejected. But realise that once she feels totally at home, she will begin to show affection — as long as you are worthy of it!

TRY some feline body language yourself. Never stare at a cat which is as submissive as this one; instead, put yourself on her level — literally. If you want to have a chat

with your cat, lie on the floor so that you don't tower over her; use a quiet, gentle tone of voice, and blink a lot — in the cat world, blinking is a sign of reassurance. Don't look at her directly, but obliquely. And if she shows signs of nervousness, leave off the conversation for another day.

Don't try to stroke her — you will know she wants human contact when she rubs herself against you or sits down on your lap.

If she seems a particularly nervous sort of cat, feed her well and give her vitamin and mineral supplements. Brewer's yeast tablets are a good source of the anti-stress B vitamins, and may help her.

Once again, patience is the answer.

COMMENT It took the best part of another year, but this cat is now a friendly lapcat. It is said that a dog is anybody's friend but you have to earn the friendship of a cat: with some, all this involves is feeding it once and giving it a friendly stroke; with others it takes years of perseverance. But just think of the sense of achievement you would feel when a cat like this begins to put its trust in you.

My cat is very frightened by the noise of household appliances. If I turn on the vacuum cleaner or the food mixer, she scoots. I've had her since she was a kitten — she was brought up on a farm — and she has always been like this.

One of the first things kittens learn is that certain noises pose no threat to them. A kitten raised in a family situation, introduced gradually and carefully to the noises of the household, will not fear those noises in later life. But a kitten raised on a farm may have lived through this vital initial learning period in a barn or outhouse, where it wouldn't experience twentieth-century noise; so when it does it will react fearfully.

The most common colour of cat in the United Kingdom is black and white, followed by black, tabby, ginger, tortoiseshell, ginger and white, tortoiseshell and white, tabby and white, white, blue, and blue and white

Anyone raising kittens owes it to the kittens, and their prospective owners, to familiarise them with any noises they may experience in their new homes, from the whirr of a food mixer to the flushing of a toilet.

COMMENT It isn't altogether a bad thing for cats to fear the noise of household appliances, as long as that fear is not disabling. Every year, many cats climb inside washing machines to investigate, or go to sleep on the clothes, and are drowned when their owners turn on the machine without checking inside first. A cat which is moderately afraid of such noises could be trained to realise that they pose no threat — but there doesn't seem much point in doing so. If your cat is afraid of the noise of certain appliances, put it outside the room before switching on.

My cat seems perfectly normal, except for one thing. She's afraid of ropes! if a rope is left lying on the ground she won't go near it. What's wrong with her?

Nothing. Your cat is behaving in a perfectly normal and natural way. Try to see through your cat's eyes and what does a rope lying coiled on the floor, remind you of? Your cat realises that any long, coiled object could be a snake and treats it with a deep instinctive wariness.

Even indoor cats, bred from generations of indoor cats, treat anything snake-like with suspicion, and this extends to ropes, garden hoses, thick twine and elasticated baggage fasteners. Any wild cat which did not have an instinctive distrust of snakes would not have lived long, and this is yet another example of how our domesticated felines retain so many of the characteristics of their ancestors.

This fear of snakes can be put to good use if you wish to deter cats from your garden: leave a coiled garden hose in full view, and most cats will not come near.

My cat is afraid of thunderstorms. At the first rumble, he cowers under the bed and won't come out until it's over. I'm not much help to him as I'm afraid of thunderstorms, too. Do you think he can be picking up my fear?

In my experience, people who are afraid of thunderstorms have cats which are afraid of them. Others who enjoy watching the pyrotechnics, have cats which will sit on the windowsill watching the display, completely unmoved by the loudest clap of thunder.

Cats are extremely sensitive animals and will often pick up their owner's moods, including fear. If you can try to overcome your fear of thunderstorms and sit quietly during one, stroking your cat on your lap, it may help you both.

Cats have other fears too, many of which seem illogical to us; though we don't always know what our cats' earliest experiences were. One of my cats is terrified of balloons, and won't enter a room containing an inflated balloon — perhaps as a very young kitten she may have been frightened by one bursting, before she came to live with me.

My cat seems to be afraid to go out of doors. There are a few big tomcats in the area which may be the reason. I hold the door open for him several times a day but he simply won't go out, and I end up pushing him out the door. I don't want him to stay indoors all the time because I think it is unnatural and cruel. How can I persuade him to go outside?

Why bother? Your cat has made his decision and he prefers your home to the dangers outside. Consider it a compliment to you, and anyway, he is much safer indoors: half of all those cats which don't live to old age are killed in road accidents; thousands of cats are stolen every year, possibly for pelts to supply the fur trade abroad; and the lifespan of the average indoor cat is about twice that of a cat which spends part of its time out of doors. It sounds to me as if you have a very intelligent cat.

As for cruelty, it is not unkind to keep a cat indoors as long as all its needs are catered for. A studio flat

with a working owner would not be an ideal situation for a house-bound cat, but if a cat has enough space to play, sleep, climb and hide in, and the companionship of another person or cat most of the day, there should be no problems.

An indoor cat will, of course, need a litter tray which is cleaned out regularly, and a scratching post. A good diet is necessary as the cat won't be able to supplement any deficiencies itself by eating herbs or prey. Some grass should be grown in a tub as cats need to nibble greenstuff to help their digestion; and they like a sunny spot to nap in.

Many pedigree cats have lived indoor lives for generations without any detriment to their health; and now, many owners are keeping their non-pedigree cats indoors too. Some become used to this from kittenhood; others adapt surprisingly well in adulthood. Some cats choose the indoor life for themselves, and should be allowed to do so.

COMMENT I have a mixture of indoor and indoor/outdoor cats. My indoor cats are perfectly happy and healthy and show no desire to go out-of-doors. My cats which are allowed out on demand only ask to be allowed out two or three times a day, and they only want to stay outside for a few minutes at a time.

I believe we overestimate the amount of time a cat wishes to spend outdoors; only if it has to supply its own food by catching prey does it need to spend more than a few minutes outside. Cats sleep for around sixteen hours a day and they prefer to do that in the security of their home.

Some cats can fear the great outdoors and may spend much of their time as high as they can climb as it makes them feel more secure

I'm worried about my cat, who walks around the house crying pitifully. She has a fluffy toy which she carries around in her mouth, making awful noises. She has only been with me a few months and has had two homes before this one. Do you think she is crying because she is unhappy?

I don't think so; I believe she is displaying maternal feelings towards her fluffy toy. You probably don't know if she has had kittens in the past, but when she walks through the house crying, she is probably calling to her young — it may sound like distress to us, but it acts like a homing beacon on kittens. Of course, such a noise could also be a cat 'calling', although it cannot be the reason in this case as your cat is neutered.

If she seems otherwise happy, don't worry about her.

TRY giving her lots of love and affection. Make sure she is well nourished, and use a good quality food to build her up.

COMMENT Just like some children, this cat was treating her toy as a security object. It is very unsettling for a cat to be moved from home to home, and her toy obviously represented her need for something unchanging in her world.

OUTCOME With plenty of affection from her owner, this cat eventually realised she had found a home for good. She settled down after a few months and although she is still very fond of her fluffy toy, it became less important to her and was no longer carried around the house.

I have a female neutered pedigree cat who is pulling her fur out in chunks. She sits down, grabs a piece of fur in her teeth and pulls it out, leaving bald patches. She also started spraying when I introduced a kitten into the household, although I keep them separate as much as possible.

Many cats develop bald patches, but few are as Phoenix-like as this one! It is unusual for cats to rip pieces of fur from their bodies, although some may overgroom themselves, licking at one spot until a bald patch appears. Overgrooming can be a sign of boredom, when a cat is not sufficiently stimulated by its environment.

Other reasons for the appearance of bald spots in the fur are: the fungal infection, ringworm; mange or eczema; or a hormone deficiency sometimes found in neutered cats, where large symmetrical bald patches appear, usually on the underside and inside of the hind legs.

In this case, the owner has seen the cat pulling the fur out itself. If boredom can be ruled out, I would surmise that this cat is easily stressed. Some pedigree cats can be quite highly strung, and the fact that she began spraying when a new kitten entered the household would seem to indicate stress. A way of easing her tensions should be sought, and anyway, it is always advisable to seek veterinary advice when bald patches appear.

I have seen my vet, who has prescribed hormone tablets. I haven't given them to my cat because I'm worried about side effects.

The pills which have been prescribed for your cat are the same as those given to breeding queens as a form of contraception — they use a synthetic hormone which prevents the queen coming into season. Some breeders have doubts about using these pills, as occasionally a queen has difficulty conceiving afterwards, but you need have no fears about side effects when giving them to a neutered cat. Indeed, they have been prescribed because of their 'side effects'.

For example, cats which are taking a course of hormones become much calmer, and in the case

57

Cats often love their 'own' children but may be nervous of others

> **My cat likes my own children, but she is never pleased to see other children. Why?**
>
> Children are sometimes too boisterous with cats. Cats, being sensible, realise this and keep out of the way. Your cat is obviously used to your children and they are used to her. But children unused to cats may be too boisterous — they may pull their tails, frighten them by making a lot of noise, and quite literally rub their fur up the wrong way. If your cat doesn't like strange children, keep them apart.

of your cat, this can only be a good thing. And if her fur is falling out (rather than being pulled out), the pills will treat the hormone imbalance which leads to this loss. Her appetite may increase while on the medication, but as long as she is not allowed to become fat, the extra nourishment should help her tensions too. Feed her several small meals a day; if she has a nap after each, she will be more relaxed on awakening.

As for the spraying, this is not unusual behaviour for a cat which feels threatened. Many people believe that females don't spray, but as you have discovered, this is a fallacy — they may be less likely to spray than a male, but will do so under stress. In fact you may be prolonging your cat's stress by keeping her apart from the kitten; she obviously knows it is in your home, and can smell it and hear it,

but she cannot find out how much of a threat it is.

So do start giving her the prescribed medication, then after a few days introduce her carefully to the kitten. She may spray again for a while, but will soon realise that a kitten is not threat, and should settle down. Having a young feline companion should also take her mind off herself; you may both find that a kitten is the best tension-reducing drug on the market.

YOU SHOULD discuss with your vet any medication he or she prescribes if you have doubts about it; that's what vets are for. You can always ask your vet for a second opinion if you are concerned about a diagnosis; or you can visit another vet for a second opinion. Then if medication *is* prescribed, give it to your cat, following the directions carefully.

Keep tense or nervous cats occupied. Regular play sessions of ten minutes each time will relax them and tire them out.

Stressed cats must receive a high quality diet and, if necessary, vitamin and mineral supplements. Brewer's Yeast is an excellent source of the B vitamins (the anti-stress vitamins), and many cats

will eat Brewer's Yeast tablets as though they are treats. There are 'nerve tonics' available in tablet form from pet stores which are specifically formulated for cats and dogs, and also homeopathic remedies for nervousness which may be worth trying. Some qualified vets use homeopathy in their practices, and there are several books available on remedies for pets.

A stressed cat can also be helped to relax by sprinkling a little of the herb catnip on the floor once a day. Susceptible cats roll in it and enjoy it, and it is perfectly harmless, although you should keep your cat indoors for half an hour afterwards to allow the effects to wear off.

OUTCOME After an initial outburst of hostility, the cat accepted her new kitten as a playmate, and they are now very fond of one another. The prescribed course of hormones had the desired effect, with the cat becoming much calmer during the course and for some months afterwards. She stopped her fur-pulling habit, though after six months it began again, but to a lesser extent. Another course of hormones rectified the problem, which several years later has not recurred.

THE PURRFECT VISITOR

My husband had been in hospital for over two months following a major stroke, when a chance remark from the Sister sparked off an idea. She was concerned to find new ways of stimulating the interest of longterm patients. Television quickly palled and many — including my husband — found it tiring to read for long spells.

'What a pity I can't bring one of the cats in to see him,' I said, and met not scandalised disapproval but a quizzical smile.

'That's a great idea. Why don't you?'

'But I thought . . . hospitals . . . germs. What about the rules?' My voice trailed away as Sister swept down the corridor, too busy to learn about my laywoman's misconceptions.

Just one hour later I was coaxing my elderly ginger boy, Thomas O'Malley, into his harness.

'Off we go to see daddy!' I said brightly, even as my confidence ebbed. 'Won't daddy be surprised?'

Thomas eyed me shrewdly, and all but shrugged his shoulders as I groped for the buckle amongst the dense fur. He brooded silently in the cat basket, but perked up as we zoomed past the vet's surgery and proceeded to comment vociferously on every gear change. By the time we arrived at the hospital car park he was peering eagerly into the darkness.

I, meanwhile, had convinced myself that the whole enterprise was misguided. Thomas would be terrified of the hospital smells; at the very least he would throw up over the unnaturally white sheets, and — worst of all — he would look at Peter as if he had never clapped eyes on him.

Once inside I let the Very Important Pussycat out of the basket and attached the lead. With tail held high the old campaigner strolled down the corridor, nodded condescendingly to the startled nurses and sniffed at a couple of particularly interesting plastic sacks.

I held my breath as I lifted him on to Peter's bed.

With a loud 'chirrup' of greeting Thomas climbed on to my husband's chest, rubbed his whiskery face against Peter's chin and settled down to sleep.

It may be a coincidence that Peter has progressed considerably since Thomas' first visit, but I don't think so. And Thomas? He knows that if that's a coincidence, the next Cruft's champion will be a ginger alleycat.

Heather Smith

Cats can have remarkable therapeutic benefits for their people

THE PSYCHOLOGY OF FOOD

Feline feeding

Nothing tells us so much about our relationship with our cats than the way we feed them. The farm cat was traditionally given a bowl of milk at milking time but was otherwise left to fend for itself, expected to live upon the vermin which it was its job to kill around the farm. The owner to whom a cat is just a cat and not part of the family throws a few table scraps into its bowl when he remembers to do so, or feeds it on bread and gravy. The caring owner compares quality and prices of prepared cat foods and also gives nutritious but inexpensive fresh food. The adoring owner whose cat is much more than a cat, feeds best chicken breasts, cod steaks and prawns.

When the gourmet petfood company Hilife commissioned leading psychologist Jane Firbank to write a psychology report on the feeding of cats, some surprising points were highlighted. Jane concluded that, for an owner, the action of feeding the cat was a crucial part of the relationship. She says:

The act of providing food is, of course, equally crucial in human relationships. Commensalism — eating together — is a vital cementing factor in social bonds, and anthropologists have theorised that the special relationship between humans and dogs and cats owes a good deal to the fact that they eat substantially the same type of food as humans and until recently lived largely on leftovers, scraps and titbits from their owners' tables.

Eating together defines the family; and this is precisely what dogs and cats do. These days the average cat is no longer dependent on table scraps, but owners still want to give their cats food of 'human' quality to evoke this sense of shared eating and shared family membership — which is why manufacturers know that it is important for their food to look and smell good

One cat demonstrating with a careful approach and a well-timed pounce that cats are less likely to be fussy feeders if there is another cat around

Good news for horse lovers

Many cat owners fear that what they are feeding their beloved pets are the remains of horses and ponies, fast dwindling whales or cute kangaroos. They needn't worry if they live in the United Kingdom.

Members of the Pet Food Manufacturers' Association account for 95 per cent of British pet food sales, and the PFMA states that none of its members uses horse, pony, kangaroo or whale meat in the manufacture of pet food.

What about the concern that your cat is depriving the third world of protein sources? According to the PFMA:

Such animal-based protein as the pet food industry uses comes almost entirely from those parts of the carcase that custom and usage dictate are unsuitable for human consumption. That material, if not used in the manufacture of pet foods, would otherwise be wasted and the rest of the carcase would be proportionately more expensive. The complex dietary, cultural and religious customs of many developing countries would rule out acceptance for human needs of much of the raw material used for pet food.

However, dedicated vegetarians point out that livestock is fed on grain, so if we raised fewer animals for their meat, there would be more grain available for people to eat.

Commercial cats

A male model of the 60s has divulged how cat food commercials were made at that time. A cat actor wouldn't eat the food it was supposed to be advertising, so the producer mixed some fish into it.

The cat preferred this dish and ate it happily. Unfortunately, it insisted on walking the wrong way to the food bowl and spoilt all the takes. So the producer tied an invisible nylon thread to the cat and dragged it across the studio to the bowl.

Thank goodness that sort of thing doesn't happen any more. . .

and have owner appeal.

Giving food — whether to people or animals — is satisfying and empowering. When the food is accepted, the feeder likewise feels accepted and has a sense of achievement. Pet therapists have found that feeding an animal is a real boost to self-esteem.

Conversely, when food is rejected, the giver also feels put down and rejected. We are all familiar with this phenomenon in a human setting but, as every cat owner knows, it also applies strongly with cats.

Feeding a cat is especially satisfying because of the nature of the food given. For reasons stemming from our hunter-gatherer past, protein is a much higher-status food than cereal or vegetables and the person who gives it feels correspondingly more powerful . . . (Even now, it is traditionally the man who brings home the bacon and rules the roast; he carves the joint and is happy to cook a barbecue even if he never sets foot in the kitchen otherwise.) Owners, therefore, get a special pleasure from feeding the high quality, pure meat or fish foods cats usually demand. Consequently, the super premium canned sector of the cat food market has seen tremendous growth.

Mealtimes with cats can often, like mealtimes with small children, turn into a power struggle. Whereas most dogs will eat anything, cats are notoriously fussy. To feed a cat successfully is often a real challenge — and the sense of achievement when the food is accepted is correspondingly great.

This is because cats often manage to turn the usual relationship with the powerful food-giver and the submissive food-

CAT NAPS

How *do* you choose a bed for a cat? One that they will sleep in? I once rushed proudly home with a cosy igloo bed for my newest arrival, Beverley, a tabby kitten. I knew a bed was called for because I live in an old, draughty place and by the time she'd finished pottering around the house in winter, the front-of-the-fire beds were all occupied.

Sure enough, I'd hardly unpacked it and put it into shape by the hearth when Beverley stepped in, turned round once and settled to sleep. She hardly left it for forty-eight hours and had 'room service' at mealtimes — her saucers on the fender. She looked for all the world like Cleopatra on her barge. The other cats, when they visited the doorway to her 'apartment', were greeted by her quiet face

and purrs; serenely, by saying nothing and nothing being said, it was understood that this was Beverley's bed.

But after all that, she decided she didn't want this little detached residence. She came out and didn't go in again. The other cats didn't want it, either. So after it had stood unused for several more days, despite my efforts to entice the others to at least take a look at the amenities therein, I brushed it surreptitiously — and took it back to the shop!

S M

Opposite:
Whatever bed you choose for a cat,
it will choose a different one

A cat caught a sparrow and was about to eat it, but the sparrow, thinking quickly, said to the cat: 'No gentleman eats until he has first washed his face.' So the cat put the sparrow down in order to wash, whereupon it flew away. Ever since, the cat has eaten first and washed afterwards.

receiver on its head. They frequently refuse food, and often remind their owners with 'gifts' such as mice that they are not actually dependent on them for food at all. Thus if anyone confers a favour in a cat-feeding situation, it is generally the cat.

Since cats are also not emotionally dependent on their owners in the way that dogs are, the result is that cat owners, unlike dog owners, can never take their cat's love for granted. Every meal is an opportunity for success — or failure. The cat plays hard to get — an effective technique for increasing motivation and attachment in any relationship.

This is why cat owners will recount with pride how fussy their cat is and boast that they have nevertheless found ways of feeding it. And it is why they expend so much thought and effort on satisfying their cat's tastes. An unfussy cat is no challenge — and no achievement.

So if you reassure a worried cat owner by observing that no healthy animal will starve itself to death in the midst of plenty, you are missing the point. What is at issue if a cat refuses its food is not the animal's health, but the owner's self-esteem.

From a psychological point of view the notorious feline fussiness is an important factor in cementing the bond between people and cats. Given that cats do not have the emotional depth and responsiveness of dogs, it may well be that if they were easier to feed they would be less valuable pets and arouse less powerful human emotions.

It is plain that the feeding relationship between cat owners and their cats has many resemblances to that between parents and children. The more the animal is seen in the light of a child, the more trouble the owner will take to pander to its tastes.

So, has Jane summed up why we become so attached to our cats? Is it true that 'if they were easier to feed they would be less valuable pets'? This does contain a great deal of truth, although I don't agree with her comment that cats are not emotionally dependent on their owners.

A great many owners 'complain' about the fussiness of their cats where food is concerned. However, it is the same sort of 'complaint' as someone saying they haven't spent an evening at home in weeks because they are invited to so many glamorous parties and functions. It isn't a complaint at all, but a source of pride; and this is immediately apparent when they are given advice on feeding their cats — because they simply don't want to know. They will continue to give their cat its preferred food because it makes them feel good to do so.

Cattery managers and vets are used to owners telling them that

At least 10 per cent of cats are overweight

their cat will 'only' eat one food. Yet so often when these cats are given another type of food, most will eat it readily. One vet was told that a cat he was keeping for several days would only eat raw fillet steak dipped in Marmite. It was religiously given this odd and expensive diet for several days, then one day was given the contents of an ordinary can of cat food. It wolfed this down with every evidence of enjoyment.

Vets don't believe that cats are fussy feeders, and have no difficulty in changing a cat's diet because they know that a cat will *not* starve to death if it doesn't eat for several days. A new food can be left in a pen, replaced daily if not eaten, and the most stubborn cats will eat it if it is the only food available, within three or four days at most; they often do so at night when no-one else is around. Owners have difficulty because they love their cats too much to see them going hungry, and give in long before the cat does.

The 'food equals love' syndrome is almost always evident when a cat has a stomach upset — often caused by overeating. Food should be withheld from a cat suffering from diarrhoea for twenty-four hours, and this is even more important when the diarrhoea has been cause by too much food in the first place. But will owners do this? No, most don't. 'He looked so miserable,' they

Cat knit

A cat-owner began to worry when her pet lost its appetite and appeared unwell. She suspected it had swallowed something unsuitable, so took it to her vet. He performed an operation — and discovered the cat had swallowed a ten-inch knitting needle. The cat made a complete recovery.

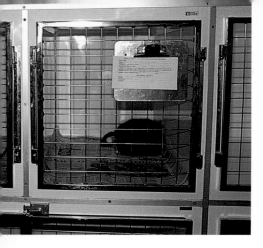

Overweight cats are usually slimmed under veterinary supervision – otherwise their diets just don't work – and may spend several weeks in veterinary pens like these

Want to attract a cat's attention? Start using the can-opener

will say, 'I just cooked him a little treat of chicken' — or prawns, or whatever. Anything to make him eat, because this increases the owner's self-esteem and gives a sense of achievement.

Vets are now noticing a 'fat cat' syndrome, and at least one practice has set up a specialised diet clinic for overweight pets; about 40 per cent of dog patients are obese, and about 10 per cent of cats. Yet cats are supposed to be 'self-regulating': according to the makers of cat food, they will not overeat and so can be allowed to eat as much as they want. Is this true?

It seems that some cat foods are unrealistically palatable, and override the cat's ability to self-regulate. Two ways of feeding are usually recommended: one is to feed a cat two or three small meals a day; the other is to leave food down at all times so the cat can eat when it wants to. In this case it will usually gorge itself for three or four days, then most will begin to regulate their intake, eating no more than they did previously. But perhaps one in ten cats will not cut down, and will eat as much as is put in front of them. Such cats become obese and require a slimming diet.

Dieting a cat is not easy, as once it has become obese, very little

Many owners forget that rabbit is a natural food for cats

food is required to maintain its current weight. Slimming diets for cats should always be carried out under veterinary supervision to ensure that the cat is not obese because of hormonal or thyroid problems, and also to ensure the success of the diet. Vets find that the most successful diets are those which take place when the cats are hospitalised and under the closest veterinary supervision — though weight loss is a slow process and obese cats may be hospitalised for six to eight weeks. There are 'F Plan' diets for cats, special weight loss diets available only from vets, which include high fibre in a canned food. Owners can use these diets at home under veterinary advice.

The average weight of a full-grown domestic cat varies between 2.7kg and 5.5kg (6lb to 12lb). However, I have seen many cats weighing between 10kg and 12.7kg (22lb to 28lb) and a few even heavier; such cats are usually immobile, unable to play (some even have difficulty in walking), and have sad, lost eyes staring out of bulbous bodies. A fat cat is very often an animal 'substitute' — be it as friend, family or child — the sole recipient of its owners' attention. Its owners are often dishonest (even to themselves) about the cause of the obesity, claiming thyroid or hormonal imbalances and insisting their cat eats little, half a can of cat food or one chicken breast a day. However, many of these cats are fed constant titbits between meals which the owners simply don't count — one 12kg (28lb) cat was regularly given packets of

Hey diddle diddle

One interpretation of why so many English hostelries are called The Cat and Fiddle is that a game called 'tip cat' (tipping or hitting a piece of wood, called a cat, with a stick) was often played at these inns while a fiddler provided musical entertainment. Another story is that the name is corrupted from the French 'Le Chat Infidèle', meaning an unfaithful cat. The 'Cat and Kittens' inns derived their names from a large pewter beer mug, called a cat, with smaller versions being called a kitten.

Mountain cat

A one-year-old black and white cat once climbed the Matterhorn, the Swiss mountain which rises to almost 15,000 feet. The cat lived with the cook at the Hotel Belvedere in Zermatt, from where many mountaineers would begin their climb. One day he followed a party which, however, he soon lost, but he spent three days climbing to the top on his own. Once at the top, he was befriended by an astonished guide, who carried him back down the mountain. The cat was named Cervinio, after the Italian name for the Matterhorn.

childrens' sweets to eat.

Part of the difficulty of dieting pets may be due to commodity size. Even if an owner knows, for example, that two-thirds of a 400g can of food is the right amount for their cat daily, they may be loathe to leave one-third of its contents overnight, so feed an entire can daily for the sake of simplicity. Another problem is bowl size. When dogs are dieted, vets recommend that owners buy a smaller bowl — people dislike the look of a large bowl with a small amount of food in the middle; they prefer giving a heaped meal in a small bowl. Unfortunately, bowl size cannot be reduced for dieting cats, because cats prefer bowls which are wider than their whiskers.

Disciplining the *owners* is the most difficult part of dieting an obese pet!

Dependence — or rather, independence — is a key word where cats are concerned. Fifteen years of dependence could become irritating or tiring, but with cats that stage is hardly ever reached — most owners suspect that their cats could fend very well for themselves if need be, and many do. Even if a cat is completely cut off from its owners, it can usually catch its own food.

A survey in the *Journal of Zoology* of cats living in an English village, collated the catches they brought home. Of eighty cats, six brought home nothing at all, while the others returned with an average of fourteen prey animals each; one brought ninety-five. Bearing in mind that these were catches *brought home* (presumably to eat later) and that many other catches were probably consumed where caught, the survey indicates that the vast majority of cats could sustain life by their own efforts.

A wild-living cat would eat a wide variety of foods, yet many owners allow their cats' fussiness to exclude all but a few, or even all but one, food. Cats which fend for themselves would eat insects, birds, mice, rats, rabbits and maybe even the occasional fish or bird's egg, as well as anything edible which they could scavenge from dustbins. Furthermore they will eat virtually *all* the different parts of the prey they catch for themselves — the brains, muscle meat and innards of birds and some of the feathers, usually leaving only the beak; and the fur, muscle meat, organs and intestines of small animals, including the vegetable matter in the stomach.

In this way they receive a varied diet, which includes meat, vegetable matter and roughage. Anyone wishing to feed their cat a 'natural' diet should study the creatures on which a cat would normally prey. For example, many cats enjoy liver, so are fed by their owners exclusively or almost exclusively on it. Cats can become addicted to it and may refuse to eat anything else — yet it is so high in vitamin A it can lead to lameness and crippling over a period of years. Study a mouse, and you will appreciate the proportion of organs to muscle meat, roughage and vegetable matter which a cat would eat if it caught its own food. A mouse's liver is tiny, and that is proportionally all a cat should be given in its total diet.

But if a cat does become hooked on a particular food, owners often give up too quickly when trying to change its eating habits. If a less palatable food is offered, it may not eat any of it and may make scratching motions around the bowl. The owner often misunderstands this behaviour, believing it is showing contempt for the offered food. In the wild, however, a cat which has eaten its fill would cover up any remaining food with vegetation by scratching around it. This is an attempt to hide it from other predators, and the cat will come back to find and eat the food when it is hungry again. So in this case, the cat is simply displaying that it is not yet hungry enough to eat the offered food, but will come back to it when it is. Usually, it doesn't have to, because most owners will immediately give in and give their cat the food it prefers, instead of holding out until their cat decides to accept the new food.

Cats will learn to eat the most surprising foods, if nothing else

Caffeineated cat

The US President, Calvin Coolidge, was a great cat-lover. It's said that he held a formal dinner at the White House where his dinner guests, unsure of their etiquette, copied every move he made. When coffee was served, the President poured half his coffee into his saucer, and his guests copied him. He added milk and sugar to the coffee in the saucer, and the guests followed suit. Then he put the saucer on the floor — for his cat.

Cats can be persuaded to eat or drink almost anything – especially if they are allowed to steal it

Opposite:
Whiskers are drawn forward in
pleasurable anticipation of an
edible treat

is offered or available. Behaviourist Zing-Yang Kuo conducted an experiment on the food habits of cats using forty-five newborn kittens. He separated them from their mothers at birth and split them into three groups; each group was then given a different type of food, first liquified, then minced, then solid. Vitamins and minerals were added, but otherwise the kittens in the first group were given nothing but soybeans, the second group only mackerel with rice, and the third group were given assorted food such as meat, fish, milk, cheese, eggs and vegetables.

After six months on these diets, the kittens were confronted with food which was new to them. It was found that the kittens on the soybean diet were unwilling to try new foods, even when very hungry. Kittens raised on the mixed diet would eat new foods readily, even when not hungry. The mackerel-fed kittens would not eat new foods either, even other types of fish, although they later became fond of canned sardines and red salmon (presumably because they too, are oily fish). The effect of these diets on the kittens' health is not recorded.

I have noticed that my own cats will eat almost anything if allowed to *steal* the food, including cooked chick peas, peppers, plain boiled potatoes, toast crusts, cooked egg whites, mayonnaise, iced current buns, bread and every conceivable vegetable. Yet if such foods are placed in their bowls, they are treated with disdain and then ignored. The answer to changing a cat's diet therefore may be to place the new food in a place where it has to be stolen before it can be eaten!

Owners spend an enormous amount of money on their cats' food. In the United Kingdom, spending on pet food is believed to be higher per animal than anywhere else in the world, and almost

Et tu?

An advert in a Somerset newspaper for a lost cat stated:
'Answers to the name of Brutus and the sound of a tin-opener.'

After a meal a cat will always
spend some time grooming itself.
This prevents any build-up of
smell from stale food which might
attract a predator

£500,000,000 — half a billion pounds — is spent on *prepared* cat food each year, most of it canned. Around 70 per cent of the average cat's diet is made up of prepared food, according to the Eruomonitor Pet Products Report; this also discovered that in the week prior to interview, 18 per cent of cat owners served fresh meat at least once, 19 per cent had served fresh fish, and 30 per cent had fed table scraps. Cat ownership is increasing, but prepared cat food sales are increasing at a much greater rate, so presumably owners are relying less on fresh food and scraps, and more on convenience cat foods. One brand is so successful that it is now the UK's largest single grocery brand.

There are a number of reasons for the growth in sales of prepared cat food. One is, of course, that busy working owners don't have much time to prepare meals so they rely more on convenience foods — for themselves as well as their pets. Another is value for money. According to the Pet Food Manufacturers' Association, the meat and bacon retail price index increased by 182 per cent between 1974 and 1987, while the price of prepared pet food increased by only 113 per cent, making it a good buy.

Other reasons may be more subtle. Powerful and expensive advertising campaigns persuade us that prepared food is what our cats want to eat — one company alone has recently spent more than £7,000,000 a year. This is half of all cat food advertising — and the company has an approximately 50 per cent market share. The two facts can hardly be unrelated.

Prepared foods are also made to look and smell attractive to the *owner* and most contain additives such as colouring and meaty scents. Therefore, three cans of different flavour but of the same brand will *look* quite different while containing the same constituents. A fish-flavoured food will be pale in colour, a lamb flavour will be a light brown and a beef flavour will be a rich, dark brown. However, the contents may be identical and may not even contain any fish, lamb or beef. In fact a cat doesn't care what a food looks like, as its colour perception is not good — but ours is, and we want a beef food to look beefy and a fish flavour to look fishy, so colourings are added to the less expensive foods to please us.

Texture is also relatively unimportant to a cat, and it will eat the hardest of dry food as readily as a sloppy food swimming in liquid. But again, texture is important to us, so foods are now made of extruded meats (*ie* slivers and scraps of meat are washed off bones and pressed together to look like meat chunks) because that is how we prefer meat to look. (The same process is used in meat pies and stews for human consumption.)

There are also foods which look like what they are, and they are deservedly popular. These are some of the gourmet, often now called super-premium, foods which contain a high proportion of the named meat — in a few cases they consist entirely of the named meat.

What does matter to a cat is smell, taste and temperature. The cat's sense of smell is more closely allied to its sense of taste than ours, and a food which smells attractive to a cat has a better chance of being eaten. Manufacturers know this and many add tempting smells to their products. But they have to find a middle line — the cat enjoys strong-smelling foods, while humans are repelled by them. Many owners have stopped feeding their cats a brand of food because they didn't like the smell of it, even though their cats enjoyed it!

Taste comes next, so manufacturers also put palatability high on their list of priorities. But palatability bears no relation to nutrition, a fact which many owners fail to understand. Just because a cat prefers one food over others does not mean that it is a better, or even a more nutritious food. For example, offer a child a stick of raw carrot and a French fry: the French fry will be chosen every time because it tastes nicer, though the stick of raw carrot is more nutritious.

The temperature of its food is very important to a cat. It prefers food which is near blood-heat, that of recently killed prey; food straight from the refrigerator may be rejected until it warms up to room temperature.

Always remember that cats don't know what is best for them, and will usually go for the food which is most appealing. Sometimes this will in fact contain pure, good protein sources, but often additives will have been used to *make* the food be more appealing.

Although many health-conscious people have tried to steer clear of additives in their own food in recent years, they have not always done the same with respect to their pets. Possibly this is due to lack of knowledge of a cat's nutritional needs, and to the success of pet food advertising. Yet cats which are intolerant to the additives in prepared foods can become aggressive or hyperactive, and this can create enormous problems — and a change of food can lead to a complete change of behaviour.

Always read the labels on the can if additives are a concern. Manufacturers who do use additives are coy about saying so, although they may state that permitted colourings have been used. Manufacturers who *don't* use additives will say so proudly; their food may cost a little more, but cat owners appear not to be worried by this. A survey by a cat magazine asked readers what their most important criterion was when choosing cat food: 54 per cent said it was nutritional value, while only 25 per cent said cost. Only 7 per cent queried the use of additives — which may mean that 93 per cent are unaware that additives are used.

If anyone coughs or sneezes while my cat is in the room, he rubs and grinds his teeth together. Any idea why?

Perhaps coughs and sneezes remind him of the noises of prey animals! A cat can be seen to chatter its teeth if it can see or hear prey which is out of reach. For example, if a cat is indoors and sees birds through a window, it will chatter. What it is doing is making the shape of a killing bite — the bite it would use to sever the spinal column of its prey — but because there is no prey between the teeth, they chatter together. Sometimes this is accompanied by growling or moaning.

Feeding, fads and fussiness

Feeding pets should be one of the easiest things we have to do, but where the cat is concerned this isn't always the case. Cats have a reputation for fussiness, yet it isn't true to say they are fussy creatures. They have a tendency to hold out for a more palatable food, and usually this tendency is more developed than in their owners, who will give in quickly to pleading miaows. Cats are highly intelligent, and they quickly realise that if they dislike a certain food they can persuade their owners to provide a tastier one just by not eating for an hour or two.

There are other dimensions to feeding a cat, though. The size of a cat's bowl, where it is sited, the temperature of the food, all affect how easy or difficult it is to get a cat to eat what you want it to eat.

And what is the best food for a cat anyway? Is it the one it wants to eat — or the one you want it to eat? I hope the following questions and answers will help you decide.

When I feed my cat he takes the food out of the bowl and pushes it all over the room. Why does he do this?

His feeding bowl may be narrower than his whiskers. Cats' whiskers are very sensitive and they hate them touching the sides of their food bowls. Try a larger bowl, and if your cat is longhaired, you will need a particularly large bowl as these have longer whiskers than shorthaired cats.

He may not like the smell of his bowl. Feeding bowls should certainly be kept clean, but they shouldn't smell of washing-up liquid, detergent or disinfectant, as these repel cats. Sterilise bowls in a solution of household bleach (sodium hypochlorite) and water, and rinse thoroughly.

Don't place his bowl too close to a litter tray; Cats don't like to eat near where they eliminate.

When a female cat has kittens, she may begin to take food out of her bowl before eating it, as if intending to carry it to her young. Others will carry their food away to prevent their kittens eating it.

YOU SHOULD provide a larger bowl.

Ensure it is clean and free from smell.

Place it at some distance (preferably in a different room) from any litter tray.

COMMENT Some cats have an allergic reaction to plastic and develop bald spots on their chins. Their plastic feeding bowls should be changed to china or stainless steel bowls.

How can I stop my cat from sitting behind the family at mealtimes and trying to grab the food out of our mouths?

Apart from closing the door with your cat on the other side? Honestly, that' the easiest way if your cat has developed bad table manners — ideally, he shouldn't have been allowed to develop them in the first

---

Is there any way of stopping cats from bringing dead mice into the house?

I don't believe, as has often been said, that cats bring mice into the house as gifts for their owners — I think they're a little more self-serving than that. Their home is their safe place, their den, where they hope they can eat their meal in peace and won't have to defend it from strange cats. It is therefore difficult to discourage them from doing so.

If you have a garden shed or greenhouse where your cat could go for his meal, preferably with a high shelf from which he can see intruders approaching, he may use that instead of your living-room as his larder.

place. It may seem cute when a little kitten jumps on the table and fights for food, but imagine your reaction when that kitten weighs 5 to 7kg (10 to 15lb) and develops an expert left hook.

It's too late to wait until your kitten becomes an adult before chastising him about his eating habits. He must learn at an early age that cats are fed from their bowls, and that he must not cast covetous eyes on your food.

Some kittens are much greedier than others, and those which refuse to behave in the dining-room must learn that bad manners equal banishment. If you are soft-hearted, you could put your cat in the kitchen with a meal of his own; though remember, if you are feeding him three times a day, you should feed him his daily ration divided by three at each meal, *not* extra calories at a third meal.

Cats living wild have to scrap for every mouthful. Your cat doesn't because you provide for him, and you are entitled to lay down the rules. Lay them down firmly.

YOU SHOULD train your cat from kittenhood not to steal at the table. If he persists, ban him from the dining-room at mealtimes. You aren't being harsh; if he lived with other cats, good table manners would be beaten into him — rapidly!

COMMENT I'm constantly amazed at the table manners which otherwise intelligent people allow their cats. At one dinner party I attended, the house cats were allowed to jump on the table as soon as the guests had finished their main course and lick the plates. Our host seemed to think that because his cats had waited until we had finished before jumping up, it proved they were well trained. In fact it is very unhygienic to allow cats to lick plates unless the plates are sterilised afterwards — which they never are. Apart from which, there are many dangers to the cats if the meal contains bones or something on which they could choke.

Longhairs have a quiet, placid intelligence

When my cat finishes eating, if there is food left in the bowl, he scratches the floor all around it. Why does he do this?

The big cats can be observed scratching around their kill when they have eaten their fill; they are simply hiding the food from other predators by scratching leaves and grass over it. This is yet another example of the deep-rooted instincts of our domestic pets which go all the way back to the wild. Your cat believes he is storing up his food for later, and the fact that vinyl flooring or carpeting is an unsuitable medium won't prevent his behaviour. A wild cat might make a kill once every few days; after eating its fill, it would want to save the remainder for when prey is scarce.

Some cats try to hide their food when the weather is hot: generally, cats don't like to eat during hot weather, so they are simply trying to keep it for later.

YOU SHOULD feed your cat less at each meal, especially during hot weather when meals should be given first thing in the morning and last thing at night.

Refrigerate leftover canned food. If you don't wish to do so, place a sheet of newspaper over the food. This will keep your cat happy and the flies away.

My Siamese cat has an unusual habit. He eats dishcloths! And I used to hide clothes, towels and dishcloths away from him. Now, however, I've had to give in to him — when he has a meal he will eat a mouthful of cat food, then a mouthful of old sweater. I'm worried about this as it must be dangerous. Is he crazy?

Not at all. In fact, fabric-eating is not uncommon among Siamese and similar breeds. It must be one of the best kept secrets of our age, and every owner with this problem seems to think he or she is the only one with a fabric-eating cat. Such people often believe *they* must be at fault in some way, and hesitate to ask for help; or if they do, little is forthcoming.

I have heard of hundreds of cats with this problem — I know of one which ate a quarter of the coverlet on a king-size bed, and another which ate most of a three-piece suite.

Yet the solution may be simple, and has been known for forty years or more. Some of the Siamese and similar breeds seem to have a high requirement for fibre in their diet; a cat living wild would receive plenty, for it would eat the skin, bones, and all of its prey, and in the case of birds, would swallow some feathers, too. The wild cat would also have unlimited access to grass and herbs which it would eat at will.

Our modern-day cats, however, are often kept entirely indoors (especially the pedigree breeds) and may have no access to greenstuff at all. And the food we feed our cats is often soft and lacking in fibre, too. So to solve this problem, try increasing the fibre content of the diet. Add a pinch of bran to each meal, increasing the amount as long as it doesn't cause diarrhoea. Inspect the contents of the litter tray, and adjust the amounts of bran as necessary.

Fibre can be added to the diet in

The pleading look outside the kitchen door makes many owners believe in cupboard love

other forms, too. Many cats enjoy cooked vegetables (including cooked potato), greens of all types, cauliflower, asparagus and mushrooms can all be added and many cats adore them. Chop up wholewheat toast or crusts; and many cats will enjoy a cereal for breakfast, though moisten with water or a mixture of evaporated milk and water which is less likely to cause diarrhoea. Many Siamese cats have a milk intolerance and react to the lactose in cow's or goat's milk, so this should not be given at all.

YOU SHOULD try adding fibre to your cat's diet — as much as he will eat without ill-effects.

Lock away all materials, if possible, until the problem is under control. It is very dangerous for a cat to eat fabric and could lead to a blocked intestine which would require surgery.

If your cat starts to chew something which cannot be locked away, spray it with a repellent spray. Unpleasant-tasting but harmless repellents are used by vets after operations sprayed over the wound to prevent the animal licking it; these can be purchased from your vet.

Ensure your cat is otherwise in good health and that worming has been carried out regularly. Give a hairball preparation as needed, especially during the spring moult.

While weaning your cat off fabric, keep him occupied. These cats are highly intelligent and become easily bored, and boredom can lead to destructive behaviour. If your cat begins to chew something he shouldn't, distract him with play.

COMMENT In my personal experience of raising part-Siamese kittens, I found they would use their mouths constantly from a very early age. At three weeks, one kitten started to suck its paper bedding; I changed this to a manmade fur fabric specifically made as pet bedding and the sucking ceased. However, they did not want to stop suckling, even when the mother had no milk; they had to be kept apart most of the time after the age of two months, and discouraged from suckling when with her by a gentle tap with a newspaper. Most sensible mother cats do their own discouraging; suckling three-month-old kittens can be painful and the mother will usually run away or give them a clout.

OUTCOME It can take a long time to wean a cat from fabric-eating, but with the addition of more fibre to its diet and extended periods of play with its owner, this cat is causing less of a problem. His owner still has to be vigilant and ensure that teacloths and towels are kept out of reach.

Is it true that a cat's affection is only cupboard love? My cat always follows me every time I go into the kitchen.

Yes, but does she follow you into the living-room, or the bedroom, too? The cat's reputation for cupboard love is an unfair one. Obviously any intelligent creature is going to become close to its provider of comfort and food, and this is its owner's role. The owner takes over from a kitten's mother when they acquire that kitten, and the kitten transfers its affection to its new human 'mum'.

At two or three months, a kitten is a selfish little creature and will demonstrate a degree of cupboard love. But if it learns that its new owner is kind, it becomes attached to the person, not the food source. Adult cats become very loyal to considerate owners, and may even refuse all food if their person is away from home. They do not automatically transfer allegiance to the holiday cat-sitter, as they would if they were interested only in food.

Certainly cats may follow their owners into the kitchen, but this is not always in the selfish hope of being fed. The same cats will follow them from room to room because they want to be with their person. As I write this, five cats are spread sleeping across the settee in my study and a sixth cat is purring on my lap. They know they are never fed in this room; they are here because I am here, and I flatter myself that they want my company.

Some cats end up with a weight problem because their owners believe that their miaowing means they want to be fed. Yet, very often, they are just asking for attention — a stroke, a fuss, or a few minutes of play.

COMMENT If a cat demonstrates no interest in its owner except at feeding times, it is more likely that the owner is at fault than the cat.

Cats which live in a domestic situation are more vocal than wild-living cats and learn to reinforce requests for food by stretching out towards it

Some owners still believe that cats are so independent that they have no use for people so they treat their cat accordingly. They will feed it and provide a home, but they give no love, warmth or companionship — and then they wonder why the cat accepts the food without apparent gratitude! With a cat, you will get out of the relationship *exactly* what you are prepared to put into it.

My cat is a very fussy eater and won't eat cat food. I have to buy him shellfish to eat! What can I do?

The easy answer is to not allow him to become fussy or faddy to begin with. From kittenhood, accustom him to the food which you want him to eat, because it is rare to find a fussy kitten.

Many owners fall into the same trap: if they put down food for their cats and it isn't eaten immediately, they assume there must be something wrong with it, and replace it with a different food. However, this not only confuses the cat but he will soon realise that if he waits

Fasting

Few owners fast their pets nowadays, but it benefits an adult, healthy pet a great deal. Fasting helps the digestive system cleanse itself of impurities, and gives the organs a chance to rest. In its natural state, a cat would be obliged to go hungry on those days when it caught nothing (though a cat which is sick or has been injured will be uninterested in food). A once-weekly, one-day fast will leave a healthy cat with a shining coat and looking in the peak of condition.

Fasting is very helpful if you wish to change your cat's food to one it doesn't like so much. One or two days without offering any food at all will encourage acceptance of any food which is offered. However, cats should not be fasted unless they are healthy adults. Queens in kitten or lactating should not be fasted, neither should kittens, or sick or old cats (unless they choose not to eat). Any cat which refuses to eat should be seen by a vet.

Choose one fast day per week and keep to that day — make it a regular routine. Ensure that there is always a fresh supply of clean water, but give nothing else: no milk, treats or titbits at all for twenty-four hours. Tell your neighbours not to feed your cat on fast days if it goes out of doors.

Most cats adapt well to a fast day. Greedy cats will continue to cry for food — but they do that even on non-fast days. Cats which are not greedy accept a one-day fast without complaint.

On the day after fast day, feed the usual amount, but in two or three small meals.

long enough, something more appetising will be placed in front of him. There are times when a cat won't want to eat everything it is given immediately. In hot weather, appetite is depressed and cats may only eat first thing in the morning and last thing at night, when it is cooler. Don't worry if this happens, and don't try to tempt your cat's appetite — in this instance he knows what is best for himself.

The most palatable food (*ie* the food your cat likes best) isn't always the best for your cat, so choose your catfood carefully in the beginning and don't change it, unless it causes physical symptoms such as diarrhoea.

There are very rare instances of cats being allergic to red meat and living on a diet of fish and chicken. However, if your cat is not being sick or suffering from diarrhoea, it is more likely that he is just plain fussy. A few cats have an undeserved reputation for fussiness because they have small appetites and are unable to eat much at one time. They should either have access to their food all day or be fed four or five small meals a day instead of two larger ones.

One trick to get your cat to eat the food you want him to eat is to let him 'steal' it. Look how cats will thoroughly enjoy unattractive food such as dry bread crusts if they

steal it from a plate when their owners' backs are turned. So keep a plate specifically for your cat, fill it with your chosen cat food and turn your back. You may be surprised at how quickly it will disappear!

Shellfish is not a balanced diet for your cat, and he will become ill if he eats nothing else. Nutritionists have spent many years developing complete catfoods, and these supply all the known nutritional needs of the cat; so do try to encourage your cat to eat a more balanced diet.

YOU SHOULD change your cat's diet gradually; in this case, mince

---

LETTER TO A LOST CAT

My dear Snowey,

You've been missing now for three weeks and my hopes of seeing you again are getting thinner. I don't know how I am going to cope without you. Every corner of the house and every tree in the garden are haunted by your presence. I see you everywhere and can still hear your loving purr.

I cry every night and I cry in the morning and cry when I come home and you are not there to welcome me back. Our family is not complete without you. I wonder if your life is lost? Thinking that you may still be alive, but suffering, destroys me.

What evil hands can do this to a lovely pet like you? Always obedient, always friendly, playful and so comforting when no-one was there to talk to. Many people loved you and yet you are gone, and I don't know how to get you back.

I pray you are well and I would not mind if someone made you more happy than I did. I'm crying as I write and my letter is soaked with tears. I am alone and there is no-one to talk to. No-one can understand how big the pain is.

Only a miracle could bring you back now, and that's what I'm praying for. You and Blackie, your best friend, disappeared together; you were always together, almost inseparable. I hope you are still together — at least you'll have each other.

I want to think of you as you were the last time I saw you climbing up the tree in the front garden.

I want to believe you are still happy, but I am so afraid that you are not, and that hurts so much it has become unbearable. I cannot stop thinking of the terrible things thieves do to animals and it is breaking my heart. I am taken over by a total sorrow; so ashamed to be part of the human race.

I send my love to Snow and Blackie. I will never forget you.

All my love,

Georgina Rimmer

Mrs Rimmer offered a £1,000 reward for Snowey's return but, six months later, neither he nor his friend Blackie, who disappeared at the same time, have been found.

the shellfish and mix it thoroughly with a canned catfood; try one of the fishy flavours as that is what he seems to enjoy. Over a period of weeks, gradually decrease the amount of shellfish in the food until you are left with none at all.

Or you could put your cat on a two-day fast, then offer a new food. An occasional short fast benefits a healthy cat and leads to easier acceptance of new food.

Ignore those pleading looks. Your cat doesn't know he is damaging his health by eating nothing but shellfish.

Do try new formulations of catfoods which come on the market — even the fussiest cat will have a particular favourite, and try different flavours, too.

Try the 'gourmet' brands which come in small containers. Although more expensive, they usually contain a higher percentage of protein than 'cheaper' brands, so your cat will eat less of them, and are delicious enough for the fussiest cat. Some of them consist entirely of various types of fish, including even some shellfish which should suit your cat, and are ideal for weaning cats off faddy diets. You will have to shop around, because not every supermarket or petstore sells every brand.

COMMENT Food fads can be extremely worrying, especially when foods such as liver are involved. Liver is extremely high in vitamin A and some cats become addicted to it, refusing to eat anything else — it may take several years, but this will result in distorted bones, lameness, deposits in the liver and kidney, tooth problems and stiffness. Surgery may be required to remove bony outgrowths.

OUTCOME This cat was definitely 'trying it on'. Then his owner tried mixing the shellfish with a fishy cat food, which he left until it was eaten — which it was. She simply had to steel herself for a short time to ignore pleading looks and miaows.

My cat won't eat cheap cat food, only the more expensive kind. How can I persuade her to eat a cheaper brand?

Everyone's idea of 'cheap' is different and, in fact, this particular brand is in the medium price range. It is an everyday cat food which is one of the many sold in 400g tins containing meat and meat by-products, and sometimes soy or cereal, rather than the small containers of gourmet foods which cost more but contain more of the named meat.

Choose your cat's everyday food carefully by reading the label to see what it contains. Most canned foods have a protein content of about 8 to 10 per cent which is perfectly adequate for a cat's needs. Sometimes the foods contain soy or cereal products which add to the protein content, but it is a lower quality protein than that derived from meat.

YOU SHOULD allow your cat to continue with her chosen diet. She is demonstrating a fair degree of intelligence!

COMMENT Compare prices carefully when shopping for cat food, and for the average adult cat, look for a food relatively high in protein and low in ash (minerals). Start at

Cats have different nutrient requirements to dogs and shouldn't be fed on dog food – blindness can result

the bottom end of the range of foods which derive all their protein from animal sources; if your cat won't eat it, work your way up the scale. Don't do what many owners do and work *down* the price range from the top, as your cat won't like it. At the top end of the everyday food market you may be paying several pence per tin for advertising and promotion, not for a better quality food. When shopping for a gourmet food, do the same thing. Most expensive is not necessarily the best.

Dog food is so much cheaper than cat food that I've started feeding my cat on dog food. He loves it, so we're both happy.

Possibly not for long. There's a very good reason why cat food is more expensive than dog food: cats have higher nutrient requirements than dogs. For example, there is an amino acid called taurine which dogs can manufacture in their own bodies; cats can't, however, so their food has to provide all they require.

Without sufficient taurine, a cat

This cat is asking to be given an edible treat. The ears are up, whiskers drawn forward and the pleading miaow is reinforced by the raised paw

Opposite below:
It may be just a toy ball but the cat's claws are gripping it firmly as it would grip a prey animal before making the killing bite

will suffer progressive retinal atrophy — over a period of years it will become blind. Taurine is also essential to keep a cat's heart healthy and to ensure healthy reproduction. Meat and shellfish are the best sources of taurine; vegetables are not a good source, and no cat will remain healthy for long on a basic (*ie* without supplements) vegetarian diet — although 'vegetarian' cats given free access to the outdoors may supplement their diet to some extent by the animals they catch. A supplement is now manufactured which when added to food is said to provide all the nutrients a vegetarian cat requires for good health.

Pet foods are specifically formulated to contain all the known nutritional requirements *of the animal they are made for,* and should only be fed to that species.

YOU SHOULD never feed your cat solely or mainly on dog food. With such a wide range of cat foods available, there is no need to do so.

If you have been feeding such a diet, change it immediately and arrange a veterinary check-up for your cat. Retinal degeneration is not obvious to an owner until the damage has occurred: once it has, it is irreversible.

My cat adores goldfish food. He climbs up to the goldfish tank and eats if off the surface. My husband says he's really after the fish but I know he isn't. Will it do him any harm? And why should he eat their food?

Because it is so delightfully smelly and tasty, and cats are attracted to strong-smelling, strong-tasting foods. Goldfish food consists of fish and their derivatives, cereal, yeasts, algae, molluscs, crustaceans, fats and oils — all foods which cats love. Stealing the occasional pinch of fish food will do your cat no harm at all.

Many worried owners have asked me about peculiarities in their cats' diets. I've listed some here, but no doubt will hear of many others from readers!

DON'T WORRY if your cat eats *in moderation* mushrooms (raw or cooked), *cooked* asparagus, corn on the cob, cauliflower, carrots, parsnips, or peeled potatoes, spaghetti bolognese, macaroni cheese or any other cooked pasta, bread, toast, cheese or yogurt. Goldfish food will do no harm and neither will stealing a little of the dog's food occasionally. None of these will harm your cat as long as they do

not form the major part of your cat's diet.

YOU SHOULD restrict your cat's intake of liver and other offal, ice cream, peas, beans or other pulses. Cats can't digest the cellulose shell of many pulses so, if they are fed, they should be mashed or puréed.

DON'T EVER LET your cat eat raw potatoes, raw fish or chocolate; do not give him dog food on a regular basis.

I have two cats, one male and one female. The male cat rushes to his food and bolts it down, but the female always takes her time. Why should there be such a difference?

It is natural for an animal to eat its food as quickly as possible. If it lived wild, it would have to eat as much as it could before the food was stolen by another animal — in the case of the domesticated cat, before the food was stolen by a more dominant cat.

Possibly your female cat is more dominant than your male, which can happen if both cats are neutered, and especially if the female has had kittens before being neutered. The male would therefore eat as fast as possible before she lays claim to his food.

Alternatively, it may be that your male cat is nearer to his wild roots than your more 'civilised' female. She possibly realises that food is a regular affair in your household and that there is no need to rush.

YOU COULD try feeding them in separate rooms. They must, of course, have separate bowls.

If a cat seems anxious about his food supply, you could feed him smaller meals, more often. Gulping food down rapidly can lead to swift regurgitation!

I've heard that cats are self-regulating and won't eat more food than necessary. So I've been feeding my cat on demand. Now she's getting fat. Is she unusual?

No, she isn't. Many cats, given unlimited food, will eat as much as possible because they retain that instinct which makes them unsure of their next meal; so many cats will overeat if given the opportunity to do so. Another problem is that some of the foods we give our cats are so palatable that they override any ability for self-regulation. It is often the pet food manufacturers who suggest feeding ad lib . . . They might, of course, be thought to have a vested interest.

An adult cat requires approximately 350 kilocalories per day, although this amount varies according to the metabolism of each individual cat and its age. The amount can treble or quadruple in the case of a lactating female. As pet foods don't usually give information about calorific values on the labels, write to the manufacturer of your chosen food and ask for it.

A good rule of thumb is to give your cat as much as it can comfortably eat at one sitting, without its sides bulging outwards — probably about one-third to one-half of a 400g tin. If this is too much, cut down the amount for the next meal. Feed this amount twice a day, but if your cat begins to put on fat, cut it down again.

Pregnant females should be allowed to eat as much as they wish as long as they don't put on *fat,* in three or four or even five small meals a day. Lactating females should be fed as much and as often as they want, which may be five or even six times a day.

YOU SHOULD discover the calorific value of the food you feed your cat and measure it out carefully. Feed less if your cat puts on fat; feed more if your cat starts to become thin.

Don't feed on demand, except pregnant or lactating females. Have regular mealtimes, preferably twice a day.

If your cat becomes badly overweight, dieting is a slow process because it doesn't take much food to maintain a cat at that weight. Fat cats should be slimmed under veterinary supervision — there are special high fibre feline diets, but these are only available from vets.

COMMENT Almost all cats in the western world are slightly overweight, and an enormous number are downright fat. Try the feline fat test: lift a fold of skin from your cat's belly. You should feel just skin and fur. If you feel fat, your cat is a little overweight. If a cat's ribs are well covered with flesh and the ridge of the backbone is not prominent, then your cat is not too thin. I have a friend whose cat's physique is perfect and the cat is fit, active and shining with health. Yet he is always being told in shocked tones that his cat is 'all skin and bone' and he should feed it more. The truth is that many of us have forgotten what a slim and healthy cat *should* look like.

My cat only wants to eat dry food and I'm sure this isn't good for his health. How can I get him to eat tinned food?

Some dry cat foods were implicated in a certain incidence of Feline Urological Syndrome, which presumably led to fears such as yours. Part of the problem was a high level of magnesium in the foods, but manufacturers claim to have decreased this sufficiently now.

Dry foods are complete foods, although the fact that they are sometimes referred to as 'biscuits' leads some owners to assume they are an additional meal. However, as long as the brand is chosen carefully and the cat drinks sufficient water, cats can live entirely on dry foods and thrive on them.

Dry foods contain only about 10 per cent water (as opposed to around 75 to 80 per cent in canned or fresh food) so your cat should drink more water. However some

don't, so watch the water level in your cat's drinking bowl—it should go down noticeably, and if it doesn't, try another brand. Vets sell carefully formulated dry foods which cats accept readily and which do not cause health problems.

Moisture in food is important to cats — prey animals, their 'natural' food, have a high natural moisture content. If dry food is fed, the moisture must be replaced by drinking water (not milk).

YOU SHOULD always make sure your cat has a bowl of clean water to drink. If your cat eats dry food but doesn't drink much, add water or gravy to the food and allow it to soak in before giving it to your cat. Water or gravy can also be added to 'semi-moist' foods if you feel it is necessary, for example when feeding an older cat.

A few pieces of dry food each day are good for the teeth and gums, so give a little dry food to cats fed mainly on tinned food.

OUTCOME This cat switched readily to a different brand of dry food, which did encourage him to drink.

COMMENT Many owners are impressed by the high protein levels in dry foods, which appear to be much higher than that of canned foods. However, the protein content of pet foods is listed on a dry matter basis: approximately 30 per cent in dry foods will equate to approximately 8 per cent in a canned food, depending on how much moisture that food contains.

I have two cats, both two years old. I feed them each the same amount of food, yet one is fat and one is skinny. Why?

Cats' metabolisms differ, just as ours do, and the amount of food which will keep one cat slim will make another cat fat. First of all, ensure that your fat cat isn't stealing from your thin cat — feed them in separate rooms if necessary. Also

make sure that your neighbours aren't feeding your fat cat — some cats are accomplished beggars. Or could your cat be taking food from dustbins? Some do, and it is a very dangerous practice.

Otherwise, feed your fat cat a little less and your thin cat a little more: *every* cat needs a different amount of food to maintain it at its correct weight. After a few months, you should begin to notice a difference in their figures.

COMMENT These cats are young, and their figures are most likely the result of differing metabolisms which vary from cat to cat and can even vary between kittens of the same litter. Older cats should be inspected by a vet if they begin to lose or gain weight, as it may be a symptom of thyroid deficiency, kidney problems, or some other illness.

When I'm on holiday, a relative comes in to feed my cat. However, she's threatening not to come in any more because my cat won't eat while I'm away and she worries about it. Would I be better placing my cat in a cattery?

If someone is willing to come in, this is usually a better option than a cattery. Although the standards of most catteries are extremely high, it is inevitably stressful for the cat, who loses not only its beloved owner but its territory as well. There is also a slight risk of cross-infection if another cat in the cattery falls ill.

So ask your relative to persevere. Cats *do* miss their owners while they are away, and one of the first signs of this is a reluctance to eat. However, no cat will starve to death in a week or even a fortnight — a healthy cat can apparently survive *six weeks* without any food at all!

Besides, your cat is probably eating something — although possibly not as much as she eats while you are at home. So tell your relative not to worry; if she continues to put food down, your cat

will eat it when she is hungry. She could also try feeding something particularly delicious once a day as a treat — although you run the risk that your cat might not want to switch back to her old food when you return!

It will help if your relative could find time to play with your cat, and spend a while stroking and fussing over it. Cats do become lonely — for human and feline company — and if it is an only cat and an indoor cat, it won't receive the companionship it needs in one or two short visits a day. The single indoor cat *might* be happier in a cattery; these are run by people who are quite familiar with the 'won't eat' syndrome, and the cats do usually manage to force down a few mouthfuls of the food which is left in the pen with them. They also have the advantage of seeing other cats, and having the attention of the cattery staff. Eating is rarely a problem in a well-run cattery.

My cat is twelve years old and seems to have difficulty eating. What should I do?

It depends on the nature of the difficulty. Some older cats find it awkward to bend down to their food bowls if these are placed on the floor because their muscles are stiff. If this is the problem, raise both food and water bowls to head height; they can be placed on a low platform or even on a couple of bricks.

If the difficulty is with chewing, see your vet. A major problem with elderly cats is gingivitis, caused when tartar builds up on the teeth where they enter the gums; it can lead to inflammation of the gums when bacteria enter the tooth sockets, resulting in severe pain and eventual loss of teeth.

Older cats need extra liquid to help their kidneys filter waste products. If your cat seems to find the food you provide too dry, add water to make it sloppy.

Remember that older cats need less protein than younger cats: too

much protein makes elderly kidneys work too hard. Add carbohydrate to every elderly cat's diet; this can be in the form of anything which your cat has shown a preference for over the years — bread, cooked pasta, cooked potato, cooked rice. The proportion should be up to one-third carbohydrate to two-thirds of meat.

YOU SHOULD make eating easier for your old cat. Keep his teeth clean and his bowls at a convenient height.

Regular veterinary check-ups will reveal gingivitis, if present.

Make sure that your older cat has as much liquid as he requires.

Always add carbohydrate to an older cat's diet, even if he or she shows no signs of old age, beginning at eight to ten years and continuing throughout the rest of its life.

If you take out pet health insurance, check that it will cover your pet into old age. Some schemes stop as soon as your cat is eight or ten years old, others will cover your cat for life — as long as the scheme is started *before* a certain age.

My fourteen-year-old cat is a fussy eater and will only eat semi-moist foods. I'm worried about this as she also drinks a lot.

When a cat is older, it is often easier to give her the food she wants to eat, but alter it to suit her circumstances. Cats don't much like having a favourite food changed, and older cats like it even less. Give her semi-moist foods if that is all she will eat, but add liquid to her meals in the form of water, gravy or meat or fish stock. Try to add some carbohydrate to her meals, mixed well in, if she will accept it. Semi-moist food is quite high in protein, and older cats need less.

Many older cats drink a lot, and this can be an early sign of kidney disease. Take your cat for a veterinary check-up if she hasn't had one recently.

YOU SHOULD take an older cat to the vet for a check-up if she begins to drink or eat more, lose or gain weight.

Add more carbohydrate to her food in the form of bread, cooked potato, rice or pasta.

Many of the more slender breeds, such as the Rex, are surprisingly greedy!

Empty coffers

A cat magazine received a letter from a cat club which said: 'Please include details of our new club in your magazine. We will eventually be spending a little money on advertising but at the moment there is nothing in the kitty. . . '

CATS AND KITTENS

Life, love and birth

The owner of a calling cat can open the door one day to find a congregation of tomcats lined up patiently outside

Many people don't realise that the kittens born to one feline mother in one litter can each have a different father: the sexually mature female (known as a queen) is an induced ovulator — that is, when sexually receptive, she will ovulate in response to each act of mating. It is also relatively rare for a female cat to mate and *not* conceive. This has obvious survival value, because if she mates with different toms and conceives with each one, it means that each litter consists of kittens from a wide gene pool — should one tom pass on defective genes, the other kittens (having different fathers) will be unaffected, so the chances of raising at least a proportion of each litter are increased.

The average litter size is around four, although the first is usually smaller, with perhaps two or three kittens. It is believed that four eggs are usually released, although not all may become fertilised. Sometimes many more eggs are released, resulting in much larger litters — the largest known was one of nineteen born to a Burmese cat, of which fifteen survived.

Oestrus can occur in the female cat as early as four or five months of age, especially in the Siamese and in other foreign breeds. Oestrus is usually referred to as 'calling' because of the noise the queen makes; it is also referred to as 'coming into season' or 'being on heat'. Although a Foreign-type female can be sexually mature (although not physically mature) at four months, other purebreds — most notably some Longhairs — will not begin to call until ten or twelve months, or even later. Non-pedigree cats will usually (but not always) start to call the first spring after they are six months old.

Duration and strength of calling varies between individual cats and breeds. Some females hardly appear to be calling at all; only the interest they arouse in entire (un-neutered) male cats demonstrates their condition. Entire toms can scent a female in oestrus

over a distance of several miles, and the owner of a queen in oestrus may open her door one day to find a whole congregation of tomcats lined up patiently outside.

For inexperienced owners, the first sign of oestrus in their females can be frightening, and the body gyrations which accompany the call can lead them to assume that their cat is badly hurt. Every vet has had numerous calls from worried owners who think their cat has broken her back or legs — in fact, the cat is not in pain at all, although she may howl loudly and roll on the ground. Some cats will push themselves along the ground on their chest, with their rear raised in the air. Others, when stroked along their back, will raise their rear into this position — the necessary position for mating.

Other cats are more genteel, and an unobservant owner might not even spot the signs of oestrus. Some cats may not be very vocal, and may just roll on the ground and behave a little more

First litters usually consist of two or three kittens although experienced mothers may have four or five

Scent will advertise a cat's sexual status to another cat

Rolling on the ground may be the first sign of oestrus

affectionately. But most queens will become restless and try to slip out of doors in search of a mate. Calling can take the form of loud and strident calls, especially at night, and the queen will lick her vulva frequently and roll energetically on the ground.

The female becomes interesting to the male several days before she becomes interested in him. Changes in body scents herald the approach of oestrus, but during this time the female is not receptive to the male and will spit and cuff at him. Only when the oestrus actually begins will she show any interest, and may then pursue him keenly.

The call will last for four or five days, or up to a week, and if the queen is not mated, she will call again within the month. A few cats, if unmated for several calls, will continue to call non-stop for a month or more. It is damaging to a queen's health to allow her to call and remain unmated over more than a few periods of oestrus, as it can lead to the development of ovarian cysts. Pedigree queens, whose matings are planned, will not usually be mated until at least their third call to allow their bodies to mature as much as possible before kittening. After kittening, the queen will be left to call at least two or three times before another mating is arranged. Theoretically, it would be possible for a queen to have four or five litters of kittens each year, but so much kitten-birth would exhaust any cat. Cats whose matings are arranged are restricted by caring owners to one or, at most, two litters per year.

Many pedigree cats will call all year round; non-pedigree cats usually have a dormant period from about October to December

This demonstrates how a calling cat will raise her rump in the air to allow mating

or January. This may be due to the decreased light levels of winter and, again, has obvious survival value — a cat which mated in November would give birth to her kittens in January when their chances of survival would be severely decreased. It is unusual to find non-pedigree kittens for sale before April in the UK, although pedigree kittens are often available year-round — their mothers, living indoors, are less affected by light levels. Early spring and late summer are peak times for mating.

Male cats are know as 'tomcats' when they are entire (*ie* not neutered) non-pedigree cats, and 'stud cats' when they are pedigree cats chosen for mating. Entire cats are also thought to be governed by reproductive cycles; although they are capable of mating at any time of year. But many stud owners report their stud cats to be uninterested in their 'work' at certain times, especially in mid-winter, and sometimes only the presence of an enthusiastically wooing female can overcome their reluctance.

Tomcats don't enjoy the same advantages as pampered stud cats, who have female cats presented to them and don't have to fight for the privilege of mating. Tomcats *have* to fight, not so much for 'ownership' of the female, but to lay claim to the territory on which she lives. The scent of a female in oestrus will carry over

Danny Puss . . .

Two cat-owners toured Bournemouth whistling 'Danny Boy' because their cat was lost: Tiger had been missing for a week when her owners thought of touring the town whistling her favourite tune. It worked — Tiger heard them, and rushed into their arms.

Catnap court case

When a tomcat called Fudge in Cumbria entered neighbours' houses and sprayed, two of them catnapped him and took him to a vet to be neutered. They pleaded guilty to criminal damage in court and were conditionally discharged for twelve months.

several miles, so tomcats will congregate from a wide area. This is why tomcats disappear for days or weeks on end; they may travel a long way in search of a female and stay in her territory for the number of days she is attractive. Whatever their size or strength, the tomcats usually suffer the same disadvantage — they are on unfamiliar territory; they must familiarise themselves with it first, then sort each other out.

They sidle up to one another, ears turned back and fur raised, growling and howling until one aims a bite at the other's neck. The attacked cat may throw itself onto its back, biting and scrabbling furiously with its hind claws, the two rolling together on the ground. Then they jump up and face one another again. This may be repeated many times until the weaker cat gives up and remains lying on the ground, a submissive position. Recognising that the other cat is no longer a threat, the victor may saunter off, to return later when the vanquished tom has left.

Thus older, weaker toms are routed, leaving the larger, stronger toms in control. However, it is the female who chooses her mate and this is not necessarily the winning cat; as the victor temporarily leaves the field of battle, she may choose the cat which remains. During the battle she will have been absorbed with her own courting display, and may have ignored the fight entirely. Furthermore, having once made her choice, she may be surprisingly faithful.

IN THE DOGHOUSE

'I'm not very keen on buying this dog.'

'Well, don't then.'

'But she's being so good and working so hard to deserve one, I feel a bit mean.'

'Let her have one then.'

'But what about the cats? They'll hate it.'

'Oooh, eee!' my husband cries, wringing his hands in despair at my perversity.

But it is a problem, isn't it? Our daughter has always been surrounded by animals: cats, ponies, goats, hens, two snakes (a Christmas present from an uncle with a sense of humour), tortoises and, of course, more cats — but suddenly she wants a puppy, and nothing else will do.

'Wouldn't you prefer a sweet little kitten, my love?' I know *I* would, so I wheedle.

No, she wouldn't. Uncle and Grandma think she should have what she wants — well, they would, wouldn't they? They don't have to face the feline fury at home. I'm out-voted, so a puppy it is.

I plan my cat survival campaign with care: puppy-free cat zones in the house, a kennel and run in the garden so there will be no strained encounters while we're out, a strict rule that, from day one, the puppy must be taught to respect the cats and leave them alone.

The puppy arrives, all soft, flopsy body and anxious 'please love me' eyes. As he was the most timid of the litter, I suggest we call him Custard. I'm overruled. My daughter insists on George Michael or Huey Lewis. As my father-in-law is a George,

Females often choose the dirtiest, smelliest, most battered tomcat of the many which compete for their favours, as scent is an important factor in their choice

Huey seems more discreet.

To a man, my five offended felines close ranks and spit hatred at the interloper. The poor puppy cowers and looks to me for comfort. Feeling beastly, I have to refuse, for that would be treason to ten yellow, watchful eyes. My daughter hugs and kisses Huey and calls me heartless.

I try to pat and fuss the cats out of their ill-humour and get growled at and scratched for my pains. This could be even worse than I'd feared.

After a day or two of painstaking diplomacy, Prince, at eighteen our oldest cat, decides to ignore the silly, quivering lump, except to spit when it looks at him. Henry, of very little brain, is torn between mothering the poor, whimpering orphan, and fleeing from its terrifying energy. Prudence, many years ago the sole survivor of a litter mauled by a dog, moves out, takes up residence in the stable and turns her back on me whenever I visit.

The young bloods, Tiger and Timmy, keep their distance, but I can see that they are intrigued. It doesn't take them long to discover that Huey is both playful and, with the swift application of claws around the nose, easily disciplined. I can see that puppy-baiting will soon rival hen-herding as their major recreation.

I concentrate on Prudence. Like the elderly aristocrat that she is, she spurns my false friendship; do I really think she can't smell the 'thing' on my hands? No, she will never darken my doorstep again, so there! She will, however, permit my husband to pat her. He, she can tell, never wanted that 'thing' in the first place.

Like a rejected suitor, I ply her with treats and woo her with trifles. Like a sensible female, she takes what's on offer and sends me packing.

Timothy and Huey become chums, so long as Timothy can share Huey's dinner dish. Tiger views Huey as exotic, but easy game; Henry still can't resolve his emotional dilemma, but takes heart from the fact that Tim and Tiger can keep the bouncing thing in order. Prince pretends Huey doesn't exist; he's not moving out for anyone.

Which just leaves Prudence and me. I'm working on us.

Jackie Short

THE PAT CAT

You may have heard of PAT dogs, which visit homes and hospitals as a therapeutic aide to patients. Well, Zowie is a PAT cat. She regularly visits an old persons' home where she is made most welcome. Zowie likes old people and walks around them purring proudly. One old lady exclaimed, 'Goodness, it's a quadruped!' Another said she had a floor mop like that.

Another, who was blind, slowly and carefully explored Zowie's face with gentle hands and described every feature. 'She has a small face with big eyes?' she asked. 'Ears are low set — with long tufts — yes?' she asked. 'She has a flattish face.' Her hands ran gently all over Zowie's body, then she said 'I can see her now. She is beautiful.'

Zowie also visits a school for physically handicapped children and they ask many questions about her. One little girl in particular is enraptured with her, and Zowie sits with her in her wheelchair and nestles against her legs. One boy said, 'I'm going to be a pilot when I grow up. Zowie will be my mascot and I will have her picture painted on my plane.' With all the innocence of youth he was planning for a future which could never be.

I asked the children what her fur felt like; here are their replies: 'like marshmallow'; 'like a white cloud'; 'like Santa Claus' beard'; and one girl said 'like my mummy's hair — all silky and smelling nice.'

Zowie has a busy life because I'm a volunteer at a charity shop and she comes along with me. She sits by the cash register and graciously allows customers to stroke her. She's also a prizewinner because she won a 'Classiest Cat' contest held by a national magazine for her charity work. It couldn't have happened to a nicer cat.

Mary Cregan

Zowie the PAT cat

Tomcats spray urine on horizontal objects to mark their territory – and to attract a female

---

Hunting

Cats are superbly patient hunters. We have all seen them crouching low, lying in wait for a prey animal, for many minutes on end without moving. Their hunting instincts are triggered by movement, and once attracted by the sight of a small moving creature, they will begin to stalk it. Depending on their distance from the prey animal, they will either approach slowly or at a run, with their bellies close against the ground and elbows high. Their tails will be held flat out behind them and the tail tip may twitch.

Having approached to within several metres, the cat will stop behind the nearest cover — which may be a clump, or even just a blade of grass. Still crouched it will watch the prey animal, and according to its distance away, will decide whether to pounce or to stalk nearer.

Before the pounce is made, the hind legs will move rhythmically up and down, the cat appearing to

continued overleaf

In his book *Cat Behavior,* Paul Leyhausen says:

In decades of observation of the free-ranging female cats we kept at home, I was able to establish that for years they always mated with the same tom . . . In my artificial communities the females always noticeably preferred one tom, but would eventually accept another if he was tenacious and energetic enough . . . Conversely, it also happens that a tom may take no notice of the most importunate offers from a female, or that he may make no approaches to a cat himself even though he drives a rival away from her. These observations show clearly that between permanent pair bonding and complete promiscuity there is many a transitional form.

The fact that the female usually chooses the dirtiest, smelliest, most battered tomcat often surprises owners, but it shouldn't: a female cat chooses her mate *not* because of his looks, but because of his smell — and entire tomcats really do smell. They spray to mark their territory — permanent or temporary — and this strong-smelling urine contains pheromones (a volatile substance the odour of which evokes a response in another member of the same species) which attracts the female. Before mating the male may even spray over the female, who does not seem to object and may even be 'turned on' by it; he is marking her with a smell familiar to him, which marks her out as his 'own'. Queens will

Hunting cat, sleek to the ground, poised ready to pounce. One ear is turned slightly to the side as she hears a noise but her eyes are still firmly fixed on her prey

continued

be generating enough energy for a spring. Then it bounds forward and attempts to land on the prey with the forepaws. If it manages to do so, it can make a killing bite immediately, grasping the neck and biting through the spinal cord with its four large canine teeth.

Prey is rarely eaten either where or when it is first killed; the cat must 'wind down' from the excitement of the chase, and will often walk away from the prey before returning to it. It will then carry it to a safe eating place, holding it by the neck in the same way that a mother cat will carry her kittens. If the prey is still alive, it will not move while being carried in this way. If it is put down and begins to move, the cat will return to the attack. Once it is dead, the cat begins to eat, usually starting at the head and working downwards. All cat owners will have seen birds or mice where the head has been eaten but no other part of the body touched.

If the cat has caught a large bird, it may pluck some feathers out before beginning to eat, although sparrow-sized birds are eaten feathers and all. It will tear out the feathers in its mouth, swing its head to the side and spit them out. After a few mouthfuls, it will lick its own fur, probably to clean off any feathers or down sticking to its barbed tongue.

Using the incisor teeth, flesh is then sheared from the carcase in long strips and swallowed whole. The cat's molars are used for gnawing bones, and its rough tongue is perfectly designed for rasping meat from bones.

spray or urinate more frequently while in oestrus, often around the house. They may even be noticed rolling around in the dirty linen basket, obviously enjoying the scent of the worn clothing.

The fact that the female's chosen mate is often the most battered simply testifies to his virility. Those ripped ears, the scarred nose and the missing chunks of fur show that he has been involved in many fights, and since he is still competing it shows that he probably won. Less vigorous toms will be unscarred; or will have scarred ankles from final 'send-him-on-his-way' swipes as they turn to run. A cat with scarred ears and face is one which stays to face and rout the competition.

When a tomcat believes his intentions are welcomed, there may begin a short courtship; he may even present the queen with a toy to attract her attention. The two will call to one another. Head and body-rubbing will follow and the two may tumble around as if playing, before the tom seizes his chance and straddles the female.

The act of coitus usually takes place out of sight, and is, as always, inelegant. A receptive female will raise her rump in the air and the tom will straddle her, gripping her neck in his teeth, sometimes so tightly that the skin of the neck is broken; as most cats' teeth are awash in bacteria, an abscess may result. Deadly viruses such as Feline Leukaemia Virus (FeLV) can be passed on in this way, and the incidence of this incurable disease is increasing among the non-pedigree cat population.

Mating takes just a few seconds, then the experienced male will run away, or leap out of reach. The tom's penis is covered in tiny pointed pieces of skin like barbs, their function, it is believed, being to stimulate ovulation in the female — they act as a trigger to release a hormone from the pituitary gland. Withdrawal may cause the female pain, for she lashes out and would bite her mate if he was still in reach. However, this may have some other cause, for calling cats which are not to be mated at that time are sometimes stimulated to ovulate (and consequently cease calling) by the careful and expert insertion of a thermometer or smooth narrow rod into the vulva. Although this undoubtedly causes no pain when done carefully by an expert, it still causes many females to growl and lash out. And, as most cat breeders will tell you, it doesn't always work, for the female may continue to call for some time.

The female will, once mated, begin to clean her fur and lick her vulva. When she is ready she will accept the same male again, or possibly even another male, and may mate several times in one day. Some queens will stop calling after two or three matings, while others will continue to call even after numerous matings spread over several days.

Matings between pedigree cats which are used for breeding are much safer and more organised. When cat-lovers buy their first pedigree kitten as a pet, they may be surprised to learn that unless it is a 'breeding' quality kitten he probably won't be allowed to let it breed. Pedigree kittens are divided into three 'qualities' by their breeders before sale, according to the looks, temperament and suitability for breeding of each one.

A 'pet' quality kitten is meant to be just that — a pet. In looks it may be enchanting, but it may not conform closely enough to the

Non-pedigree cats arrange their own lives

With this paw . . .

A mail-order minister from California performs a wedding ceremony between cats. She holds a specially written ceremony under a bow-bedecked nuptial arch. Flowers are provided, along with a photo album and a wedding certificate. The bride and groom are expected to 'love, honour and obey — and keep the fleas away'!

'Standard of Points' for its breed: this is a sort of blueprint of how each breed should look; it is drawn up by the cat club formed to promote the breed, and is accepted by a cat registration organisation as the description of the perfect cat of that breed. For example it would be considered a 'fault' if a kitten of a short-nosed breed had a nose rather longer than it should have. Or if a kitten of a slender breed had a compact, chunky body — although many would consider those very faults made the kitten look much more attractive than its sisters and brothers who conformed more closely to the Standard of Points. As a pet quality kitten, it will cost less than a kitten sold for breeding, but the new owner must agree to neuter it at the relevant time, and only then will its pedigree certificate be handed over. The breeder will also place the kitten's name on the non-active register of their registration organisation, which means that no offspring from that cat can ever be registered as pedigree.

So a cat for breeding is selected as being suitable at a very early age, and the new owner will start investigating possible matings when it is just a few months old. Many breeders start off with one or two queens but find it best not to purchase a stud until they have built up a bigger harem — two females would give him the opportunity to mate, at most, four times a year — hardly enough to keep him happy! Some breeders even persuade inexperienced purchasers to buy a breeding pair (a compatible male and female) without thought for the natural urges of the poor male! Most owners of queens begin by using males which are at public stud; contacts with stud owners are made through cat clubs and shows, where the owners of queens have an opportunity to see a variety of males and choose the one they feel to be most suitable in looks, temperament, and breeding.

Stud cats rarely live indoors. Because they are entire they usually spray, and even if they are not habitual sprayers, the proximity of visiting and calling queens will encourage them to do so. So most live in stud houses, which can be both functional and luxurious — large, enclosed runs with sleeping accommodation at one end, with their own heating and lighting systems and plenty of playthings as well as climbing and lounging areas. It could be a lonely life, so a good stud owner will spend a lot of time with her cat, often sitting in his run and reading, or dealing with correspondence.

It is sometimes said that stud cats become vicious: although this undoubtedly happens occasionally, I have never come across an example of it. If one does, something in his life is making him so. A correctly kept stud cat, fed on the excellent diet he needs, with plenty of human company and female cats to service regularly, living in good accommodation, won't become vicious or difficult to handle.

When a mating has been agreed between owners, the next step is to ensure that both cats are in good health. Both will be inoculated yearly, and the stud will be tested for FeLV regularly — hopefully at least twice a year. When the queen next calls, she will be taken to her vet for an up-to-date FeLV test; the result will be known within a day and, if negative, she will be taken to stud. If she is lucky there will be a suitable one nearby, though breeders think nothing of driving several hundred miles to a particularly good stud.

The queen always goes to the stud cat; he never goes to her. It is vitally important that the male is in his own familiar territory or mating may not take place. Unfamiliar territory upsets some queens but not to the same extent. They may go off call (and some go off call as a result of a long journey to the stud) so the owner may have to bring her home again, or, more likely, leave her where she is until she settles down and calls again.

A careful toilette is always carried out after mating. The queen will lick all over the lower part of her body

Putting the bite on

An American inventor has come up with a unique idea for a cat contraceptive in the form of a collar. The collar is said to stop the tom biting the queen's neck, its preliminary to mating.

Feline Leukaemia Virus (FeLV)

Feline Leukaemia Virus has been described as the cats' AIDS. It is slowly increasing among the non-pedigree cat population, and slowly decreasing among the pedigrees. FeLV depresses the cat's immune system in the same way that AIDS suppresses the human's, making the sufferer more vulnerable to other diseases; the longterm outlook for a cat with the virus is therefore poor.

The reason that FeLV is decreasing among the pedigree cat population is that no reputable breeder will allow a queen or stud cat to mate unless a recent certificate showing a negative result for an FeLV blood test is produced. Non-pedigree cats, which arrange their own matings, do not have that advantage.

Although it is believed that the virus is not transmitted sexually, as such, it is probably transmitted in the saliva, by biting, licking or sneezing. As the male cat grips the female's nape of neck in its teeth during mating, often breaking the skin, the disease can be passed on in this way.

Symptoms of FeLV include lack of appetite, weight loss, fever, general malaise, swollen glands and blood in the faeces. There is no cure at present, and any cats with FeLV must be

continued opposite

If the queen is a stranger, the stud owner will inspect her pedigree certificate when she arrives, and will ask to see inoculation certificates and FeLV test results. The queen will be placed in her quarters to settle down; she shouldn't be placed immediately in the stud's house, but in an adjacent pen where both cats can scent one another and become interested in each other before meeting.

It may be the following day before the stud owner introduces them, and they will supervise the mating to ensure that neither cat is hurt, and to give assistance if a virgin queen is nervous, or if the stud cat is inexperienced. It is usual to place new stud cats with experienced queens at first, or experienced studs with virgin queens. For example, a queen may climb onto a high shelf where the stud has difficulty reaching her. If he grips her low on the back instead of on the neck, the mating will not be successful — the stud owner may help disengage his teeth and move him further up the queen's back. But most cats don't need much — or any — assistance.

After mating, the queen will either be taken back to her quarters or, if the two cats have settled down happily together, will be left with the stud. She will stay with him for three to five days and may be mated six or eight times during this period.

The queen's owner will then return to pick up her cat and will pay the stud fee, which can vary from about £50 to £150, according to the breed of cat. The stud owner should provide a certificate of mating: this gives dates of the matings and the pedigree of the stud cat, which will be needed to complete the pedigree certificates of the resulting kittens.

As can be seen, free-living cats arrange their own lovelife in a simple and uncomplicated way, but the breeding of pedigree cats is an expensive and time-consuming hobby. There are as many as 20,000 registered cat breeders in the UK alone, most of whom consider breeding to be a hobby, with an ultimate goal of improving their chosen breed and producing the perfect pedigree cat.

The gestation period of the cat is around sixty-three to sixty-five days. In general, cats are extremely fecund and it is fairly safe to assume that a mated cat is pregnant. The first apparent sign is at about three weeks, when the queen may 'pink up': maiden queens have small nipples which enlarge and become pinker under the influence of the hormones of pregnancy. Queens which have had several litters of kittens will have enlarged nipples anyway, so pinking up may not be apparent. Although it is rare, a few queens may suffer from morning sickness.

At four weeks, a vet may be able to feel the kittens in the uterus by gentle palpation. This should not be attempted by anyone not medically qualified as, inexpertly done, it could cause damage to the kittens or the queen. Ultrasound scanners are now being used by some veterinary practices to 'see' the kittens in the womb and check their progress.

At five or six weeks, the queen's abdomen will be visibly swollen, although with some Longhairs this may not be immediately apparent. The queen's appetite may increase and she may become more friendly and loving. She may also slow down, and even become rather lazy, so should be encouraged to exercise gently. Her muscle tone needs to be good to help her through kittening, so the owner should roll a ball for her to chase or trail a ribbon, ensuring she gets at least two gentle five-minute 'workouts' daily.

About one week before she gives birth, the kittens can be felt moving and kicking. The queen seems to find it most comfortable at this stage to lie flat out and, if she is lying along an owner's lap, their kicks can be clearly felt. The uterus is shaped like a horseshoe, with kittens on either side of it, and it is often possible at this stage to tell how many there are. The kittens are born alternately, first from one side of the horseshoe, then the other.

Scientists will undoubtedly disagree, but I believe it is often possible to tell what a kitten's personality is like before it is born. One with an active, assertive kick will turn out to be lusty and demanding; those which, in the womb, are quieter and less active have a much more laid-back attitude to life when born.

A mother cat will search out a safe nest in which to give birth. It must be dry, warm and enclosed, safe from predators, and protected from the weather and natural (or even man-made) disasters. Cats possess a remarkable instinct for finding such places even when not in kitten — when pregnant, or with young kittens to care for, this ability becomes almost supernatural.

A domesticated cat will accept as a nursery a clean cardboard box lined with warm paper or fabric, particularly if it is carefully sited: in a warm position, and away from prying eyes and noisy areas of the household. Failing ideal conditions, the cat will often choose to give birth in a place which is awkward or inaccessible to its owner, but ideal from its own point of view. Airing cupboards are often chosen for their warmth, darkness, soft padding and the fact that they are high above the ground; cats always feel safer at a height than at ground level. Otherwise a sideboard may be chosen, or the top of a wardrobe, or under a bed.

For cats living in a domestic situation, a nursery should be set up several days in advance. This should provide a large kittening pen, left open at all times for the mother cat to enter and leave at will, with a bed or large cardboard box lined with many layers of newspaper inside; then there should be several layers of paper towels or washable bedding material which can be changed

continued

isolated from all other cats, and should not share their food or water bowls, or their litter trays. Euthanasia may have to be considered for affected cats.

FeLV vaccines are available in the USA and parts of Europe, and cats are vaccinated at nine weeks, twelve weeks and twenty weeks; thereafter yearly boosters must be given. Vaccine will protect only around 65 per cent of cats; 10 per cent of vaccinated cats may suffer side effects, with ½ per cent experiencing serious side effects. For this reason, the vaccine has not been accepted in the UK at the time of writing (1991).

There is a similar, although unrelated virus of cats which is also causing concern. It was first called Feline T-lymphotropic Lentivirus (FTLV) but is now more often called Feline Immunodeficiency Virus (FIV). It was 'discovered' in 1987, although it had probably been in existence for many years without being identified. Symptoms and transmission are as for FeLV, and there is no treatment at present.

It is important for owners to realise that, although these viruses are life-threatening for their cats, *it is impossible for a human to catch leukaemia, AIDS , FeLV, FIV or any similar virus from cats.*

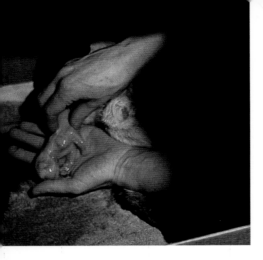

A newly-born kitten, still wet and unmoving

Code of Practice

Although non-pedigree cats have to arrange their own sex lives, the growing number of pedigree cat breeders abide by the codes of practice laid down by the cat clubs to which they belong. For this reason, should you ever wish to buy a pedigree cat, you can get a list of reputable breeders from a club. Cat clubs are of two types: breed clubs, which specialise in a particular breed of cat; and area clubs, which cover a specific area of the country and have members who breed many different types of cat. Contact the registration organisations (addresses at the back of the book) for information on cat clubs.

Most clubs insist that their breeder members comply with their own code of practice. For example, members' queens should not have litters more often than once every six or eight months; the breeders should be in attendance when the kittens are born; prospective purchasers should be checked for

continued opposite

regularly, and allow even new-born kittens a good grip with their claws. Another large cardboard box can be upended over the top to simulate the natural conditions of an enclosed nest. A small hole cut in the side allows the queen to come and go as she wishes. The upended cardboard box can be removed in case the owner needs to assist at the birth, for daily checking of the kittens and for changing the bedding.

This imitates the nest which would be made by the feral mother — she would find a small uninhabited cave, or the shelter of an overhanging bush, and would give birth on dry leaves or grasses. Such mothers may even pluck fur from their own bodies and line their nests with it. She will have chosen a site near a food and water source as she will not leave the nest for long during the first few weeks. If the water source is a river, lake or pond, she will want to be well above water level.

Most cats give birth with relative ease, although some members of pedigree breeds which have been developed for certain features — for example, a large round head — may have more difficulty. The queen may begin to pant or purr when birth is imminent and as her pulse rate increases. She will usually lie down and perhaps brace herself, using her paws, against a vertical surface. Contractions can last for half-an-hour or even longer, but a healthy, fit cat will often produce her first kitten within ten to fifteen minutes.

A cat living wild, or anyway living amongst other cats, may be assisted by other female members of the group who will help her clean and dry her kittens. Pet cats which are very attached to their owners will insist on their presence, and if the owner is asleep, will waken them or give birth to their kittens on the bed. Many cats will become very agitated if their owner leaves the room, or moves out of the cat's range of vision. She may get up to follow, even trailing a kitten along by its umbilical cord, if the placenta has not yet appeared.

Each kitten is born in an individual birth sac. Many owners will refer to kittens as twins if two are born in a litter, but they are not true twins unless they have shared one birth sac; this only happens about one in every hundred births. When the mother's fur is light-coloured the birth sacs are pinkish-white; and black when it is dark. Each sac is remarkably delicate, taking less effort to tear than the finest sheet of tissue paper. The queen will lick the sac which will tear, and will continue licking the kitten, which is wet when it is born. Licking its nose and mouth will clear it of mucous, allowing it to breathe, and the kitten will respond almost immediately by squeaking in a constant high pitch. However, the squeaking can unnerve a first-time mother who may even shrink away from the kitten; an owner who is assisting can help calm her

Five-day-old kittens instinctively huddle together for warmth. These are patterned by the Himalayan gene and their points are already beginning to darken

Ten-day-old kittens. Already their eyes are opening and they are more mobile but they still keep close together

continued

suitability; and only healthy, inoculated kittens, at least twelve weeks old, should be sold.

Owners of stud cats may also have to abide by certain rules: for example, they must have been breeding cats for at least three years before purchasing a stud; they should keep the cat in comfortable accommodation, and spend as much as two hours each day with him; they should accept only properly registered queens, and be prepared to educate the owners of the queens if they are novices and give free advice if required; and they should follow up the progress of any resulting kittens.

From the above, it is obvious that club members should place the welfare of their cats before all financial considerations. Members failing to meet such high standards can be thrown out of the club. So treat warily any cat breeder who is not a member of a cat club.

until she returns to look after the kitten. Fortunately, this reaction is rare as most cats know instinctively what to do.

The birth sac is attached to the placenta (or afterbirth) by an umbilical cord approximately 8cm (3in) in length. The queen will continue to lick the kitten before dealing with the umbilical cord, which she will shear with her teeth. She may not do this until five or ten minutes after the kitten has been born and, indeed, there is no urgency to do so. She may shear the cord before the placenta has appeared, or afterwards, when she will continue eating along the cord and will eat the placenta as well. This has a dual function; it is believed that it stimulates the flow of milk, and it also keeps the nest clean, and obviates smell which would attract predators. Some mothers are over-enthusiastic, and may eat the cord all the way down to the kitten's belly; an umbilical hernia can result when it is left too short.

Many people don't realise that cats do, of course, have a 'tummy button' because the circular bald patch is later hidden

amongst the fur. All cats, male and female alike, also have nipples, just as we do, although they have no function in the male.

It can take half an hour or more for a placenta to appear and if the mother has not sheared the cord, the kitten may be trailed around the nest, often being trampled on by the mother — though surprisingly, this doesn't usually appear to cause injury. If the cord has to be cut with scissors (which is never as efficient as by the mother's teeth) it is important that no pressure is applied otherwise an umbilical hernia may result; yet few umbilical hernias ever seem to result from the weight of a kitten, dangling from its own cord.

A constant concern for the mother cat at this time is to keep the nest clean so that predators are not attracted by the smell, so between contractions she cleans the kittens and herself, and disposes of the placenta. If a kitten is born dead, she will eat it — she cannot leave a body to decompose in the nest, and it is, after all, a good source of protein. There are also recorded instances of mother cats eating a kitten which has survived birth but died several days later.

The mother cat is also remarkably sensitive about illness in her kittens, and although they may appear perfectly healthy she will often know if something is wrong — perhaps a sick kitten's suckling is not so vigorous, or it may have a certain scent. We don't understand the process involved, but the mother cat will often take it out of the nest and hide it away. In the wild, that kitten would die, and the mother cat will not have wasted precious energy in trying to raise a sick kitten, one which might infect the rest of her litter. In a domestic situation, a human will rescue the missing kitten and put it back in the nesting box — though you generally find the mother cat will hide it again. By the time the rejected kitten displays recognisable symptoms of illness, it is often too late to do anything to save it.

Newborn kittens are about the size of hamsters and look more like rats than cats. They weigh approximately 50 to 75gm (2 to 3oz), although the larger breeds such as Ragdolls or Maine Coons can commonly weigh 85 to 90gm (3½oz). Kittens are born the colour they will remain throughout life, with the exception of cats patterned by the Himalayan gene: Siamese, Balinese, Birmans, Colourpoints and Ragdolls. These kittens are born white, and their coloured 'points' — their extremities — darken with age, beginning at the age of four or five days. Not everyone realises this, and sadly there have been stories of breeders of Himalayan-patterned cats who, when faced with their first, all-white litter, have believed that a mis-mating has occurred and have euthanised all the kittens.

Kittens are born with their eyes closed, though on rare occa-

Cost of loving

In the 1940s, the stud fee for a Champion Persian or Siamese cat was two guineas (£2.10) 'plus carriage'. The pedigree offspring were sold for five guineas (£5.25) to six guineas (£6.30). In the 1990s, the equivalent stud fee would be £50, with Persian or Siamese kittens selling for around £100.

sions some are born with them open; these kittens must be kept in darkened conditions — after a few days, the eyes usually close, only to reopen at the normal time. Newborn kittens are unable to hear well. They are born without teeth, but have fully developed claws, which they are unable to retract into the claw sheath, as an adult cat can.

As soon as the kitten is licked dry — which takes ten to fifteen minutes — it will try to reach its mother. Although kittens are born with a good sense of smell, they probably find her by the warmth of her body as much as scent because an important priority is to keep warm. Newborn kittens can lose heat rapidly, and if allowed to chill will become sluggish and eventually comatose. The queen will curl around her first kitten as the second is born, and will purr almost continuously; this presumably helps the kittens find their way to a teat and the rich first milk, the colostrum. Queens vary in the time it takes them to produce milk; some may have milk while they are giving birth or even before, for others it may take some hours. The kittens will nurse anyway, and their sucking and kneading will help stimulate the milk flow. This kneading (paddling) movement of the paws on either side of the teat as it nurses as a kitten is a behavioural characteristic a cat will perform throughout its life when happy. Its earliest memories are of the comfort and succour of its mother's teat, so happiness will stimulate it to perform the movement which originally made the milk flow — it may even dribble while doing so. Indeed, suckling must be such a comforting behaviour in itself that, until about three weeks of age, a kitten will also suckle from a female without milk. And many kittens continue to suckle well into adulthood, mouthing their owner's skin, clothing or the teats of other (even male) cats, if allowed to do so.

Newborn kittens are unable to walk for about three weeks so at first they move around using a crawling, paddling movement; their hind legs push their bodies along while they paddle their front legs like oars.

The queen has eight teats, in four rows of two, and always initiates feeding during the first four weeks when she will climb into her nest and lie on her side for her kittens to feed. She will do so in response to squeaks of hunger, or when her milk builds up and the pressure becomes uncomfortable.

The teats nearest her head and tail are often not as well-formed or large as the others, and in my experience it is the four teats in the centre which are the most sought-after. Nor do I believe that any particular kitten lays claim to any particular teat: rather feeding seems to be something of a free-for-all, with all the kittens heading for the middle of their mother's body (which is warmer anyway) and once there, moving upwards. Kittens have to raise

At three or four weeks old, kittens are ready to climb out of their kittening box to explore

themselves up to the level of the lower teat, and if they miss it, they just keep climbing until they reach the teat above. Sometimes they miss that one too, and end up on top of their mother, or fall down the other side. Loud squeals will then result until it manages to paddle around itself, or the mother paws it around to the correct side. Meanwhile the remaining kittens will be trampling over each other to reach a teat, the weaker brothers getting knocked off by the stronger ones, which will continue to grow bigger and stronger, sometimes at the expense of the smaller littermates.

During these early days, some queens will be fiercely protective of their kittens, and become distressed if they are handled, especially by strangers. Owners should ensure that there is a 'no visitor' rule for the first week or two after kittening. If a mother feels her kittens are threatened she will try to move them to a safer place; for the domesticated cat this may be to a spare bed, hiding them under the bedclothes, or to some other dark, hidden place. This can hurt the kittens, as not all mothers are particularly skilled at picking them up and carrying them — normally she grips the scruff of the neck, leaving the legs dangling, but sometimes she grips some other part of the body, and her teeth may puncture the skin. The dangling extremities may hit against obstacles, and the kitten can be quite seriously hurt.

Yet many queens will allow a trusted owner to handle her kittens, only becoming concerned if the kittens begin to squeal continuously. Some kittens will always do this when picked up, while others squeal rarely — it is an early indication of their temperament. Studies have shown that kittens handled and stroked regularly during the first few weeks develop more quickly, opening their eyes earlier and leaving the nest earlier than unhandled kittens. G.W. Meier (1961) discovered that handled Siamese kittens even developed their distinctive coat pattern earlier than those which had not been handled.

Cats are excellent mothers, and for the first four weeks the mother does everything for her kittens. She not only protects them, keeps them warm and clean and feeds them, but she helps them eliminate their waste products, something they are unable to do for themselves at first. After a feed she will lick them all over, and her licking of the area under their tails stimulates excretion. The queen will swallow everything which is excreted, which means that she in turn will have a lot of extra waste products to dispose of. Although the thought of this is distasteful to many, it keeps the nest clean and free from smell, which would attract insects, leading to illness, and predators.

Some cats won't excrete for several days after giving birth, and a domesticated mother cat which has just given birth won't use a litter tray which is too near its nest because of its instinctive fear of attracting predators. And some won't leave their kittens for the length of time it takes them to use a tray which is placed some distance away. So an owner has to find a happy medium: far enough away to be acceptable, but not so far that the cat feels she is out of reach of her kittens. This instinct must make life very distressing for those pedigree cats which are kept locked in small pens with their kittens, their food and their litter tray.

On the rare occasions a feline mother cannot look after her kittens, humans come to realise just how much work a litter can be. The kittens need feeding every two hours around the clock, using a specially formulated reconstituted milk — a queen's milk contains 41.3% protein with an energy content of 142 kcal per 100g (Baines, 1981), and neither cow's nor goat's milk has sufficient protein or energy content to sustain young kittens.

Besides this regular feeding, the newborn kittens must be kept at a temperature of 30–33°C (85–90°F); and after every feed, their abdomens and bottoms must be gently rubbed and any expelled waste wiped away. So it's not surprising that owners of 'orphaned' kittens usually try to find a feline foster mother for their kittens. Other lactating queens will usually readily accept strange newborn kittens and will look after them as if they were their own.

The new kittens may hiss as early as two days of age if a stranger approaches their nest, but this is pure bluff; purring can begin as early as the fifth day. On average eyes open between the seventh and tenth day, although it can take up to sixteen. Kittens raised in darkened surroundings open their eyes earlier than

In the news

Seen in the *Shropshire Star*: 'Free to good home. male and female tomcats. . .'
From the *Croydon News*: 'For sale; female, inoculated Burmese kitchens. . .'
In the *Pulmans News*: 'Eccentric home wanted for aggressively unsocial ginger tom (neutered)). Answers to the name of Misery Guts.'

Playing with its mother's tail begins to develop hunting skills. It is the movement of the tail which attracts

those raised in bright surroundings; female kittens open their eyes before males, kittens of young mothers before those of older mothers, and fathers pass on early (or late) eye-opening to their offspring. Vision is not good at first, but continues to improve until the third or fourth month of life. The kittens' crawl becomes more ambitious and some can stand at two weeks, although they are not truly mobile until three weeks or so. Milk teeth begin to erupt at two weeks.

From birth until around two weeks many kittens will squeal loudly if picked up; at three weeks kittens are able to walk —

CAT SUMMER

I remember the day well when I first met Cat. I was a sickly child, and it was the first warm day after a long hard winter. Mother said that the sunshine would do me good, and if I promised to stay in the small front garden, I could stay outside. It was a rare treat for me, living as we did in a top-floor flat.

After Mother had left me, I felt very small and frightened on my own. I sat on the step and watched people pass by. After a while, I became aware that I was being watched. Sitting in the next-door garden was a little black cat.

Oh, how I wanted him to come to me. I sat very still, and very slowly he came towards me. We looked at each other and liked what we saw. He came closer and climbed into my lap. Gently I stroked him, and deep within his throat a rumble came, that grew and grew until it erupted in a purr. I did not know then that it was a purr, only that the cat was happy and so was I.

From that moment on I had found a friend. Mother came downstairs to bring me in and found me cuddling the cat. At her approach, he fled. My friend had gone; I cried.

The next day, he came to meet us when we returned from the shops. I begged to stay outside again, and was in seventh heaven cuddling Cat and listening to the lovely purr that came from deep within him.

For the next two days the rain come down, and from my high window I watched the people with their dripping umbrellas hurrying along the busy road. I wondered what my friend was doing and hoped he was as warm and dry as I.

The next day was warm and sunny and I was allowed to take my toys outside. I sat playing with my dolls and wondering where Cat was, when he came wandering down the road. When he saw me he started running and jumped on my lap. Gently I hugged him and felt and heard the lovely sound only cats can make.

That summer I was no longer lonely, as Cat was never far away. As time went by, he would sit in my pram and I would wheel him up and down the path. I loved him dearly and wished he was mine so I could be with him all the time.

Then another bout of illness kept me indoors. How I longed for Cat and missed him so. One day, returning from the shops, Mother found him on the doorstep. Thinking he would cheer me up, she carried him upstairs to my bedroom.

I thought I was dreaming when I awoke to find him on my bed singing his lovely song. Mother found him a saucer of milk and I watched his pink tongue lap every drop.

I was so happy that summer, watching him eat, sleep and listening to his purr. Alas, nothing lasts. Mother discovered he had fleas and I was banned from playing with him.

I never knew where he came from, or where he went. He was just not around any more. I'll never forget Cat, or the warm friendship he gave to me that summer of my childhood.

G. Pollington

Although this kitten has never seen a real mouse, he has grasped his toy mouse firmly and is attempting a killing bite on the back of the neck

although sometimes this is with a comical-looking drunken gait — and they begin to play with their littermates. At first they will simply bat one another with their paws, but within a few days they are pouncing on each other and on anything that moves, undoubtedly learning the rudiments of hunting skills. At three and a half to four weeks they are able to use a litter tray, which most kittens take to with alacrity.

At this age the kittens will begin to pursue their mother when they are hungry, instead of her deciding when to nurse them, and queens vary in their reaction to this. Some will selflessly nurse their kittens for months to the possible detriment of their health, others will run away and perch on a high piece of furniture and only return to the nest when they wish to. Between four to five weeks of age the kittens should be receiving their first solid food — at this stage the feral queen would return to the nest with small, dead prey animals so her kittens could accustom themselves to the smell, touch and taste of their future diet. Within a few weeks she would bring live prey for her kittens to catch and eat, calling to them to come and share her spoils. Paul Leyhausen has reported that mother cats have distinct calls depending on the type of prey they are bringing back to the nest. For example, there is one call for a small and relatively harmless prey animal such as a mouse, and a different call for something larger and more dangerous like a rat.

An expert hunting cat kills its prey with one bite by severing the spinal cord with its large canine teeth. Interestingly, the distance between an adult cat's canine teeth makes the cat adept at killing rats whose neck dimensions ideally suit the size of the cat's jaws. Two-month-old kittens have canines which are ideally spaced for killing mice. A kitten which is an expert mouse-catcher may have more difficulty as it grows because its teeth no longer 'fit' its prey.

Kittens will still be suckling when they begin to eat prey animals, and their first experience of prey may be sucking on a

Supercat

A Derbyshire farmer heard squeaking coming from an abandoned magpie's nest. He investigated and, six metres above the ground, found a litter of kittens. The farm tabby had chosen the cosy nest as the perfect kittening place.

Cats' eyes

The cat's eye is proportionately about four times larger than the human eye; it has a much wider field of vision, and better sight in the dark than we do, but less colour vision.

A cat can see more than a semi-circle without moving its head, and because the eyes are on the front of the head, the field of vision of each eye overlaps the other by about 44 degrees. Because of this binocular vision, a cat can judge distance very accurately. A hunting cat can be seen to sway its head slightly which is an additional help to it when judging distance.

The cat's eye is more curved than the human eye, and has a deeper-set lens — this enables it to see an object five times more brightly than we can. It also has a pupil which enlarges to a circle to permit more light to enter in dark conditions. When the light is bright, the pupil contracts to a slit to cut down on the amount of light entering the eye.

A human eye has four rods (which respond to light) to each cone (which responds to colour); the cat has twenty-five rods to each cone, which makes the cat's eye light sensitive but limits colour vision, especially in the dark.

Cat's eyes 'glow' in the dark because of a mirror-like structure behind the eyes called the *tapetum lucidum* which reflects back any light which shines on it.

dead creature brought back to the nest by their mother. Later on they will eat whatever is left after their mother has eaten, and in this way they learn what prey is. Kittens which have not been presented with partially eaten prey animals grow up without associating prey with food — they may catch a mouse or a rat, but they don't realise it is edible until it is cut up for them. Many cats upset their owners by catching prey, and then add insult to injury by not eating it. But if these are cats which have never learned to

recognise prey as food, they will simply have been following their instinct to chase anything which moves — and they don't know what to do with it once it stops moving.

Kittenhood, like early childhood, is a time of learning, and a kitten has become what it will remain in adulthood by the age of six or eight weeks. The experiences it gains from the humans around it and from its mother are therefore vital to its subsequent development.

After four weeks of age, kittens will pursue their mothers in search of food. This kitten's mother doesn't lie down to suckle but holds the kitten at bay with her tongue

Queries on Kittens

There are so many questions about kittens. For many owners, a kitten is their first excursion into the complex world of the cat, yet that sweet, sleeping little bundle they chose bears no relation to what they discover they have when they get home. Instead of the 'easy' pet they thought they had acquired, they find a creature with a will of its own, with its own preferences as to food, sleeping places, companions and just about everything else in its world.

The lucky owners (with lucky kittens) ask the questions *before* they buy. Those less fortunate work out the answers afterwards. If you haven't acquired your kitten yet, read The Contented Kitten (p22) first; you may just find it makes life a little easier for you — and your kitten.

I want a kitten but I'm just about to move into a new house and I will be buying new furniture. I don't want the furniture scratched. What can I do to prevent it?

One of the reasons cats and kittens strop on furniture is to make it smell familiar. They have scent glands on their paws and stropping transfers their scent to whatever they strop on. New furniture is particularly at risk because, to a cat, it will smell strange and foreign. A new settee may have no scent that we can distinguish, but a cat will be able to identify the smells of the fabric and the chemicals used in the filling, the furniture store and delivery van, and those of eve-ryone who has handled it. And when it was delivered, a passing tomcat may have anointed it with spray — something which your cat will not appreciate at all. Just watch how a cat will sniff all around anything new which comes into a house.

To a cat then, a new item of furniture is a foreign and possibly threatening object, and it will want to imprint it with its own scent as soon as possible. It will probably do this by stropping, although in a few rare cases it may spray on the furniture too. Thankfully, with a young kitten, spraying should not be a problem.

It may help to ensure that new furniture smells of *you* as quickly as possible. Imprint for example a settee with your scent by sitting on it, lying on it, rubbing your hands over it; if your kitten has built up a relationship with you by this time, the settee will then become less threatening.

Is there anything else I can do?

Training your kitten in the rules of your household is possible *and* desirable. Rule one is that the kitten should not strop on the furniture, and it must be made to realise this. The owner, however, must do his/her part by providing an alternative: buy or make at least one scratching post, and if your kitten strops the furniture, immediately say 'NO' in a loud, firm voice — remove the kitten and take it to its scratching post, and demonstrate. Yes, demonstrate! Get down on

My cat is neutered but he still gets the urge! Why?

He may be reacting by instinct. One of my neutered males will adopt a mating posture occasionally with a calling queen, but then realises he doesn't know what to do next and walks off looking puzzled. A few cat breeders are fortunate enough to own neutered males which *can* mate their females, but without being able to impregnate them. These males are most useful when a breeder doesn't want the queen to continue calling — or have her take hormones to prevent calling.

In a few rare instances when a tomcat is neutered, some testicular tissue remains which continues to release the male hormone, testosterone, into the bloodstream. In these cases, the males may continue to behave like entire tomcats, including spraying.

your knees and run your fingernails down the scratcher, and this will almost always stimulate the kitten to copy you. If it does, stroke it and praise it using a warm and loving voice.

Kittens are highly intelligent creatures and one loud 'NO' is usually lesson enough for many of them, though others may take a little longer. But cats and kittens will still try their luck, looking over their shoulder as if to say 'Will I get away with it this time?' The answer should be no; if a kitten is forbidden once, it must be forbidden every single time, otherwise it will continue to strop because it knows it will sometimes get away with it.

YOU SHOULD provide a scratching post, even if your cat or kitten can strop on a tree outside. It will want to strop indoors, too, and it is vital for it to have somewhere it can do so.

TRY training. It's your responsibility, and your most potent weapon in the battle of the shredded settee.

Try making any new furniture smell familiar, by sitting on it and using it before your cat has access to it.

Settees — favoured stropping items — often come covered in plastic. Leave the plastic coverings over the arms at first; cats won't scratch plastic as they hate the feel of it under their paws.

Choose furniture which doesn't encourage your cat to strop: steer clear of loop-pile carpets, wickerwork, hessian or textured wallpaper and heavily textured coverings for settees and chair coverings. Smooth, silky fabrics and painted walls are rarely scratched by cats.

Don't buy a Siamese or other Foreign breed, all of which love to strop.

COMMENT Never smack a stropping cat; it is behaving naturally and won't understand the punishment. You may just end up with a very nervous cat which still ruins the furniture.

Be prepared for the fact that even the best trained cat will strop on the furniture occasionally. If this really is a problem for you, buy a goldfish!

Cats and kittens need to strop. This cat is scratching a bush, then sniffing the scent markers it has left behind

Littermates often don't get on well together once they mature

Opposite:
A kitten's waking moments are full of exploration and learning

I've never owned a cat. Now I want a kitten but I'm at work all day. Should I buy two kittens, to keep one another company?

Felines are social creatures. A kitten which has just left its mother has been completely dependent on her company and that of its littermates, and to be brought to a strange home where it is left alone all day would need a massive readjustment: no-one to cuddle up to, no-one to play with, it would suddenly find the world a cold, bleak, unloving place.

The company of another kitten or cat is therefore an absolute must if an owner is at work all day; it isn't enough to provide a cat flap and leave the kitten to find its own friends. First, a new kitten should not be allowed out of doors until at least a week after its second inoculation. Which means a non-pedigree kitten has to endure at least a month of solitary confinement. Second, your kitten is very small and inexperienced, and should not be allowed out on its own all day to fend for itself; it will have to battle with full-grown and possibly aggressive cats even in its own garden.

I suppose I should buy two kittens from the same litter because they'll be more likely to be friendly?

In my experience this doesn't work very well. After a certain age, littermates usually show signs of disliking one another — as do mother and offspring — and often spend most of their time fighting. Sibling kittens born wild would disperse once they were mature enough to do so, and so would adult females and their offspring. Possibly this is a deep-rooted instinct, for close relatives which stayed together would eventually interbreed, to the detriment of the health of their descendants. Even the neutering of pet cats is not enough to overcome the resistance many close relatives obviously feel against staying together once past maturity.

So buy two unrelated kittens, but try to ensure that their temperaments are compatible. For example, you wouldn't want to buy a very dominant, assertive kitten as company for a timid, nervous one.

Buying unrelated kittens also gives you the opportunity to get to know one feline at a time. If you haven't had a cat or kitten before, you won't realise how big a difference it can make in your life, how much care and attention it requires. Buy your kitten when you can take some time off work so that you can keep it company and help it settle down, before the second kitten arrives.

YOU SHOULD provide company for your cat or kitten if you are away from home for long periods.

Before bringing a second kitten into your household, ensure it is completely healthy.

Introduce the two correctly to help them become friendly (see pp 29–32).

COMMENT Many working owners realise they can't cope with a dog so turn to the cat as an easier pet. But it isn't — it requires companionship just as a dog does, and not only for the first few months, but for fourteen or fifteen years. Many of us look to pets for companionship without appreciating that our pets look to *us* for companionship too, as well as all their other needs. Working owners, especially those who also enjoy an active social life or long holidays, should think very seriously before buying a cat or kitten. Some cat breeders won't sell kittens to a prospective owner who is at work all day.

I bought a Burmese kitten, but after a little while it became destructive so I had to take it back to the breeder. I've since had other breeds of pedigree kittens, at different times, which have also become destructive, so

they've had to go back too. While I was at work, they shredded the wallpaper and the carpets and generally wrecked my flat. I've heard that longhaired cats are more placid, so I think I could keep a longhaired kitten without it turning destructive. What do you think?

I think that any breed of cat, no matter how placid, will become 'destructive' when treated in this way — this owner was at work all day long and left each kitten, completely alone, shut in a small flat, without any form of stimulation or company. Although kittens will sleep for as long as eighteen or twenty hours a day, their waking moments are full of exploration and learning, and they have remarkably high energy levels. Kittens want to explore and play, and this owner was not providing anything whereby each kitten could work off its excess energy or its natural curiosity.

Without companionship or playthings, each kitten began to 'play' with what was available: cushions, wallpaper, carpets. They didn't know they were being 'destructive' — tearing feathers out of stuffing and chasing them was far more fun than sitting around staring at the walls. Longhair or shorthair, kittens are kittens; and although an adult longhair may be a placid lapcat, longhaired kittens are active and playful, too. Even the most placid breeds of cat will become unhappy and bored if left alone all day.

These kittens were in the feline equivalent of solitary confinement without any remission for good conduct. And when they behaved in a way their new owner found inappropriate, they were sent back to their breeders, and then expected to make another huge adjustment to another new home.

YOU SHOULD take your responsibilities seriously if you acquire a kitten (or a cat). Understand its needs and realise that it isn't a

stuffed toy, to be cuddled at bedtime but otherwise left to its own devices.

COMMENT This person was intelligent and caring — she simply didn't understand a kitten's requirements. When I explained her kittens' behaviour, she was devastated at the thought that unwittingly she had been 'cruel'. She said, 'Why didn't the breeders explain all this before I bought their kittens?' She was quite right; breeders have an enormous responsibility to find the most suitable homes for each kitten they breed. Unfortunately, when vet-

BILLY AND THE FLYING BOMBS

Our family has always been interested in cats, and with a lifelong love and acquaintance with these beautiful animals, I never cease to wonder at their ability and intelligence in reacting to unusual circumstances.

Billy was a green-eyed British grey shorthaired which I bought in 1941 as a kitten. He learned between 1944 and 1945 how to discriminate between the infernal racket produced by a flying bomb — colloquially called a Doodlebug — and that of an ordinary aircraft. He had learned from bitter experience that the former noise usually ended with an earth-shaking explosion — bad news for cats!

The house we were living in at the time was an old, well-built, converted farmhouse with very stout walls. In the dining-room fireplace we kept a large, steel-bound chest, and if he heard a Doodlebug, Billy would scurry to the space between the chest and the back of the fireplace. It was the safest place in the house — for him at any rate.

The major point is that Billy's keen hearing far outweighed our own, and he was off to his hidey-hole long before we heard the approaching bomb ourselves. He was our four-minute-warning system, and when we grew more accustomed to the antics of these weird weapons, with such warning we could decide whether it was safe to watch the flying menace or whether it was wiser to take shelter. A benefit which those who did not own cats could not share.

Tony Lawton

RISKY – THE KAMIKAZE CAT

When I bought Risky she was so tiny that I hid her in my jacket pocket from my children. She had no fear of anything whatsoever, and I've never known a kitten get up to such antics.

I hadn't realised at first that she was deaf. . . but that never bothered her at all. She would scale up the curtains and leap squirrel-fashion onto the wall unit, then from ceiling height launch herself onto whichever lap she had selected. When she was spayed, the vet said to keep her indoors for several days, but that same evening she was stuck on a bungalow roof (she often travelled along our road via the rooftops).

One day when she was doing her acrobatic act from curtains to wall unit, I noticed her hind leg was swinging in all directions — yet she had shown no signs of pain or discomfort. I rushed her to the vet who confirmed a broken leg; this had hardly mended before she arrived home injured again, this time with an airgun pellet through her other hind leg.

Her favourite pastime was to sit on our garden wall and leap down and dash towards any car which approached. One day I was fortunate enough to spot her stalking a steam-roller. If I hadn't seen her I think she would have been a 'flat cat'.

One day she went missing; being deaf, it was pointless to call her. After two days, my son found her under a shed, her face smashed. As soon as the vet saw her, he said she couldn't survive. She had obviously been hit by a car and her lower jaw was totally smashed. He said he could attempt wiring it, but didn't think it would succeed. He rang the next day to say he had wired the jaw but was not too hopeful for her.

When I took her home, I was told to feed her on a liquid diet of essence of chicken. She was ravenous; as I put the spoon to her mouth to try and pour in a little liquid, she opened her mouth so wide and grabbed the spoon that the wiring all came away. I couldn't believe such a thing could happen after all the vet's work on her. He told me the jaw could not be rewired and she'd have to take her chances. Needless to say, her jaw set, but crookedly, which gave her a really evil expression.

Sadly, Risky was put to sleep eventually, for she developed cancer on the tip of the ear which spread, a not-uncommon occurrence with white cats. But she lived until she was eighteen, a good age for a cat, and she had lived her life to the full, using up all of the nine lives God had granted her.

Audrey Philps

erinary and food bills mount up, many are only too willing to sell to kind, if misguided owners. Now that this person understands the problem, she has decided she will wait until she retires, in a few years time, before buying another kitten.

Several months ago I gave a home to a kitten which came from a rescue shelter. It is a little nervous and it has a very strange habit — although I provide a litter tray it won't use it — it will only go to the toilet in the greenhouse. I think it was kept in a shed before going to the rescue shelter. Is this the reason?

Kittens and cats are creatures of habit. Being kept in a shed without human company would explain this kitten's nervousness; also why it looks for a shed-like structure in which to go to the toilet — as a kitten, it learnt that this was the 'right' place. Patience is always required when looking after a feline which has had a poor start in life.

TRY placing a litter tray in your greenhouse. Most cats take to a litter tray readily, as long as it is kept clean. Keep an indoor tray too, and place a very large, up-turned box over it with a small doorway cut in the side. This will give your kitten the security it felt in the shed. When it begins to use the covered tray, the large box can be replaced with one which is smaller. Many kittens and cats prefer to use litter trays which are covered in this manner; it makes them feel more secure from attack.

OUTCOME The kitten happily used a litter tray in the greenhouse once it was provided. Later, the owner placed another covered tray indoors and, after a few days of explorative sniffs, the kitten used it too. Once it was using it regularly, the tray in the greenhouse was removed. If possible, always allow your cat a degree of choice in the siting of its litter tray.

My neutered male cat is very dominant, and really likes to be the boss. I want to buy another kitten for company for him but I'm worried in case it would be bullied. Although I will have the kitten neutered at the appropriate time, which would suit my cat best, a male or a female kitten?

As you intend to have it neutered, the sex of the kitten isn't nearly as important as its temperament. An entire male would grow up to be dominant to a neutered male in the same household, and would probably upset your present cat who would lose his 'boss cat' status. However, neutered cats rely on their temperament rather than their sexual status to work out a hierarchy.

Either a male or a female kitten would make an equally good pet for you. Some people believe that males are more loving, but this isn't necessarily so. If your cat is very dominant, he will want to remain so, so don't choose a very assertive kitten — if one immediately rushes towards you and begins fighting with your shoe-laces it would probably not be the ideal choice. Nor would a quiet, shy little kitten which holds back or even hides from the sound of a strange voice. Choose a middle-of-the road kitten from the litter; one which shows a kittenish degree of curiosity and friendliness without acting like a tearaway.

If I chose a pedigree kitten, would any particular breed be more suitable than another?

One advantage in choosing a pedigree kitten is that to a large extent different breeds have recognisable personalities: generally, the longhaired pedigree breeds are friendly and placid, shorthairs are quite catty cats, while the foreign types are very active and adventurous. So, armed with a basic knowledge of the temperament of different breeds, you can therefore choose a kitten to suit not only

My mother has a sanctuary for cats. A large number of them lived together for some time without breeding, but as the older ones died the younger ones have begun to breed. Why is this happening?

It is possible that overcrowding prevented an increase in numbers. In the wild it is found that many groups of animals will not expand beyond the number that the territory can support and feed. It isn't usual for the cat to be self-regulating in this way because, when numbers increase too much, some animals move on to a new territory. In a sanctuary, however, the cats cannot move on.

Or it may be that one of the older cats was mating all the females without result. If he has since died, the younger cats would move up the hierarchical ladder and have their turn at mating the females. Ideally, cats which live in a cat sanctuary should all be neutered to prevent an increase in their numbers.

yourself, but your present cat, too.

Another advantage is that a pedigree cat breeder should not only have an in-depth knowledge of the cat type she breeds, but should also know each kitten in each litter — because although temperament varies with breed, individual temperament varies from kitten to kitten. Even the most placid mother produces kittens which can vary in character. So explain carefully to the breeder exactly the sort of kitten you are looking for, and don't be afraid to ask for advice — good breeders are always looking for the best homes for their kittens.

Breeds of pedigree kittens have varying, and to a large extent, recognisable personalities

YOU SHOULD choose a kitten to suit your cat, particularly if it is very dominant or excessively retiring. Don't choose a kitten just because it is a pretty colour and hope that its personality will change: it won't. It is particularly important to acquire a non-pedigree kitten from a source where it has been living as part of the family; then the family can advise you about its temperament. Rescue shelters can give invaluable advice on this subject; pet stores less often; and kitten farmers know nothing whatsoever about the temperament of their charges.

COMMENT As always, introduce cat and kitten carefully. Remember that the new kitten is for your cat; it isn't for you — at least until your cat has made friends with it. Proper introductions can set the seal on a rewarding friendship, while the wrong introduction can put your cat's back up — literally.

I bought a kitten from what I thought was a reliable source. The breeder seemed so nice but my kitten isn't what I expected her to be at all. She was healthy but very nervous. I think she'd been kept in a pen all the time. I also discovered that I'd been overcharged for her by several hundred pounds. Also, although I bought the kitten nearly a year ago, I haven't had her paperwork — her pedigree certificate hasn't been sent to me. Where did I go wrong?

This sort of problem is unfortunately more common than it should be, and it's often because most prospective owners don't know how to go about finding a reputable source for either pedigree or non-pedigree kittens.

It is vital that the purchase of a kitten (or any living creature) is not a matter of impulse. Just as you would choose a new car by studying

models, comparing prices and investigating the dealer's reputation, so you should ensure that the type of cat you want will suit you.

Where is the best place to acquire a kitten? If you want a non-pedigree kitten and no friend's cat has recently had kittens, approach your local rescue shelter or ask your vet; if you want a pedigree kitten, find out months before you purchase who has a reputation for fair dealing and good, healthy kittens.

Never take the kitten home on the day you first see it — indeed, no reputable breeder would allow it. Instead, go home and think about it, and don't be pressured by the thought that if you don't buy the kitten someone else will snap it up. Few kittens have waiting lists and even for those which do, a caring seller will allow the prospective owner a day or two to consider. If you buy a kitten from a rescue shelter, you will be checked out by a shelter volunteer to ensure that you are providing a good home, before the kitten is released to you.

I don't want anyone else to have the problems I've had with this breeder. So what can I do?

Some unscrupulous breeders survive simply because unhappy owners think there is nothing they can do, or shrug the whole thing off as a bad experience. Within days they come to love their kittens even if they aren't as expected, so again they do nothing, feeling it is somehow a rejection of their kitten to take action against the breeder. However, for everyone who does nothing, another dozen new owners fall for the same ploys, unscrupulous dealers make money, and many cats may suffer.

YOU SHOULD report your grievances about any pedigree cat breeder to the organisation which registers her or his cats. In the UK this will be the Governing Council of the Cat Fancy or the Cat Association. Ensure you have received a proper receipt at the time of purchase, and forward a copy of this and any other documentation you may have.

Complain to any newspaper or magazine in which the breeder advertises — even one justified complaint may be enough to stop the press accepting advertising.

If the breeder is a member of a cat club, inform the club's secretary or chairperson. Each cat club has rules which breeders must adhere to.

Don't forget organisations which exist to help the consumer, local Trading Standards Officers, the Citizens Advice Bureau, your solicitor. And notify the Royal Society for the Prevention of Cruelty to Animals if you believe that any animals are being treated cruelly or neglected.

COMMENT Breeders can be banned for life by their registration organisations from registering their cats with them in the case of misconduct. However, although this is sufficient to stop many bad breeders it doesn't stop them all; only by reporting abuses to the registration organisation can these people be weeded out. So if you haven't had a fair deal, do something about it: every time you let it pass, you let down an animal which can't speak up for itself.

My cat had kittens eight weeks ago. The kittens have been eating solid food but are still suckling from their mother. They all eat together from one bowl and mum lets the kittens eat first. When they finish, she has her meal. Now she is being sick after every meal.

Most feline mothers defer to their young kittens over food, and consequently may not receive enough to eat at a time when the energy demands on their bodies are enormous. Lactating mother cats need three to four times as much food as they would normally eat, and it should be of high quality (vets sell specially formulated foods). They will also benefit from a multivitamin and mineral supplement specifically for cats — available from vets and pet stores — and a calcium supplement while nursing of 100mg daily.

Your cat may not be receiving enough food if she allows her kittens to eat first. Feed them separately, then the amount each is eating is clearly apparent. Your female, through hunger, may be bolting her food and a rapidly eaten meal on an empty stomach can cause vomiting. However, continued vomiting by any cat, whether nursing kittens or not, is a cause for concern and veterinary advice should always be sought without delay.

At eight weeks, the kittens should be fully weaned. Your cat has expended a great deal of energy on them for the past four months — two months gestation and two months nursing and caring for them; this represents about 1/45 of the average cat's life, and equates to a human mother carrying a foetus and breastfeeding a baby for a total of more than eighteen months. The feline mother — who may have five or six kittens to care for — is therefore in need of a rest.

If a cat is used for breeding and is to have another litter at some time in the future (preferably not for at least another six or eight months), it is very important that she is given sufficient rest between litters. Although theoretically capable of producing four or five litters per year, the fittest queen should not be allowed more than two litters a year, and ideally one. Most kittens start eating solid food at around four weeks and should have correspondingly less access to their mother's milk. They should be weaned away gradually, because if they don't suckle, she will feel very uncomfortable. She will produce as much milk as is needed; so if her kittens are allowed to suckle for a short period for perhaps three times a day during the fourth week, twice a day during the fifth week, and possibly twice a day for a shorter period during the sixth week, her milk will slowly decrease. By the seventh week, normal, healthy kittens will be thriving on good quality cat food, kitten food and some fresh food.

Even the best feline mother will have had enough of feeding her kittens by the sixth or eighth week (though some wild-living cats may continue for nine or ten months) — their sharp little teeth and claws will be hurting her, and she will be relieved when you take over as 'mum'. Don't expect a vote of thanks from the kittens though — they will resist the change as long as possible!

TRY Separating the kittens from their mother at night. Place them in a large kitten pen with their food, water and litter tray. They'll eat solid food readily when mum isn't available, and mum will get some well deserved peace and quiet.

COMMENT We may be guilty of treating many mammals the same way we treat the cow, which we expect to produce milk year-round under very unnatural conditions. Perhaps we don't stop to think what a strain it is for any creature to suckle its young and keep producing milk month after month.

I've just had some advice from my vet which surprises me. My new kitten, eight weeks old, has diarrhoea. I'm feeding him a well-known brand of cat food and my vet says his diarrhoea may be caused because I'm feeding him different flavours of the same brand of food. He suggests feeding just one flavour. Could this be causing the diarrhoea?

It is always best to allow a vet to check over any kitten suffering from diarrhoea as young kittens can become dehydrated very quickly. There are a number of possible causes, including worms, which a vet can advise on.

However, I doubt that feeding different flavours of the same brand of food would cause diarrhoea. Although the gourmet or super-premium brands of cat food contain large proportions of the meat named on the label, most everyday cat foods contain little or none. For example, 'salmon' and 'lamb' flavour may be virtually identical in composition, and neither contain any salmon or lamb at all. The contents of 'everyday' canned or dried foods can include offal from abattoirs and poultry factories, frozen and dried blood, fish trimmings and ground bone. To the resulting gloop are added the minerals necessary for health, colourings to make the product appeal to the consumer's owner (not the

PARIAH PUSS

'Mum! Mum! Come here quickly!'

'What's the matter?'

'It's Timmy. He's growing horns!'

'Horns? Don't be silly. Cats can't grow horns.'

'Well, he is!'

I look. In front of each ear is a perfectly round, slightly scabby, hairless patch that is vaguely reminiscent of a recently de-horned goat kid.

'See!' my daughter continues. 'It's probably because he's such a devil, killing birds and voles.' She smiles at her joke.

Purring, Timmy looks up at me, all love and melting eyes.

'Have you kissed him, Stephanie?' Her name is not Stephanie but she is fourteen and has just reached the 'Why didn't you give me a more romantic name?' stage and this month it's Stephanie.

'No,' she replies.

'Has he nuzzled you under the chin?' It's one of his favourite endearments.

'Hmmm, a bit. Why?'

'Go wash your hands and chin very thoroughly. I think it's ringworm and it's catching.'

She drops poor Timothy like a hot stone and rushes to the bathroom.

I inspect the four other felines. Timmy's sparring partner, Tiger, has two small 'horns', too. Henry, Timmy's surrogate mother, has one, just in front of his crumpled ear. Oh, dear.

In my vet box I find half-a-dozen tablets and some antifungal powder, both at least six years old, from the last ringworm plague. They'll have to do until I can get to the vet.

I mix the powder with water and bathe the offending portions. I get out the pills.

Timmy and Tiger, the young bloods, take theirs like lambs; grab the scruff, open the mouth, pill at the back of throat, gulp.

Henry, the passive, mild-mannered, elderly gentleman, fights like a tiger. I wrap him in a blanket; he jams his jaw shut, but I manage to prise it open half an inch. I push the pill in through the large gap between his three remaining teeth and clamp his jaw shut. Head back, throat massage, gulp. Hallelujah! As I let him go, a very moist pill shoots out of the side of his mouth and he makes a bolt for the cat flap.

After three repeat performances and one disintegrated pill, I give up. My daughter puts her head round the door.

'All done?'

consumer itself who doesn't care what colour its food is), and flavourings to make the food palatable.

The basis of the everyday foods is virtually identical until a flavouring is added, and unless your kitten is allergic to any particular one — which is possible but unlikely — feeding several flavours of one brand of cat food is unlikely to give it diarrhoea. However, feeding different *brands* of cat food may. When you first buy a kitten, ask the breeder what it has been eating and continue to feed that food for several days. If you then wish to change its food, do so slowly to prevent a stomach upset. Add a spoonful of the food you have chosen to your kitten's regular food. Then increase the percentage of your chosen food at the same rate as you decrease the regular food until your kitten is eating 100 per cent new food. Young kittens require a higher protein intake than adult cats so the best thing to feed them is kitten food, not cat food; there are several brands on the market, and there is one available from some pet stores which has no added colourings or flavourings — it is made from chicken and fish, so is very bland. Vets also sell foods specifically formulated for kittens.

What other causes of diarrhoea are there?

Giving cows' or goats' milk most commonly causes diarrhoea in young kittens, apart from change of food; kittens don't need milk once they are weaned, and many are allergic to the lactose in it which they are unable to assimilate. Anyway, cows' or goats' milk is a very poor substitute for queens' milk.

Overfeeding will cause diarrhoea, too. Give your kitten three or four small meals a day; however, if food is left on the plate, or your kitten has bulging sides, or passes faeces more than two or three times a day, you are probably overfeeding it. Cut down on the amount, though not the number of times fed — kittens have small stomachs and need regular topping up.

Intestinal worms can cause diarrhoea, so a kitten should be wormed for roundworms at around four weeks of age, at eight weeks and at around fourteen weeks. However, if your kitten has diarrhoea, don't worm him until the diarrhoea stops.

COMMENT There is one brand of canned food which seems to cause more stomach upsets than any other. If you think the cause of diarrhoea is the brand of food you are feeding your cat, try a different brand to see if the diarrhoea stops.

'No, Henry's outwitting me. His pill's melted.'

'Henry?' she echoes in disbelief. 'Oh, mum, you are a wimp. I'll give it to him.'

I don't argue, it's not worth it. Besides, I'm a great believer in the discovery method of education. I hand her a dry pill and she goes Henry-hunting.

Unsuspecting, he is lured by his sweet, friendly young mistress. I stand clear. Suddenly the trilling endearments cease, and she grabs him by the scruff.

'Now, Henry,' she commands fiercely. 'Take your pill or I'll smack you!'

'Daphne!' I cry, horrified.

'Stephanie,' she corrects.

'Whoever you are,' I continue hotly, 'don't you dare smack him!'

'Of course I won't, mum. I'm just telling him. You've got to master animals.'

With this she wrenches open his jaw and shoves the pill down his throat. It vanishes. She pats his hard little head and he purrs. What was that about babes and sucklings?

The vet confirms my fears, blames me for encouraging hedgehogs, and gives me a cartload of pills. I decide to treat the hedgehogs too, as they are a source of infection.

'It'll be a long haul,' he says.

At least I won't have to bathe them all once a week in anti-fungicide as I recall doing last time.

That treatment has, happily, fallen from favour in the interim, the vet says. Just as well. I've still got the scars.

'Ringworm!' my husband cries. 'They'll all have to stay outside.'

They are confined to the utility room. I warn my neighbour with the longhaired Cream. She is not amused.

I buy up the Co-op's entire supply of washing soda and six pairs of rubber gloves. I wash every washable surface with a very strong soda solution. We all start adding disinfectant to our bath water and inspect every skin blemish with suspicion.

The weeks pass. Henry cowers whenever he sees me but his patch vanishes. Tiger's patches fade but Timmy, now re-named The Ringworm Kid, still looks as though he's growing horns. As he spends many happy hours in the stables massacring rodents, I begin to worry about the goats and they, too, have to endure regular inspections.

Our friends, hearing the news, shun us. My daughter moons around the house at weekends as her friends won't visit, either.

'Cheer up, Tiffany,' I say.

'Stephanie!' she yells. The isolation is affecting her nerves.

I'm nearly out of pills and 'The Kid' still has his horns. Oh dear, when there is a plague on your house, it *is* a long haul.

Jackie Short

How not to visit your vet too often

Self help?

A seven-year-old Bourne-mouth cat started acting strangely, leaping in the air and staggering about. A vet said he believed that someone locally had been growing marijuana plants which the cat had eaten. The cat had to undergo the indignities of a stomach pump.

Preventative medicine is a very popular concept nowadays, and it can apply to your cat just as much as it can to you. Veterinary bills can be expensive, especially over a long course of treatment, so keeping your cat fit and well will save you both heartache and money. All it takes is a little time and forethought — and visits to the vet can be kept to a minimum if we look after our cats as well as we should look after ourselves.

The timetable opposite is a guide to keeping your feline fit, though some items may have to be altered to suit individual cats. For example for a Persian, daily grooming, not weekly, is essential. A hunting cat will require worming more frequently than an indoor cat. And if you have wool carpets, flea treatments may need to be more regular than if you have nylon carpets.

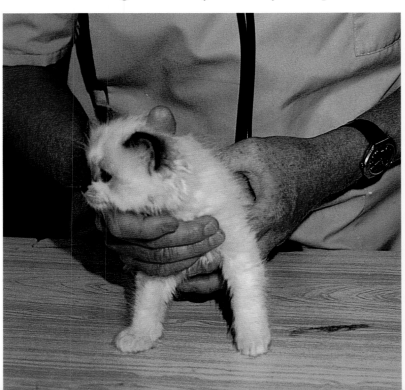

Inoculating your cat or kitten gives your vet an opportunity to give it a general health check-up

THE FIT FELINE TIMETABLE

Yearly	Inoculate against feline infectious enteritis and feline respiratory disease (combined inoculation)	*These diseases are fatal*
One to three -monthly	Worm against roundworms	*Worms can cause a serious loss of condition and damage to liver and lungs*
	De-flea	*Fleas cause loss of condition and can carry fatal diseases. Many cats develop an allergy and can lose fur*
Monthly	Use a hairball treatment, if necessary	*Hairballs may require surgical intervention if allowed to build up*
Weekly	Groom	*Swallowed hair will lead to hairballs*
Daily	Play with your cat	*Play keeps cats fit and helps expend unused energy*
	Water	*Fresh, clean water should be available at all times*
Twice daily	Feed	*Good-quality food keeps cats healthy*
	Clean litter trays	*Cats will not use a dirty tray and consequently may not urinate frequently enough, which could lead to urological problems*
Nightly	Keep cat indoors	*Cats are more likely to be lost, stolen or injured during the hours of darkness*
Constantly	Keep your home safe and know where your cat is	*Cats are easily poisoned by everyday products, injured in falls, trapped by curiosity, or lost*

Stress in the cat can take many different forms and can be caused by something as simple as erratic mealtimes

The cat under stress

Few people realise, as they see their cat relaxed and purring, that stress is a major problem for felines. Any deviation from the normal pattern of their day may cause them to become stressed, which lowers their tolerance to illness and may lead to behavioural problems such as soiling or spraying. What are the causes of stress in cats? Taking a cat to compete in a show is one, which is why no cat is allowed to compete more often than once a fortnight. Yet despite the long journeys usually involved and being penned for ten hours in an unfamiliar environment, a seasoned show cat may be less stressed by the experience than a cat, unused to travelling, which is taken on a five-minute car journey. Listed overleaf are some of the factors that cause cats to feel stress, the major

continued overleaf

continued

stresses coming first and the less stressful situation last:

Going to live with a new owner (adult cat)
Moving house
Divorce of an owner
A death in the family
A journey by aeroplane
Going to live with a new owner (kitten)
A new pet joining the household, dog or cat
Having to share a home with three or more other cats
Remaining entire (un-neutered)
Excessive overweight
An unsympathetic owner
Having a serious illness or a broken limb
Builders or decorators in the home for more than a few hours
A new baby in the house-hold
A new cat on the territory
A family member leaving or an adult joining the household
Staying in a cattery while an owner is on holiday
Competing in a cat show
A long journey by road or rail
An owner on holiday while the cat is looked after at home
Erratic mealtimes or lack of routine
Loneliness and boredom
A visit to the vet for a check-up
A short journey by road or rail

What can you do if your cat is suffering stress? First, be understanding and patient. If you know when your cat is likely to be upset it makes dealing with any consequent problems that much easier, because you know that the problem will cease when the cat feels secure and unthreatened again. Have regular play

continued opposite

COUNTDOWN TO HEALTH

Yearly: Inoculations

Feline infectious enteritis and feline respiratory disease (often referred to as 'cat 'flu') don't sound particularly serious but are both fatal to the majority of cats which contract them. Yet both illnesses are easily preventable — all it takes is one combined inoculation once a year. Kittens are protected by the antibodies in their mother's milk for the first two months of life, but should be given their first inoculation at nine weeks with another at twelve weeks. Thereafter, one yearly booster inoculation will prevent cats from suffering from either illness — yet only 8 per cent of cats in the UK have boosters on a regular basis. Those of breeding queens should be up-to-date at the time of conception in order to pass on antibodies to their offspring. Queens in kitten should not be inoculated with live vaccine, but with a 'killed' vaccine, so always inform your vet of her condition at the time.

The yearly booster is an opportunity for your cat to have a general health check-up, which a good vet will do without being asked; perhaps the early stages of an illness can be diagnosed and corrected — possibly even before you knew your cat was unwell. Also, you can ask your vet questions about any aspect of your cat's health, and can stock up with worming tablets, and flea or hairball treatments, all of which are sold by most vets.

These inoculations (for FIE and FRD) are the only ones currently given in the UK; in other countries, both Feline Leukemia Virus (FeLV) and rabies inoculations are available. The former is not available in the UK at the time of writing due to fears about its efficacy and the risk of side effects; and rabies inoculations are not yet necessary as the UK is currently (1990) rabies-free.

One- to three-monthly: Worms

The most common type of intestinal worm found in cats is the roundworm. These live in the intestinal canal so they prevent the proper absorption of food, and cats with worms will become malnourished; poor condition of the fur and a loss of weight is frequently the first sign of worm infestation. A wormy cat may be off its food, have a pot belly, will have either diarrhoea or be constipated, and may vomit or cough.

Regular worming is vital to keep a cat in tip-top condition. Kittens may be born with roundworms, or become infected via their mother's milk — the larvae will have been dormant during pregnancy, then develop under the influence of the queen's hormones to infect her offspring. Adult cats can become infected by eating prey whose bodies contain encysted larvae, which develop into worms when eaten.

Worming and flea treatments go hand in hand: cats may swallow fleas while grooming, and if the fleas have worm eggs in their systems, they will develop in the cat's body. However, treatments for worms and for fleas should *not* be given at the same time, as together they can prove toxic. Leave at least four or five days between the two.

If your cat hates taking pills, palatable roundworm tablets are available. Many cats will eat these whole, like treats, and all will eat them if mashed up and mixed into their food. If you have more than one cat, feed them a very small meal one at a time, making sure they eat every morsel so that they get the proper dose.

Kittens should first be wormed for roundworms at around four weeks of age — worms are particularly dangerous to young kittens. Repeat this a month later, then a month to six weeks after that. Adult cats can be wormed every three months or so (even though many worming products recommend monthly worming) though hunting cats should be wormed more frequently than those which stay indoors; queens should be wormed before mating and during the last few weeks of pregnancy. In the case of young kittens and pregnant females, ask your vet's advice for the best and safest product to use.

You may never see a tapeworm, although your cat may be suffering from them. They are rarely seen in faeces, and are less common than roundworms, but they are often viewed with more revulsion because bits of their segmented bodies may break off and be seen wriggling on the fur around the cat's anus, looking like brownish grains of rice. A specific drug to kill tapeworms is necessary ; a roundworm preparation will not kill them. A cat

An off-colour cat may have worms. Regular worming is vital to keep a cat in tip-top condition

continued

sessions with your cat because exercise is an excellent way to unwind. Once a day, sprinkle a little catnip on the floor for your cat to roll on, as this herb will help your cat relax. Spending a quiet time with your cat on your lap, stroking it until it purrs, is as good as a massage for releasing tension.

For extremely stressed cats, a vet may prescribe tranquillisers; just as with humans, these have enormous benefits when used intelligently, but should be considered as a last resort. Altering your cat's lifestyle to eliminate the stress it is feeling should always be your first priority.

To trim your cat's claws, press gently with thumb on top of the paw and fingers below to bring the claws out of their sheaths. Trim off just enough to blunt them, without cutting into the quick which runs through the centre of the claw

If you think your cat has fleas, comb it thoroughly while it stands on white tissue paper. Then dampen the paper. If the black debris turns red, it is because there are flea droppings present which contain your cat's digested blood

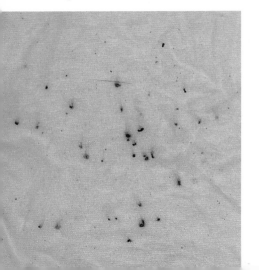

which hunts can be wormed for tapeworms every two to three months; an indoor cat less frequently. If tapeworms have been seen, burn your cat's bedding as segments will have dropped off there, and keep your cat free of fleas as they can start a new infestation.

One- to Three-monthly: Fleas

Fleas are very easy to control — once you know how. They are also nothing to be ashamed of, as all cats will have fleas at some time in their lives. A female flea can be responsible for around 250 offspring *every month,* so the pet owner must wage war against not just the adults but the young at every stage of their life cycle. Understanding that life cycle can help win the war.

Fleas don't spend all their lives on their cat hosts, so simply spraying the cat will not kill all the fleas. Also, they lay their eggs in warm, undisturbed surroundings such as in carpeting, around skirting boards and in corners, and sometimes in stuffed furniture. So when buying a flea spray, buy two different types, the second type being an environment or surface spray for use on your cat's living areas.

Surface sprays are very powerful and should be used according to instructions. Spray one room at a time, first of all removing all living creatures, including fish (which can be killed by flea spray), and all food and water bowls. Spray all carpeting thoroughly, along walls, in corners, and especially under radiators; fleas like warm spots. Spray soft furniture thoroughly — though check for staining on an out-of-sight corner first, if you are worried. Then close the door and leave the room for the recommended amount of time. Try not to breathe too deeply while spraying, and wash all exposed skin thoroughly afterwards. Air the room before allowing anyone — feline, human or piscine — back into it.

If you fail to do this regularly, you may have to call in the local pest control officer to do it for you; and although surface sprays are not particularly cheap, they still cost less than having professional pest control treatment. Treatment will also disrupt your household routine, as you will have to leave home for around six hours. All in all, it is to be avoided, if possible.

Fleas seem to be particularly fond of natural fabrics — wool carpets and feather-stuffed pillows — and largely scorn man-made carpeting and foam furniture. I once had a dreadful flea infestation in a settee with feather cushions, and to eradicate it, had to spray it thoroughly, cover it with plastic sheeting and leave it overnight.

Although cat fleas will bite humans (especially around the ankles and wrists), they will not live on them, preferring the tastier cat.

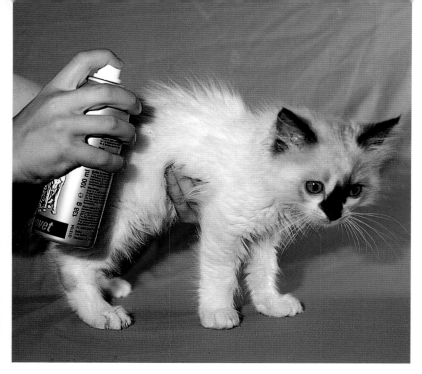

To de-flea your cat, use a spray formulated for cats — *not a surface spray:* first, grasp your cat firmly by the scruff of the neck, without pulling its paws clear of the floor. Rub its fur up the wrong way, so that the spray reaches its skin, and quickly spray a two-second burst along its back. Then, lifting it clear with your hand under its chest, spray a two-second bust along its tummy.

Most cats detest being sprayed and owners dread de-fleaing — but it has to be done. And four seconds of discomfort every month or two are much better than suffering the result of fleas. Ask a friend to help; one person can hold the cat while the other one sprays.

Cats hate de-fleaing because they are being sprayed with a *poison* — it has nothing to do with the hiss of the spray. Cats will instinctively avoid most poisons, so to be sprayed with one is distressing for them. But if any manufacturer manages to invent a non-poisonous flea spray, you can be sure it won't kill the fleas; they are extremely tough little creatures, with hard outer shells, and a product has to be strong to be effective against them.

If you can't bear to spray your cat, vets can now prescribe either tablets which it can take daily, or a product which can be added to its food; these keep the fleas off the cat altogether.

How do you know if your cat has fleas?. . . If it is scratching, especially around the ears, under the chin or at the base of the tail. You have to be quick to see a flea; they are tiny reddish-brown insects which move extremely fast, and in fact the only indication of their presence may be their droppings, which look small, black and dirty. These are easy to see on light-coloured cats, but very difficult on dark cats — especially black ones because they have

I had two cats but one was killed on the roads. The younger cat has now taken on the personality of the older cat. Why?

Cats react in different ways to the loss of a feline companion. Some appear to go through a grieving process, when they stop eating and mope around looking lost, sometimes for months; others take on a new lease of life. These are cats which have been dominated by their companions, and have had to take second place when food or comfortable sleeping places have been disputed. With the loss of the other cat, the subservient feline becomes top cat — and enjoys it.

Many cats show their new joy in life by becoming more friendly towards their owners, and may lie on laps they have ignored for years. The behaviour of some will alter drastically; for example one cat — the least-favoured of a pair — pulled chunks of its own fur out for years. When its companion died, the habit ceased immediately so obviously the stress it had suffered while being undercat had caused the fur-pulling in the first place.

Scratching is often the first sign of fleas, especially around the ears or under the chin

dark skin, too. If you suspect the presence of fleas, comb your cat while it is standing on a sheet of paper. Dampen anything which drops off with water: if it turns red, it is flea dirt; and flea dirt turns red because it it composed of your cat's digested blood.

Which spray to use? Ask advice from your kitten's breeder or your vet. I know of two sprays with identical active ingredients, yet in my experience one is very effective at killing fleas and the other isn't.

Why sprays? Because I think they are the most effective and, in the long run, the least damaging to your cat's health. Flea collars work by spreading an insecticide over the cat's fur, which means that it is constantly in contact with a poison. An RSPCA survey showed that, of a sample of 569 cats wearing flea collars, 408 suffered from dermatitis around the neck and 161 *were injured or died* through wearing collars. (Remember, collars can become hooked on bushes or trees and may throttle your cat.)

If you insist on using a flea collar, remove it for several hours each day (better still, overnight) to allow your cat's skin to breathe — and always take collars off if they get wet. They needn't be worn constantly because of the residual effect of the insecticide on the fur; they also take a day or two to be effective after being put on.

How often to use a spray treatment? If you are an observant owner, I would say 'as necessary': when you notice your cat scratching, or when you seen flea dirt in your cat's (regularly combed) fur; or you may notice a circular, raised, red and itchy lump on your own skin. If you are an unobservant owner, you may notice nothing: in which case, spray regularly — every month or two, depending on the time of year. Spring used to be the peak time for fleas, but now the problem is almost year-round because with central heating we make our surroundings more comfortable both for ourselves and for fleas, which consequently thrive. Certainly, peak times are still springtime and when the central heating is switched on, so spray then, and as necessary in between. During very hot summers it may be necessary to spray every few weeks.

Flea powders can be used, and often are, by those who believe their cat's dislike of de-fleaing is because of the hiss of the spray. Powders should be puffed onto the *skin* (rub your cat's fur the wrong way to reveal it) and then thoroughly brushed out. Powders have the advantage that they can be used on cats which won't tolerate sprays. If a cat objects to powders too, place the powder in an old pillowcase, insert your cat with its head clear of the top, and rub the powder into its fur through the case. Or there are special applicators, brushes with hollow spikes, which distribute powder through a cat's coat. These are often sold at cat shows or are advertised in cat magazines.

Why does my female cat walk around with her tail in the air when my other two cats don't?

She does it because she's a happy little soul. A tail held high in the air is a sign of a cat at peace with the world. It would be more interesting to find out why your other cats *don't* have their tails in the air!

If you are a nervous owner, don't be embarrassed at asking for assistance; the trick is to be quick and firm (but kind). Remember that your vet will assist you with any problems you may have, including de-fleaing, and will teach you how to do it yourself; and your cat's breeder, or any local breeder of cats, will also assist you and teach you how to do it yourself.

Of course, there are other methods which don't involve poisonous substances. Cat owners used to get rid of fleas by combing their cats with a fine-toothed comb; each time they combed out a flea, they would burn it in a flame, or drown it in liquid (it's a waste of time trying to squash a flea in your fingers — they're too tough). Even today there are owners who never use flea treatments, because thorough daily combing gets rid of them all. But do you have time for a thorough daily grooming?

Herbal treatments can be effective in repelling fleas; they won't kill them, but they will keep them off your cat as long as they are continually used. Garlic is said to repel both fleas and worms; an infusion of lemons, rubbed on the coat, is said to repel fleas, as is Wormwood (*Artemesia absinthium*), a perennial herb which yields a bitter oil. Grow it in your garden or in a window-box, dry it, rub it into the coat and brush out. There are now herbal flea-repellents available in the form of cat collars, powders, liquids and sprays.

And an ultra-sonic device has been invented, which a cat wears around its neck on a collar. The ultrasonic waves are said to be inaudible to humans and to cats, but their vibrations make it impossible for fleas to attack your pet; however, recent research in the USA has cast doubt on their efficiency; according to the scientists, fleas are deaf!

Monthly: Hairballs

Hairballs — or furballs — are caused when a cat swallows an excess of hair when grooming. Often the cat disposes of the hair itself by passing small amounts in faeces or by sicking it up; and if you brush your cat regularly, hairballs won't be a problem at all.

If the cat is unable to eliminate them, however, expensive surgical intervention may be necessary.

The cat's tongue is like one of those combs which is used for backcombing hair, and a cat uses it to groom its fur; but once hair (or anything else) is stuck on its barbs, the cat is unable to spit the hair out and must swallow it. Swallowed hair can build up internally into a hairball, and if this is not eliminated, it causes a blockage and the cat is unable to eat. This is when surgery is necessary to save its life.

Therefore comb or brush your cat at least once a week, and if it is longhaired, comb it more often than that. If it is a Persian or

---

Is it possible to train a cat not to cross busy roads?

Probably not. You would have to accompany your cat each time it goes out, and discourage it from crossing by using an angry voice or slapping the ground in front of it. However, this may startle it and it could run into the road — the opposite effect to the one you want. If you are worried about traffic, consider the possibility of keeping your cat indoors, or fencing in part of your garden as a safe run.

I believe that cats are often safer living in the vicinity of very busy roads than they are when they live down quiet country lanes. A quiet road can lull a cat into a false sense of security and it may not hear a car until it is too late. On the other hand, busy roads are so noisy that most cats keep well away from them — unless chased by a dog or another cat.

Babylonian curse

The pet cemetery in Kensington Gardens contains the body of a cat poisoned in Victorian times, with a headstone laying a Babylonian curse on the poisoners. It's said the authorities wouldn't allow the curse to be engraved in English.

any other breed with extremely long hair, comb it daily. And comb an elderly cat several times a week, as ageing muscles can't cope with expelling hairballs or with the contortions necessary to groom a fur coat adequately. When cats of any description are moulting (usually in spring and early summer) comb them more often. And if you have a shorthaired cat which licks your other cats, watch that it doesn't end up with a hairball problem.

Especially during the moulting season, feed an oily meal once a week. Sardines or pilchards in oil will lubricate any swallowed hair and help pass it through the digestive system. If this is not sufficient, a hairball remedy will help. You will know if one is necessary if your cat crouches down with head low and makes a dry, rasping, 'honking' noise. It may also be off its food, looking miserable, or unable to eat much food at a time (though this, of course, may be a symptom of other problems). Hairball treatments are available at some pet stores and at all cat shows. They are

THE WOMAN WHO LIVED IN A SHOE

She came to be known as The Woman Who Lived In A Shoe and she will never know how we treasure her philosophical gem, delivered with artless honesty in a single, throwaway sentence.

Promoting spaying and neutering is a vital part of the Cats' Protection League's work and, true to the League motto, we help where we can. But with funds forever threadbare we must be selective and weed out cynical spongers like the shark who drove his 'penniless' aunt's cat to the vet, at our expense, in a gleaming Mercedes.

There was no Mercedes outside the house in the modest terrace in one of Belfast's poorest areas. The door stood ajar. When Audrey and I rattled the letterbox, a boy stuck his tousled head round the lintel.

'Hello, is your mother in?' I asked.

'Aye. Hey, ma — there's two big women wants you.'

Ma waddled down the hall, her contours proclaiming the imminence of a Happy Event.

'Are youse from the cats' home? I'm awful glad yis called. Like I told the lady on the 'phone, we have a wee problem.'

That was a typical Ulster understatement. The tiny living-room swarmed with cats. Kittens frolicked on the floor, the chairs and the hearth. Furry shapes dived from the top of the television and swung joyously on the curtains. A fireguard draped

with steaming nappies swayed crazily, then fell in a soggy heap. Stuffing sprouted from the side of the settee, where two coal-black feline charmers were having a ripping time.

I stared round in despair.

'We'll never find homes for all these in a month of Sundays.'

'Sure, I've got homes for them, love. A lot of the neighbours is havin' them an' my cousin in the country that was under the doctor with her gallbladder, she's takin' six. It's a farm, but she's good to her cats, feeds them outa proper tins and lets them sleep in the kitchen. It's not them wee kittens bothers me. It's Maggie and Bessie and Sadie.'

She pointed to the corner by the fire where two homely tabbies and a black-and-white lay placidly surveying the fruits of their labours.

'They're only strays that came to us, but God love them, you couldn't see them starvin'. We'd keep them if they were spayed but if they'd more kittens. . .'

We took her point.

'It's an awful lot of money to get them fixed, you see, an' Him Upstairs hasn't done a hands turn these years past.'

She jerked her thumb towards the ceiling.

'Spends half his time in the pub an' the other half in bed.'

Her rollicking laugh held no bitterness. Life, she

All cats should be groomed at least once a week to help prevent them swallowing loose hair

implied, was like that for a woman and one simply accepted it.

There was no doubt in our minds. This was a deserving case.

'You've done so much to help these cats, the least we can do is pay for their operations,' I told her. 'Leave it with us and we'll make the arrangements.'

'Thanks, love. That's good of yiz.'

From above echoed a series of alarming crashes. Our hostess reacted with a foghorn bellow.

'You come down here this minute or I'll skelp the living daylights out of yiz,' She grimaced. 'Jumping off the beds again. My head's turned with them.'

The house shook as if a railway train had thundered through it. Into the room burst the boy who'd greeted us. Behind him was a smaller boy, a larger boy, another smaller boy, three even smaller girls and a plump toddler, followed by a baby crawling furiously on all fours. Him Upstairs may have been workless, but you couldn't call him idle!

'We'll get those queens to the vet before the end of the week,' I assured Ma. 'Otherwise they'll be on their way again.'

'Aye, like me.' She patted her enormous stomach.

The children crowded onto the doorstep, chattering like starlings. The baby grabbed Ma's ankle and tried to bite it.

Ma sighed. Turning her eyes skywards, she uttered her immortal truth.

'By God,' she said, with a depth of feeling straight from the heart, 'I shoulda sent that oul *fella* of mine to the vet years ago!'

Lorna Gulston

Terraced life for a Belfast cat

extremely palatable, most being flavoured by malt, and cats will lick them up from their dish. However, the active ingredient is usually mineral oil, which coats a cat's stomach and intestines and hastens the passage of food through the stomach. It therefore robs the cat of nourishment, and so should never be given more often than the recommended dosage on the packaging (and preferably less often).

If no specific hairball treatment is available, medicinal liquid paraffin can be given. Give a teaspoonful once a day for three or four days, or until the cat expels the hairball — though for the same reason as given above, never for more than a few days. In any case, it is not easy to administer, as cats usually object strongly; it should be given very slowly, a drop at a time, into the *side* of its mouth. A medicine dropper is better than using a spoon, but in either case, care should be taken not to allow the liquid to enter the cat's lungs, or permanent damage could be caused.

Another alternative is petroleum jelly, rubbed onto a cat's paws. Any cat hates having sticky paws, so it will lick it off, though the same caution still applies, as above.

It's easier not to allow hairballs to develop in the first place. Keep combing, and stock up on hairball preparation at any cat show you might visit.

Weekly: Grooming

'But cats groom themselves,' say some mystified owners. 'They don't need our help.' Oh yes, they do! Especially if they are longhaired or elderly; and all cats receive enormous physical and emotional benefits from grooming by their owners.

Some owners never groom their cats; others groom daily, or every time their cat lies down on their laps. Kittens are used to being groomed when their mothers lick them, and an owner's stroking and combing is an extension of this and should be enjoyed; furthermore a cat which is regularly combed should not suffer from hairballs, and may not even suffer from fleas. I know someone who has groomed her cat daily since she has owned it and says it has never had a flea, despite it being normally attractive to fleas when it had a previous owner.

How do you groom a cat? It's easy if you have had your cat from kittenhood, because you take over the grooming role from its mother. But kitten or adult, introduce your cat to the process by just stroking it with your hands. All cats which are used to human company will enjoy this, and you won't be able to groom a cat until it enjoys being stroked.

Once it is used to the pressure of your hands, stroke it with a comb using short strokes. If it objects, stop. And if it begins to play with the comb, stop. It mustn't associate the comb with an

Opposite:
Cats have tongues covered in barbs. Once hair is stuck on the barbs, cats must swallow it

What does a cat cost?

It doesn't matter what a cat cost to buy. You may have spent £500 on a top quality new breed, or you may have been given a free kitten. Either way, the cost of looking after it for the next fifteen years will be exactly the same. The following estimated cost table for keeping a neutered cat for its average lifespan is based on today's prices, in the suburbs. If the cat is to be used for breeding, the cost could be one-sixth to one-third as much again. In large cities such as London, the cost of keeping any cat will be higher than that shown here.

Essential veterinary fees, neutering and inoculations	£215.00
Veterinary fees and drugs for one *minor* ailment or accident per year	£300.00
Veterinary treatment — one major accident or illness in 15 years	£550.00
Food:canned	£1,150.00
dry	£100.00
fresh — fish, offal, some chicken, eggs etc	£1,250.00
Mineral/vitamin supplements	£75.00
Litter	£500.00
Equipment: beds, scratching posts, climber, litter trays, combs etc	£500.00
flea and worming treatments, shampoos etc	£200.00
miscellaneous — toys, catnip etc	£150.00
Cattery fees: two weeks per year for 15 years	£500.00
Total:	**£5,490.00**

objectionable experience or confuse it with a play session. Try again when it is in a more receptive mood. Evening grooming sessions are often best, when a cat is relaxed and sleepy.

Start and finish on an area your cat enjoys having groomed, such as under the chin or behind the ears. Keep areas your cat doesn't enjoy, such as the tail or tummy, for the middle of the session, and do these quickly. Use a metal-toothed comb for cats, and if your cat is longhaired, use a specially designed comb with alternate long and short teeth. You can finish off with a brush if you like; natural bristles will prevent static building up.

It's a good idea to begin any grooming session by stroking your cat with your hands; not only does this get it in a receptive mood, it also enables you to feel any matts which may have appeared since you last groomed. Comb the favourite areas first, then along the sides, holding the comb at right-angles to the cat's body and using short strokes. If the comb meets any resistance, stop instantly; don't try to tug out any tangles as this will hurt, but tease them apart with your fingers. Some cats are relaxed enough to lie on their backs while their bellies are being combed; others will have to be dealt with standing on a table. The cat's backbone only has a thin covering of flesh, so it is best not to comb this area at all.

Generally cats don't get too matted or dirty, but if the fur does become heavily tangled, matts will have to be cut out. One or two can be done with round-ended scissors — cut upwards, from the skin towards the end of the fur so as not to cut your cat; or cut the matt across, ensuring you don't nick your cat's skin. Although the resulting baldish patch will not look particularly attractive, the fur will grow back. In a bad case the matts may have to be dealt with by complete shaving, under veterinary anaesthetic, which is not only expensive, but as with all anaesthetics carries a slight risk. Matted fur hurts a cat because as the matts tighten, they pull the skin; so as always, prevention is better then cure.

Although cats rarely need to be bathed, their only way of cleaning themselves is by licking, so if they get covered in something which might make them ill, bath them before they can groom themselves.

Bath your cat in a sink rather than in a bath (where you will have to do it on your knees) in warm water a few centimetres deep. The water should be the temperature of a baby's bath — test it by dipping your elbow into it and it should feel comfortable. Pour in a little shampoo; this breaks the surface tension and makes it easier to wet your cat down to the skin. Have several jugs of warm water ready to rinse it and place a piece of old towel at the bottom of the sink to stop it slipping about. Most cats will object, so put on a collar or harness so you can keep a grip on it (don't use a flea collar which should never be allowed to get wet while on a cat). Put an apron on yourself and take a deep breath.

Making as many soothing noises as possible, place your cat gently in the water. Stroke it and calm it down, then start by wetting the bottom of the flanks and working upwards. Don't pour water over the face or head; use a damp cloth. When the cat is wet, pour a little shampoo onto its back and start lathering. There are many shampoos made specifically for cats; otherwise use a very mild baby shampoo. Don't use a dandruff preparation for humans, or detergents, or anything containing lanolin which may make your cat's fur sticky.

When you have lathered up the fur, pull out the sink plug and start rinsing off using the jugs of warm water. When all soap has been removed (usually one lathering is enough or as much as any cat will stand) wrap your cat in a warm, dry towel. Always shampoo in a 'waterproof' room such as a kitchen, as your cat may shake itself dry. Rub it through the towel, and when that one is wet, wrap it in another dry towel. Your cat should then be completely dried off in a draught-free, very warm room and kept indoors for the rest of the day. A cat's fur has wonderful insulation properties, but damp fur makes it very cold indeed. You'll be surprised how skinny your cat is, too, when its usual thick covering of fur is stuck flat to its body.

If either you or the cat are nervous about bathing, a helper will

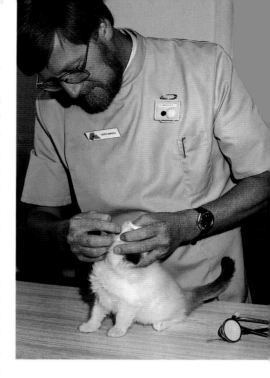

Veterinary fees are just one item of a total cat-keeping cost of around £5,500

Persians' coats can easily become matted if they are not thoroughly groomed every day

be a godsend. If your cat is likely to lash out in fear, trim its claws a little and remember to speak soothingly to it all the time you are bathing it.

For fur which has got just a little grubby, use a dry shampoo. For white fur, talcum powder (preferably unscented) can be sprinkled on and thoroughly brushed out; or use ground up Fullers' Earth (the grey type of cat litter) or bran *warmed* a little (not heated) in an oven, both of which must be thoroughly brushed out.

Daily: Play

Bored cats can become destructive cats — yet cats have always been considered animals which can amuse themselves. Certainly there is plenty to occupy the cat living in a large, rural territory, with feline friends in the area and an owner to chat to when wanted.

But most cats nowadays live in urban settings, with tiny territories which may already belong to unfriendly felines. Consequently they are unwilling to go out of doors so are more restricted to their homes. And what it the typical home of the average feline these days? It is an empty house or apartment, with owners at work. Some cats are totally restricted to an indoor life, which can be safe and happy if all their needs are provided for, but like a solitary confinement if they are not.

Cats must 'play', and play to a cat is virtually indistinguishable from its natural behaviour of stalking and hunting. And if a cat no longer needs to hunt to survive, we must replace those instincts with something else: play.

Although many owners will play with kittens, they seem to think this is no longer necessary as their cat matures. Yet play sessions will keep a cat fit and healthy, and will use otherwise unexpended energy; it also strengthens the cardiovascular system and lessens stress. The owner who plays with her cat isn't woken at 3am by a bored and yowling animal, nor does she return home to find the wallpaper shredded from the walls. A strong bond will be forged between them, and she will enjoy the play sessions as much as the cat does.

Many of us lead sedentary lives these days, so we have to make a special effort to keep fit, working out at the gym, or playing squash. Cats nowadays also lead comparatively sedentary lives, so should also be encouraged to 'work out'.

So how do you play with your cat? Once (or better still, twice) a day, set aside some time for play, preferably not immediately before or after a meal. Start off and finish gently; and always collect safe, attractive play items. Roll objects for your cat to play with and chase — table tennis balls, or plastic golf practice balls

with holes cut into them which allow your cat to hook them into the air. Try also plastic eggs, pine cones and wine corks, which are oddly shaped and will roll erratically — your assistance will be necessary to retrieve these from under and behind furniture. If your cat enjoys playing in a cardboard box, place one of these rolling objects inside.

Basically, all it takes for play to start is for you to start the ball rolling — literally. Cats are attracted by movement and will ignore most stationary objects, so roll the ball and off you go!

Remember: don't roll balls or other objects *towards* your cat: prey animals of course run *away,* a*nd so should any play objects.

You can also trail something about for your cat to chase and pounce upon — use a dressing-gown cord or a cord which won't shred and be swallowed. Again, trail it away from your cat or dangle it from above so your cat can jump up at it. Never allow your cat to play unattended with string or wool; if it swallows some of it, it won't be able to spit it out and will continue swallowing it.

Play sessions keep cats' cardio-vascular systems healthy. This kitten is treating a soft ball like a prey animal and enjoying its 'capture'

Further growth

When a thirteen-year-old cat lost nearly all her fur, her vet suggested that an increased fat intake might help. Every day for three months, her owner covered her with melted margarine, which the cat licked off. Her fur grew back again.

Every time I use bleach my cat is ecstatic. He rolls around on the wet floor and licks it. I can't stop him from trying to bite through the bleach bottles under the sink.

Some cats adore the smell of bleach and react in the same way as they do to catnip. However, rolling in catnip will do your cat no harm, whereas rolling in bleach is very dangerous. It will burn your cat's tongue if he licks it off his fur, and it will burn his pawpads if he walks on it. So keep your cat *out* of the room until the floor is dry. And move those bleach bottles to a high, safe cupboard; if your cat succeeds in biting through them, the bleach could kill him.

Adult cats shouldn't be given milk – even though they may enjoy it – because many cats are allergic to milk

Daily: Water

Water is essential to every creature's survival. Forget about milk — like us, cats don't need it once they are weaned. In fact, a surprising number of cats can't tolerate the lactose in milk after the age of about twelve weeks — it gives them diarrhoea. So always keep a plentiful supply of clean water for your cat to drink. Many cats will prefer a large container, as this is more like the natural waterhole they would drink from in the wild; this is why many cats will drink from fishtanks in preference to their drinking bowls — and they are really *not* trying to eat the fish. They will also drink from puddles of rainwater, where again, they are using a natural waterhole; they may also be seeking water which has not had chemicals added to it.

Chlorine and other chemicals in water can be off-putting to cats. However, these chemicals disperse in water which has been standing for a few days. — another reason why fishtanks are favoured. Unfortunately, drinking bowls can't be left for days between replenishings because, at floor level, they pick up so much dust and dirt. To encourage your cat to drink, supply filtered water or still mineral water; or bottle some tap water and use it a day or two later.

It is particularly important that an ill cat should drink; cats can survive for several weeks without food, but they must drink. To encourage it to do so, make a weak stock of bones or meat, then

A well-fed, healthy cat will have shining fur and eyes

drain, and place the cooled stock water in your cat's bowl, a little at a time. Or add a little honey or glucose to plain water.

A cat which loves milk can be encouraged to drink water by adding just enough milk to the water to colour it. Otherwise milk can be discarded as a drink for any weaned cat.

Some cats, especially those suffering from urological problems, must be encouraged to keep their liquid intake high. A little salt added to their food will make them thirsty and drink more without adversely affecting their health.

Twice Daily: Food

Nowadays, most cats are fed almost entirely on canned complete foods. Although this causes a guilt complex in many owners, who wonder if they are doing their best for their cats, canned complete foods are balanced nutritionally, and are much better for a cat than a home-produced diet which may be unbalanced if an owner hasn't time to prepare the necessary variety of foods. There are teams of skilled nutritionists working for the pet food companies, ensuring that complete foods *are* complete in every known nutritional requirement.

My cat insists on waking me up at 4am, and isn't happy until all the household is awake. How can I change his habits?

The first step would obviously be to keep him out of your bedroom. Some cats with this habit spend their nights in the kitchen, with a cosy bed and a litter tray. However, many owners like to have their cats around at night, so if you want him to sleep on your bed without waking you up, you could try the following:

Make sure your cat doesn't go to bed full of energy — play with him in the evening to tire him out. Feed him his last meal of the day just before bedtime, so he is more likely to sleep for longer; and make sure the meal is sufficiently large to keep hunger at bay until a reasonable hour the next morning. Then if he still wakes you at 4am, throw a pillow at him — but otherwise ignore him. Under no circumstances should you get up to feed him or let him out. If you do, he will realise he just has to persevere and he will get whatever it is he wants.

Cats can be trained from kittenhood not to bother their owners too early in the morning with the pillow ignoring treatment; and cats have a good sense of time — mine don't wake me until 8am on weekdays and 8.30 on weekends!

135

My cat ran away six weeks ago. Do you think after this length of time she will return?

It is always possible, so don't give up hope. In fact, cats rarely run away. If she has not been injured or killed in an accident, or stolen, she may unwittingly have hitched a lift. Frequently, when vans or lorries are loading or unloading, a curious cat will investigate the inside of the vehicle. When the driver comes back, the cat will hide, and is often locked in the van which may travel hundreds of miles before stopping again; once it is opened, the frightened cat runs out. Cats can be remarkably clever at finding their way home.

I know many instances of lost cats which turned up on their owners' doorstep, several years after going missing, walking into their homes as if they had just been for a five-minute stroll around the corner.

So how do you choose a canned cat food? There is a wide range available, but choosing a good food for your cat is simple. First of all, the 'everyday' foods *ie* for daily feeding: these are in the medium price range, usually packaged in cans of around 400g. Nowadays they are usually referred to as 'premium' foods, though as none is particularly special I feel the designation 'everyday' is more accurate. They are usually complete foods (check the label) which means they contain everything which is known to be necessary for good health in the average, adult cat. A 'supplementary' or 'complementary' food does not contain all the necessary nutrients, and a vitamin and mineral supplement will have to be given in addition.

For the average, adult, neutered cat choose a brand which is relatively high in protein (all levels are found on the labels) and low in ash (mineral content). Ideally, the food should have little or no cereal or soy content — although this adds protein to the food it is of lower quality than meat protein; it is also cheaper, which is why it is usually found in cheaper foods. Therefore select the brands which offer the best nutrition and value, and try to persuade your cat to eat the cheapest of them. Prices vary by several pence a can, and the more expensive everyday food is not necessarily better. Nor is your cat's favourite canned food necessarily the best; it is simply more palatable to the cat.

Gourmet cat foods (also called super premium foods) are increasing their sales. These are often sold in little cans or tubs, but cost around the same as the larger cans of everyday food. However, while everyday foods will be only *flavoured* with the meat named on the label, gourmet foods actually contain a large proportion of the genuine thing — some brands have 100 per cent of the named meat, others no more than around 25 per cent. Again, read the labels to see what the food contains, and to compare package sizes, as some are substantially heavier than others. Gourmet foods are higher in protein than everyday foods, so a cat will require less of them to feel satisfied.

Dry foods are convenient and economical; they are sometimes referred to as biscuits, but in fact are a complete food, unless they are 'treats' in which case they can be given occasionally as 'treats' and not used as a complete diet. A few pieces of dry food each day, sprinkled on top of other food, exercises teeth and gums. If your cat eats mainly dry food, make sure it is drinking plenty of water as it will not be receiving sufficient moisture in its food. Dry food can always be fed soaked in stock or water if this is a problem.

In addition there are semi-moist foods and chubs, though these are not big sellers in the UK; chubs are large, sausage-shaped plastic cylinders containing meat, but are usually not complete foods — and I view with suspicion those which are said to be suitable for cats *and* dogs. As the nutrient requirements of the two animals are quite different, cats should be given food made specifically for them.

For the same reason, cats should not be fed dog food on a regular basis. Dog food contains less taurine (an amino acid) than cat food because a dog can manufacture taurine in its own body; a cat cannot, and if constantly fed a diet deficient in taurine, it will develop progressive retinal atrophy and will eventually go blind. It may take some time before any problem is noticed, but by then the blindness will be irreversible. Taurine is also necessary for healthy heart function and for reproduction. Cat foods contain sufficient taurine; dog foods and vegetarian foods usually don't. Cats cannot remain healthy on a basic vegetarian diet because the levels of taurine and other nutrients are insufficient; this is compounded if they cannot supplement their inadequate diet through hunting.

However, a supplement is now produced which is said to supply the taurine, preformed vitamin A and arachidonic acid which are necessary for a cat's good health. The supplement is also suitable for vegans because it contains no animal products whatsoever, utilising such sources as algae and blackcurrant seeds. The supplement can be added to foods such as chickpeas, rice and soy beans, potatoes or lentils, and recipes are given with the product. Many of these include yeast and soy sauce for extra palatability. Although my own cats are not vegetarian, I have certainly found no resistance amongst them to eating chickpeas, lentils, rice and potatoes — provided they can steal them from my plate.

What about home-cooked food? This can cause problems if the owner isn't careful. For example, liver is often fed because cats enjoy it and it is inexpensive. However, it contains an excess of vitamin A which will lead to lameness, stiffness, distorted bones and other health problems if fed too often; the biggest problem is that some cats become addicted to it and refuse to eat anything else. So don't feed liver more than once or twice a week. Liver-*flavoured* canned foods are not a cause for worry because they may contain little or no liver at all.

A diet of home-cooked fish will not provide all the nutrients required for health either, although one or two meals of fish (both white and oily) a week is fine; similarly scraps can supplement your cat's diet. Cats don't suffer from coronary artery disease, so cooked fat cut from chops and cutlets can be given in moderation, as can the cooked skin and dark meat from poultry, as well as small amounts of leftover cheese and chopped vegetables.

Should you wish to feed your cat an entirely home-cooked diet, variety is essential, and try to keep as near to the cat's natural diet

---

My cat cries to go outside, but as soon as I let him out he cries to come back in!

Cats like to go out of doors for a little relief of several kinds: some prefer to excrete out of doors and, once having done so, like to come back indoors to the comfort and warmth of their homes. Others ask to go out just to check what has happened in their territory since their last visit. They sniff around to check which other cats have passed that way and, having reassured themselves, ask to be let indoors again. Some cats simply want to stretch their legs, or have a good strop on a bush or tree.

Don't overestimate how long a cat wants to spend out of doors. Despite that warm fur coat, indoors is always more comfortable and cosy, and cats, being intelligent creatures, would rather be inside than out.

Older cats – this one is fifteen – should have a restricted-protein diet

as possible. For this reason, fowl of all types and rabbit are good basic foods. Feed all of the meat and skin, including the organs, but do not give your cat cooked bones which will shatter and could cause choking. Fowl and rabbit are better thoroughly cooked because cats can suffer from salmonella poisoning and may die if the raw or undercooked carcase is contaminated.

Fish and liver have already been discussed; cheese is a good protein source, though too much of it will make many cats sick. Lightly cooked eggs (or well cooked if salmonella poisoning is a risk) can be given occasionally. Meat such as pork should always be thoroughly cooked, and ideally should not form part of the diet at all. Small amounts of beef are always enjoyed; and from time to time add some chopped, cooked vegetables.

Always remember that kittens, pregnant and nursing queens, and cats under stress have higher nutrient requirements. Vitamin and mineral supplements specially formulated for cats and available from vets and pet stores, should be given in accordance with the directions on the packet.

Older cats need less protein than the average adult cat, and more carbohydrate — cooked peeled potato, rice, bread and particularly pasta can be added to their regular food. Start off with very small amounts and build up the quantity until it is about one-third of the total. A high-protein diet makes the kidneys work hard and in an older cat the kidneys are often the first organs to fail.

Remember that feeding is a valuable training aid. If your cat is outdoors and you call it in for food, it will be eager to respond to your call; this is especially convenient when you want it in for the night. Therefore give your cat its last meal of the day just before bedtime; a later meal will also encourage your cat to sleep.

Twice Daily: Litter Changing

Providing a litter tray and keeping it clean will encourage a cat to use it. It will not only prevent 'accidents' happening on your carpets, but will help keep your cat healthy because it is eliminating its waste products more frequently.

The most commonly used litter is dried clay, which may be grey, white or pinkish in colour. The grey litter is usually the least expensive, especially if bought in quantity from pet stores. It is extremely absorbent and will hold moisture up to 125 per cent of its own weight; pour it into the tray to a depth of about 6cm because liquid will then form a solid ball which can be easily lifted out. Clay litters have good natural odour-absorbing properties (especially the grey), though a few have deodorant added; some cats don't like this — they may have an allergic reaction to it, and may even refuse to use it or may start sneezing if given it to use. Litter deodorants can also be purchased to sprinkle on a non-deodorised litter, though

My two cats run around like mad things together at certain times of the day. I'd like to know why.

What you are describing is referred to as a 'mad spell' by cat owners; some cats have a 'mad spell' every evening, some rarely do. It isn't caused by any mental imbalance, simply an excess of energy. Domestic cats don't often experience the intense bursts of activity required to catch their own food, so they indulge in these 'mad spells' to use up the energy which has no other outlet. Anything may start them off, a sound, a small movement or a companion cat showing a willingness to play.

many cats have the same reaction. If your cat refuses to use one, and if you are worried about odour, try sprinkling baking soda (which has odour-absorbing properties) on the litter. But odour needn't be a problem if the litter tray is carefully sited, kept clean, and litter used to the recommended depth.

Wood-based litters are pellets made from softwood sawdust which are extremely absorbent — they can absorb up to 300 per cent of their own volume — and have a pleasant, natural pine scent. Their odour-absorbing qualities are good on liquid waste, but not so good on solid waste. Wood-based litters should be used in a shallow layer as they expand when wet.

Both types of litter can be flushed away in small quantities or placed on the compost heap. Wood-based litters can also be burnt.

Today there is a new type of litter which is reusable. It is made of pellets of natural material covered in paraffin wax, and utilises a new design of litter tray with slots in the bottom and a collecting tray underneath. Liquid waste passes around the pellets, without wetting them, and collects in the tray which can be regularly emptied. This offers little or no smell from liquid waste, but it has no odour-absorbing properties for solid waste. The litter is washable, so can be used for many months. This type of litter is very useful if a vet asks you to collect a urine sample — simply pour it out of the lower tray.

Another new litter, currently available in the USA, is made by combining fibres from natural grasses and then drying them in the sun to make them absorbent. Apparently the litter controls odour well, doesn't cling to a cat's fur, and is also biodegradable.

Of course before cat litter, there were other litter mediums — shredded newspaper can be used, but in thick layers to prevent

I'm moving to an eighth floor apartment with my cat, who is very used to going out of doors. The apartment does have a balcony, but no access to the ground for my cat. How will he react to our new home?

When cats move house, they don't enjoy going out-of-doors at first anyway. They have lost their familiar territory, and the new one holds many fears and dangers for them. Your cat will be too concerned at first about *this* change to be aware of his newly restricted lifestyle.

When you have settled down, you may find that he adapts surprisingly well, especially if you have provided everything he needs to be content, and ensure that he has plenty to occupy himself. He will probably enjoy lying on the balcony, especially if it catches the sun, but make sure it is safe for him. Many cats are killed by falls from balconies and windows, despite their reputation for sure-footedness. You might consider fencing in the entire balcony with wire mesh to keep him safe, if it doesn't contravene building or fire regulations.

An indoor litter tray is cleaner and more healthy for your cat – and the neighbours will appreciate it too

Don't keep your cat out-of-doors for long periods and especially not at nights. At night, a cat will have to spend much of its time trying to keep warm and dry

your cat getting its feet wet; afterwards if can be burnt or placed on the compost heap. Garden earth or sand can be used too, and composted afterwards. Some cats will use a tray containing small smooth pebbles, which can be drained and washed regularly. I've even heard of one owner who, when he ran out of cat litter, filled his cat's tray with breakfast cereal! His cat ate the sultanas, and used what remained in the expected way.

Litter trays should be sited carefully, or a cat may not use them. A quiet spot, and away from food and water bowls (cats won't use trays sited near their food) is best. For those cats which like privacy, covered litter trays are available, or you can cover an ordinary tray with an upended cardboard box with a hole door cut into it. This will also prevent litter scattering over the floor.

140

Nightly: Keep Your Cat Indoors

You'll keep your cat safe by keeping it indoors at night; outside they are more likely to be injured, run over, lost or stolen. They aren't so easily seen in the dark, and may take chances on roads which they would not cross during the day.

At one time it was almost a tradition to put the cat out at night, but most owners now realise that this is not only unsafe, but unkind. Cats don't always have a very pleasant time if left to their own devices; they have to spend most of the night trying to keep warm and dry, with the constant threat of having to fight off not only feline trespassers, but dogs, foxes, rats and pet thieves, too. Cats will expect to spend their nights indoors if this is what they are used to from kittenhood. Serve the last meal of the day just before bedtime, provide a litter tray, water and a comfortable bed, and your cat has everything it requires. Cats used to spending the night outside *can* be converted, though they may complain at first. Until they are used to the idea, shut them in a room such as the kitchen with all their requirements and a few toys; then leave them there until next morning, ignoring any irate miaows. They will usually adapt very quickly and will appreciate the new comfort, especially if elderly.

Sober thought

Actuaries have compiled a league table showing the drinking habits of members of different professions. They've discovered that vets are the least likely of all the professions to be convicted for drunken driving. Not many people know that.

Garden chemicals can injure your cat. Keep them to a minimum and weed by hand

My cat retrieves other people's belongings from washing lines and wherever else she can find them. She is very proud of herself for doing this. How can I stop her without telling her it is wrong?

You could enlist a neighbour's help — which they may be only too glad to give if they are constantly having to retrieve their underwear. A gentle booby-trap may be the answer. Ask your neighbour to hang a few socks on the line, and inside each sock place a small plastic container full of water; if your cat pulls them off the line, she will get wet. Cats don't like that and she should desist, although it may take several soakings to get the message across. The best thing about this plan is that your cat will associate the socks with her soakings and won't blame you — which is what I think you're concerned about.

Constantly: Keep Your Home Safe and Know Where Your Cat Is

Thousands of cats are seriously injured or killed each year in their own homes. The old saying 'curiosity killed the cat' has a great deal of truth in it, for cats are curious about anything new in their environment and this can lead them into danger.

For example, cats will climb into washing machines to sleep on the clothes inside, so always check before switching on as many are killed in this way.

Don't open windows on upper floors more than a few centimetres. Many cats have fallen to their deaths after chasing an insect across a room and out of the window, and they are *more* likely to be injured by quite short falls — one kitten fell less than a metre and broke its neck. A longer fall from a greater height in fact gives a cat time to adopt a more aerodynamic position, to turn around and land on its feet. Cats should not be allowed to sleep on high windowsills as they can roll off in their sleep.

Many cats chew wires and flex. Train yours not to by removing it each time and saying 'NO' in a firm, loud voice. But don't take chances, cover flex with flex protectors, and unplug all unused appliances. And make sure your cat never jumps onto cooker hotplates as they may not have cooled down: train it to keep away from the cooker. Better still, keep cats out of kitchens while cooking.

Keep cleansers and chemicals out of reach. A cat which has swallowed poison may stagger, have fits, diarrhoea, or may vomit. Place it in a secure, darkened room while you telephone your vet. If you know what your cat has swallowed, take the container to the telephone so you can report the contents, and he or she can prepare or recommend an antidote.

Diluted household bleach is the safest cleanser to use in a household containing cats, though it should be left to dry thoroughly before a cat is allowed back into the room. Otherwise its paw pads will be burnt by the bleach, as will its tongue if it tries to lick it off.

Don't leave wool or string lying around, or threaded needles. A cat will play with any of these, and if it gets them into its mouth, it won't be able to spit them out again because of its barbed tongue, and will have to swallow them. Cats never swallow needles which aren't threaded.

In the garden, all chemicals should be kept in lidded containers rather than sacks which might split — slug pellets are a particular danger as cats often find them attractive to eat. Place pellets under upturned flowerpots; some cat-loving gardeners kill slugs and snails by sinking shallow containers of beer into the soil. The slugs drink it, fall in and drown. However, cats should not be allowed to drink alcohol either — some have become quite drunk and ill after imbibing the alcoholic slug bait.

If using sprays or poisons in the garden, ensure your cat is indoors and don't allow it out again until the area has dried completely. If a dew has fallen, the area will still be wet and a potential danger. Keep your cat indoors if a fence is being creosoted; it is corrosive, and will burn any skin it touches, including your cat's mouth if it tries to lick it off its fur. Hand cleanser such as that used by car mechanics will remove creosote from fur, but must be thoroughly rinsed out. If your cat has swallowed any creosote, milk should be given to neutralise the acid effect and the vet called immediately.

Dispose of anti-freeze carefully: it is poisonous, yet its taste is attractive to cats and dogs.

Take particular care of your cat at Christmas. It can choke on pine needles or turkey bones, be cut by tree ornaments made of glass, chew the flex of the Christmas tree lights, or be poisoned by poinsettias, or mistletoe, or holly berries.

If you can keep track of your cat, your chances of keeping it safe are increased. Cat-flaps allow cats to enter and leave at will, so many owners don't know where their cats are. In fact most cats just want a quick trip around their territory from time to time, so it is safer to open the door for your cat and let it in again a few minutes later. Then if it goes missing, you will know almost immediately and can begin your search.

My cat is very well-behaved indoors, but when he goes outdoors he goes mad and attacks everything in sight. Why?

He's probably playing at being the big game hunter. Cats' hunting instincts are triggered by movement — they lose interest in prey which ceases to move. Out-of-doors your cat will see many things moving — grasses, leaves, flowers and insects — and he is probably 'pretend-hunting'. It is nothing to worry about; just ensure he has enough to keep him occupied indoors.

In high light conditions, the cat's pupil narrows to a slit to cut down on the amount of light entering the eye

Feline fitness

You can help keep your cat fit and well by following the recommendations in the previous chapter. But still vitally important is your knowledge and awareness of your own particular cat.

Cats are such stoic creatures that they can be seriously ill before you notice anything is wrong with them. I've said this already, but the better you know your cat — its moods, habits and ways — the sooner you will notice a change in behaviour, and the sooner you can take action.

So observe your cat closely. Don't feel you are 'wasting time' by watching your cat play, or eat, or sleep: in fact you are storing up knowledge of your individual cat's behaviour. You will notice if it is scratching, if it looks thin (or fat), seems listless or overactive, needs grooming — and a hundred other things you may not even notice you are noticing.

Your cat has only a limited number of ways in which it can let you know if it is feeling under par. So watch, see and act — you owe it to your feline friend.

When you suggest that 'immediate' veterinary attention should be sought, how immediate is immediate? I work all day, so if my cat is a little off-colour, can she wait until evening surgery before seeing a vet?

Maybe she can, maybe she can't. Do you want to take the chance?

As an example, one of my own cats had what seemed to be nothing more than a sore paw; I took her to my vet at 9am and he (and I) believed there was nothing more wrong with her than that . At 7pm the same evening, she died. She was seen by four vets during the course of the day as her condition worsened, but she deteriorated too rapidly for anything to be done for her. Although this was an extreme case of a rare illness, it does make an important point.

I was with her all day and able to seek veterinary attention immediately it was apparent it was necessary. Some illnesses are so rapid in their course that nothing can be done anyway, as in my case, but it is important for a loving owner to know that everything possible was done. If I had gone out for the day at 9am, I could have returned to find her dead. Grief when a pet dies can be hard to cope with; if it is combined with guilt, however misplaced, it can be overwhelming.

YOU SHOULD never take chances with your cat's health. A cat which appears off-colour may simply be off-colour, but it may be displaying symptoms of a serious or even fatal illness.

See your vet at the first sign of *any* behavioural change or any physical symptom, even a sore paw. If you are not able to do so because of other commitments, try to get someone else to take your cat for you. If finances are low, ask if your vet will send you a bill, rather than paying on the day. And in the UK, the Peoples Dispensary for Sick

What's in a name?

Some veterinary practices are in the habit of attaching the names of their animal clients to their owners' surnames. This can cause amusement as some owners choose their cats' names to compliment their own. Embarrassed vets are sometimes to be heard calling for Tupper Ware or Fluff Ball.

Animals will treat, free of charge, any animal whose owner is in receipt of State benefits.

My cat hasn't been very well recently and as I am a great believer in homeopathic medicine, I would like to treat him homeopathically. What homeopathic treatments would you recommend for cats?

I would no more recommend a homeopathic treatment for an ailment than I would a conventional treatment. Every ailment should be seen and diagnosed by a qualified veterinary surgeon. Homeopathy undoubtedly has its place in medicine but it has one great drawback — it allows people who are not medically qualified to buy and administer it, and unwittingly, they may treat the symptoms of an illness rather than the illness itself.

A qualified homeopathic practitioner will never make a blanket recommendation for a treatment for, say, nervousness in a cat, because that nervousness can come from a variety of causes. The qualified practitioner will attempt to discover its cause; only when in full possession of the facts will it then be treated. A homeopathic vet will use homeopathic remedies if he or she feels they are called for; fortunately they will also be in a position to treat the problem with conventional medicine if he or she feels it is more appropriate.

There are a number of qualified vets who also practise homeopathy; their names can be obtained from the Royal College of Veterinary Surgeons. However, *please* don't attempt to be your own vet. I am horrified by the number of cat breeders who now turn to the pills in their medicine cupboard instead of seeking qualified help.

YOU SHOULD NEVER diagnose and treat a cat's illness yourself, unless you are a qualified vet. By self-diagnosis you are acting as judge and jury to to your cat; the sentence could be death.

My cat has the occasional flea. He hates being sprayed so I don't bother too much about it. But now I've been told I could be risking his health. Is this true? Surely one little flea isn't going to cause much damage by a bite?

Tiny and innocuous though it may look, one bite from a flea could cause a fatal illness in your cat. Fleas transmit disease from cat to cat; if a flea bites a cat suffering from (for example) feline leukaemia virus and then bites yours, the disease could be transmitted to him.

So although many cats (and owners) find regular flea-spraying stressful, the alternative is much worse. Take no chances; keep fleas under control. There is a wide variety of products which are manufactured for their eradication, and it could save you a lot of heartache — and expense.

Older cats need our help with grooming. Fur may become grubby and talcum powder can be used as a dry shampoo

Is it true that you can't bath a cat? My cat is filthy!

It isn't strictly speaking true, although with some cats it's more difficult than others — some will not submit to it at all, and will scratch everything and everyone to shreds in their efforts to get out of the tub.

If your cat's fur is dirty, is there a reason? Has it been ill recently? Sick cats often cannot make the effort to keep themselves clean, yet dirtiness is distressing to them. Or is your cat old? Older cats often

The cat's covering

A cat has around 60,000 hairs per square inch on its back, and 120,000 per square inch on its belly.

Guard hairs, as their name suggests, guard the softer parts of the coat and are often coarser than the rest. It is believed that some guard hairs throughout the coat have sensory functions, allowing a cat to 'feel' its way.

Awn hairs are the topcoat that we can see, being finer and shorter than guard hairs; they are relatively weatherproof. Down hairs comprise a type of undercoat which can't be seen on most cats except when brushing them; they provide insulation.

In cold weather, the fur is fluffed out by contraction of the muscles at the roots; this traps a layer of air which helps keep the cat warm. Cats moult in spring which enables them to keep

continued opposite

lack the suppleness to keep themselves looking spruce.

If your cat is already stressed through illness or old age, and is not used to being bathed, don't put him under additional stress by bathing him. Brush or comb him regularly, preferably several times a day, which will make him feel better and may encourage him to begin grooming himself again. Try a dry shampoo if necessary (see p132), and help keep his spirits high with plenty of your company and love.

If your cat has rubbed up against some harmful chemical, you will have to bath him before he licks it off. But grubby fur can be dealt with in other ways.

My cat moults dreadfully in the springtime and her fur gets all over the furniture. Why do cats moult?

In springtime, the fur thins to help keep a cat cool. This is not triggered by warmer weather, but by the lengthening daylight hours. Cats also moult when under stress, when ill and when old.

Cats can end up swallowing a lot of loose hair at this time, so regular grooming is vital. Both long- and shorthaired cats should be groomed regularly by their owners, but particularly when moulting. If necessary, use a hairball prepara-

tion — but not too frequently.

Cat fur can be removed from furniture with a clothes brush, sticky tape or — what I find most efficient — a damp scrubbing brush.

My cat loves climbing a tree which is in my garden. The first branch is about eighteen feet above the ground, and although he can climb up, he can't get down again. I'm fed up with rescuing him from this tree and one day I left him there for twelve hours. He still couldn't get down so I had to rescue him again. How can I stop him climbing the tree?

Cats usually can get down; leaving him up the tree for a day was a good idea because most cats will climb down themselves when they become hungry or realise that no-one is going to heed their cries. There are occasions, however, when cats become genuinely stuck.

Your cat can be prevented from climbing the tree by several means: place a cone of half-metre wide wire mesh around the tree at a height of about two metres; he will not be able to jump or climb past it. Or, place something sticky or slippery in a band around the tree: a half-metre wide band of honey or treacle would discourage him, as cats hate getting their paws sticky; unfortunately, this would also en-

The cat's coat is composed of three types of hair with as many as 120,000 hairs per square inch in some areas

Cats feel much more secure when they can climb high

continued

cooler in summer; the moult is triggered not by warmer weather, but by the extra hours of daylight.

Because the cat's coat is of such good insulating material, cats will often sit too close to sources of heat, quite unaware that their fur is scorching because the heat won't have reached the skin.

Cats also spend many hours each day grooming their fur; this not only keeps it in good shape, making the hairs lie in the same direction, but it has a soothing effect too. A cat's early memories are of being licked by its mother, and licking (or grooming) can become a comforting displacement activity in adulthood. For example if a cat tries to jump a gap, fails to do so and falls, it will often sit down and give itself a few hard licks. This has a calming effect, and gives it a few moments to get over its shock.

courage flies and wasps. Soap or washing-up liquid spread around the tree — again, in a half-metre wide band at a height of two metres — may prevent any further climbing because of its slipperiness.

Your cat may be enjoying the security which the height of the tree gives him; ground level is fraught with dangers for animals, and the higher they are, the safer they feel. He has an excellent vantage point, and can easily fight off any aggressors. So he might be happier if he is allowed to continue climbing the tree — but has some way of getting down again. Why not lean a ladder securely and permanently against the tree? Most cats will learn to use one, and it should save future rescue attempts.

My cat is eighteen years old. He was always very clean but now his fur is grey instead of white. I don't want to bath him because he has never been bathed, but how can I stop him looking so dirty and unkempt?

Help him a little. An old cat isn't as supple, and can't bend and stretch to groom himself as a young cat can, and can't reach all the areas he used to. This often causes great distress to an older cat, because they all like to keep themselves well groomed.

All cats should be helped because there are a few spots — behind the head and under the chin — which no cat can reach, and knots and matts can otherwise result in these areas. Owners should comb or brush their cats at least once a week throughout their lives, and more frequently for longhaired cats and in the spring moult. As a cat gets older, he should be groomed more regularly — daily if he enjoys it.

Many older cats are reluctant to groom themselves because they are less able to reject the resulting hairballs; their muscles lose tone and are unable to expel foreign objects. If you groom your cat regularly, he is less likely to pick up and swallow loose hair and so have a hairball problem.

CHIA AND CASEY

At one time I didn't think my Siamese cats, Chia and Casey, would make it to three years of age. Their first year was a very healthy year, without any problems, but in the summer of the second year they started what became known to my vet and me as the long vomit!

He couldn't identify the cause. Their normal food made them ill; so did fish and so did chicken. For three weeks the only thing they could take was beaten egg white mixed with a little glucose solution, put into them by dropper, and only about three drops every half hour.

By the end of three weeks they could keep down well skimmed chicken broth. It was fully six weeks before they were back to normal, running around and playing, and able to eat without being sick. I had a long questionnaire to fill in from one of the veterinary colleges which was investigating the digestive problems of cats. Most of the questions were revolting!

That year the attack started late in June. Then they returned to their normal healthy state and we forgot all about it until early June the following year, when exactly the same problem hit them. Again, it lasted for six weeks. Again I had two very sick little cats, who didn't much care what went on around them.

Again they were fed every half hour with a few drops of beaten egg white mixed with glucose solutions. They had injections and antibiotics on both occasions but these seemed to have little effect.

Then all was well for the rest of the year.

The following year I took them, as I always did, in the second week in May, for their feline enteritis preventive injections. Before I had gone two miles on my journey home, I heard ominous sounds from the back of the car. I stopped to investigate.

Casey was being extremely sick; so sick that he was on the verge of collapse. I drove straight back to the vet. By the time I reached there, Casey was obviously a very ill little cat indeed and Chia had started to be sick.

This time they were far worse, and it was touch and go with them; but in the end we won the battle. I keep a diary, so looked back over the past two years. The first time they were ill had been six weeks after the injections for feline enteritis; the second time had been three weeks; this was instantaneous.

So, no more preventive injections. They never had the same symptoms again, though on one occasion I thought it had recurred. However, that time it proved to be Warfarin poisoning from eating mice that had been poisoned — Vitamin K injections and lots of nursing got them both over it.

I have never heard of any other cats reacting like that to their preventive injections, but there was no doubt whatever on that last occasion as to the cause.

After that, both cats became allergic to beef protein! Mince or any proprietary catfood with beef in it made them instantly ill. I had to prepare my own diet for them. This has been adapted as Chia has grown older, as she has a digestive problem and can suffer from constipation. Then she has to be given a remedy for the problem.

I never thought I would inspect her litter tray with anxiety each day and heave a sigh of relief at an object that, shown to the vet, was pronounced 'beautiful'! But then vets have different ideas as to beauty.

One gets very basic with animals. My farmer friends peer intently at everything their sheep and cattle produce, as it is a major diagnostic aid to health. One told me that if a dog produced an object that could be picked up without staining the hand and thrown over next door's fence it was ideal. Too soft was a sign of overfeeding; too hard, underfeeding or too many bones.

I might add that I have never attempted this!

Joyce Stranger

Cats which have become used to combing by their owners over the years enjoy it, because the combing motion is so like being stroked (and the licking motion of another cat).

If a cat's white fur has become grey but he is not used to bathing, don't stress him by immersing him in water; give him a dry shampoo instead. White fur will come up white again if sprinkled with talcum powder (use an unscented variety if possible) which is then brushed out completely. Also, ask yourself how your cat is getting dirty. Most golden oldies are happiest when allowed to spend most of their day by the fire. Are you locking your cat out of the house for most of the day? If so, allow him to spend more time indoors. Old bones feel the cold, and old cats are less able to defend themselves against marauding younger cats in the same territory. You may be subjecting your cat to a high degree of stress by expecting him to spend as much time outdoors as he did as a youngster.

You say he should spend more time indoors — but he has become dirty, so I want him to spend a lot of time out-of-doors. I don't want him messing in the house. What should I do?

So give him a couple of litter trays: if you live in a house, place one upstairs and one downstairs; if you live in a large apartment, place a tray at each end. Older cats don't have the control over their muscles which younger cats do; your cat will try to get to the nearest tray or outdoors, but if it is too far away, or if he has to negotiate stairs, he won't be able to reach it in time. In fact, this will distress your cat more than it does you, because the fastidious cat hates to soil its home.

Don't ever reprove an elderly cat which hasn't reached its tray in time. It isn't his fault — it's yours. Place a tray nearer next time.

YOU SHOULD put yourself in your cat's place. An eighteen-year-old cat is like a centenarian human, and is no longer able to look after himself as he once did. He's been a friend to you for a long time, so be a friend to him. Groom him daily, keep him clean and comfortable, and give him a couple of litter trays.

Don't expect to have him euthanised because you think he's a nuisance, as some owners try to do. Vets should only euthanise cats if they are in pain, suffering an incurable disease, or if their quality of life is so low that death is a preferable alternative.

My cat is 17 years old and has very smelly breath. He has also lost some teeth. Is this the reason for his bad breath?

No, but loss of teeth and bad breath can both be signs of gum problems in the older cat. Tartar, or scale, can build up on teeth over the years, especially if cats are fed a soft diet. The tartar eventually inflames the gums and can cause bad breath, dribbling and difficulty in eating. If left untreated, teeth may fall out.

Cats with tartar on their teeth need veterinary attention as the teeth will be descaled under anaesthetic. They should also have a veterinary check-up as the gingivitis may be symptomatic of an illness such as kidney disease or leukaemia.

YOU COULD try cleaning your cat's teeth once a week from kittenhood. Once a cat is elderly, it is probably too late to start as he may not tolerate it.

Always give a cat a little hard food each day to exercise teeth and gums; some raw meat occasionally will perform the same function.

Have a health check-up for your cat at least once a year, and preferably every six months when it is over the age of ten years.

In the golden years, our cats depend on us more

THE MIST
AND THE SPINNING WHEEL

Blue Mist of Valletta is a most unusual Blue Angora. Unusual, because her fur is combed out, spun and knitted into beautiful sweaters by her owners, Roger and Peggy Sear.

'Angora is one of the easier cat furs to spin,' Roger says. 'It has no undercoat so it doesn't matt, and the Angora will shed almost continually all year, instead of having one yearly moult. The Angora's hair structure is unusual, too — it's similar only to the Turkish Van.'

Roger combs the Mist twice a day, and in that way collects half an ounce of fur from her each week. To be suitable for spinning, cat fur must be at least one-and-a-half inches long and some of Mist's fur is as long as four inches. A fortnight's collection of fur takes an hour to spin.

'The fur is about one-fifth of the diameter of human hair,' Roger says, 'yet it's remarkably strong. A two-ounce hank, after spinning, will take a strain of more than five tons. It's very strong, but not as elastic as wool, and it's much more difficult to spin.'

The beautiful sweaters knitted up by Roger's wife, Peggy, are made mostly of sheep's wool spun by Roger, with decorative patterns picked out in different coloured wools, and cat or dog fur. Recently, Peggy finished knitting a child's bolero made entirely of cat fur, believed to be the only one of its kind in the world.

As well as using fur from Mist, Roger and Peggy's friends collect fur from their cats. Roger has used combings from a Colourpoint, Chinchillas, and from Red and Blue Persians.

Spinning cat fur requires a special technique which Roger has developed over the years. He says that great patience is needed to adapt spinning technique to fine fur, and he has to spin with his fingers dampened with oil — neatsfoot or olive. The yarn is too fine to be produced on commercially made spinning wheels, which Roger says don't have sufficient balance or control.

So Roger also makes the wheels on which to spin the fur. He makes about four each year, and the one in the photograph is made of Brazilian rosewood, inlaid with every known type of oak and with mother-of-pearl decoration. The Mist's favourite spinning-wheel is made of olive wood, for the wood attracts many cats in the same way as the herb, catnip. While Roger was making the olive-wood wheel, Mist sat in his workshop, purring non-stop.

Roger believes that the spinning of cat fur goes back to the time of the ancient Turks — at least as far as 1,000BC. He has collected another eight ounces of Mist's fur which will go towards the next cat fur sweater. 'I use the Mist's fur to make sure that she remains with me forever — whatever happens,' Roger says.

Blue Mist of Valletta – the cat who made a bolero

TIGGY – THE CARING CAT?

Tiggy is a cat who will live forever in my heart. I had the horrifying shock of the police coming to my door one day to inform me that my husband had died suddenly. I wondered how I would live through the night, being now quite alone.

Tiggy knew how upset I was. Although her bed had always been downstairs she would not settle. She miaowed and clawed at the door to be allowed upstairs. Finally I gave in and she curled up on my bed.

As can be imagined, I was sobbing. Tiggy walked up to my pillow and sat there licking my forehead and gently stroked my face with her warm, soft pawpads for many minutes. In feline language I know what she was saying: 'Don't worry, you still have *me*.' She was a wonderful, caring cat who helped me get through that dreadful night.

Peggy Farrington

CATS ABOUT THE HOUSE

Cat behaviour and what it means to you

For most of us, a cat means a creature reclining on the fireside rug, or on our laps, or draped over the best chair. Our experiences of our cats are in our own homes. But how much do we know about the life of the cat about the house? Do we understand what they are telling us? Why they do what they do?

Most of us work for eight hours, sleep for eight hours and spend the remaining eight hours relaxing; how does a cat spend its day? Even if you've spent all your life with cats, you might be surprised if you worked it out.

THE CAT'S DAY

Average, well-fed, adult domestic cat

Sleeping	16 hours
Grooming	5-6 hours
Sitting around	1 hour +
Patrolling territory	15 minutes
Playing, fighting and hunting	15 minutes
Eating and drinking	10 minutes
Eliminating	5 minutes

The cat's predilection for sleep and its ability to 'cat-nap' are always used as examples by those who prefer to see it as a lazy creature; in fact, both characteristics make it a superb survival machine. Sleeping is an excellent way of conserving energy; for a cat which had to provide its own food would expend a great deal of energy in short, sharp bursts of hunting, and the ability to totally relax and conserve energy between bursts of effort would therefore be invaluable.

A home-living domestic cat, with no need to hunt, will sleep as

Opposite:
Half-closed eyes show contentment or lack of threatening intentions

Opposite top:
Sleeping – a sixteen to twenty-hour a day occupation. Sleeping conserves energy for when it is needed

Opposite below:
In warm weather a cat will sleep stretched out to allow the passage of cooling air through fur

Feline courtesy – when joining a companion, a cat will give an exploratory lick to see if it is welcome. If it is not, the other cat will hiss

much as sixteen hours a day. A kitten will sleep longer than this because it is using up an enormous amount of energy in play, learning the skills needed to defend itself and hunt for its food. Newborn kittens will sleep almost all the time they are not suckling, and a few even seem to have developed the ability to suckle and sleep at the same time!

Suckling is the first pleasurable experience of a kitten's life and occasionally appears to be revived in an adult cat's dreams. The mouth will be open with the tongue protruding slightly over the bottom teeth in the suckling position (the tongue would lie along the bottom of the teat and curl partly round it), and the cat may make sucking motions with its mouth, the throat moving as if swallowing.

Cats *do* dream, and not all their dreams are pleasant ones. You may see your cat lying, fast asleep, with legs twitching as if running, breathing heavily, with its face twisted into a grimace of fear or aggression. Behind closed eyelids, its eyes will be moving rapidly from side to side. 'Rapid Eye Movement' (REM) sleep is observed in humans, too, and appears to coincide with the dreaming state in deep sleep — in cats this is believed to be about 60 per cent of its sleeping time (in humans it is 20 per cent).

A cat may settle down to sleep with one paw, or sometimes its

Are cats cruel?

'Cats play with their prey. They're cruel animals.' How often have you heard that statement? It isn't true, and it shows a basic lack of understanding of the cat's behaviour when hunting.

'They catch something and let it go only to catch it again.' The reason they do this is that the cat's hunting instinct is triggered by movement. Should the prey animal play dead, the cat may lose interest in it; also, it may not be able to see it very well if it is right under its nose, because at close range a cat's eyesight is poor. Once the prey animal starts to move again the cat can see it, and again its hunting instance will come into play.

'Cats beat their prey and toss it about.' If a cat corners a rat, one bite from that rat could be fatal; the cat must therefore prevent it biting, and does so by hitting it on the head to make it lower its head — then the rat cannot bite the cat because it cannot see its target. Tossing prey in the air is done for a similar reason: to disorientate it and stun it so it is unable to bite back. As soon as the cat manoeuvres the rat into a position where it can effect the killing bite and finish it off, it does. And cats can't moderate their behaviour according to the type of prey; all prey must be considered potentially dangerous, so it must all be treated in the same way, whether a rat or a robin.

continued opposite

tail, curled over its nose. This not only keeps the nose warm, it also cuts down the supply of oxygen and so hastens sleep. A sleeping cat will also indicate the ambient temperature by its position: a warm cat will sleep with paws stretched out and belly or sides exposed to the air; a cooler cat will sleep in a tucked-up position; whereas a cold cat will be curled into a tight ball.

As a cat warms up it likes to stretch out; if it cannot do so, it will move to find a place where it can. This is one of the reasons why many cats won't use the beds provided for them, preferring rugs or chairs. If the bed is too small, the cat can only sleep curled up. While it is happy to do so while it is feeling cold, as soon as it warms up it will want to stretch out to cool off and cannot do so without leaving the bed.

Newly introduced cats won't sleep or eat close together, though as they begin to accept one another they will slowly approach, and will eventually sleep curled up together. This is a powerful incentive to acceptance, though in fact the 'cuddling' often observed — when one has its paws around the other — is rather to restrain the other cat. The dominant cat will usually settle down to sleep by licking its companion's face or head to show its dominance, while holding it still with its paws, and it will keep its paws around the less-dominant cat's body until one of them moves.

Cats have a well developed body language. If a cat wishes to join another which has already laid claim to a bed or a comfortable chair, it will not simply jump up and settle down, it will give the other cat an exploratory lick. If it doesn't react, or reacts by blinking or returning the lick, the cat knows it can then settle down. If the other cat doesn't wish to have company, it will hiss or stare at the interloper, who will then jump down and find somewhere else to nap.

A cat settling down to sleep with its owner may lick or nibble

Domestic cat or tiger – both are superb hunting machines

*Only cats or kittens which know
each other well will sleep close
together*

continued

**'Cats keep on playing with
their prey after it is dead.'**
A cat is a superb athlete,
and has to be in order to
catch anything which
doesn't want to be caught.
No human athlete is ex-
pected to finish a race and
then immediately take up
their embroidery where they
left off: an athlete has to be
'psyched up' for a race, as
does a cat to hunt, and after
it is over, it takes time for
both to wind down. The cat
does so by continuing its
hunting behaviour; this also
ensures the prey animal is
dead. After all, would you be
able to tell the exact moment of death of a rat?

**'Cats don't even eat what
they have caught.'** They
don't if they're not hungry,
and most domestic cats are
kept well fed. Nor do cats
eat their prey where they
have killed it. If they became
hungry and a meal wasn't
forthcoming, they would
then probably eat what they
had caught. The house-cat's
frequent response is to bring
its dead prey back to its
home; this is not as a gift to
its owners, but an attempt to
keep the prey somewhere
safe until it is hungry
enough to eat it.

157

LUKE OUT!

Luke is my five-year-old ginger cat who is a lovely companion and wants lots of love and attention. One summer I was rushed into hospital and Luke missed me very much., When I returned home he became upset if I went to sleep in a chair at the wrong time of day — so much so that he discovered a way of attracting my attention and waking me up.

I have a Lifeline telephone which means I can call for help just by pressing a button. Three times when I was asleep I was woken by an urgent voice calling my name and asking if I was all right. Three times I said I hadn't called for help.

I was about to doze off one day when I saw Luke jump onto the telephone shelf and deliberately sit on the alarm button. At last I had the explanation of why I had appeared to cry 'wolf' three times! Luke had found a sure-fire way of waking me up.

Phyll Chappell

his/her chin, and this is often seen as a sign of affection. However, it may also be a throwback to suckling, or a demonstration that the cat believes itself to be dominant! As many as 90 per cent of owners allow their cats to sleep on their beds, which suits both parties. Cats enjoy the human body warmth, and owners admit they feel safer because they know they would be warned at the first hint of danger because their cat would run away.

Cats with owners who are away from home for most of the day will spend a larger proportion of that time sleeping. Yet a cat has an almost uncanny ability to distinguish the sound of its owner's footsteps or car engine from amongst all others, and will rush to greet him/her at the front door — despite the popular misconception that cats are indifferent to their owners' whereabouts.

A cat has its own welcoming miaow which it will use only for its owner; other people, even companion cats, will hear a different miaow as their greeting. The cat will then rub against the owner's legs, and may accompany this with a trilling or chirruping noise of greeting. It may bounce on stiff front legs, back slightly arched, with ears pricked up and tail held high.

Cats rub like this because they have scent glands around their chins and lips (and also anus), and when they rub they transfer this scent onto whatever they have touched, making the object or

Above left to right
A cat rubs against objects to transfer its scent. First, this cat looks around the surrounding area for any possible dangers, then it rubs against the post, then checks its scent has been suitably impressed

Opposite:
When cats first meet, they sniff one another's faces

159

Cats and the elderly

Although many elderly people would love to have a cat as a pet, they are often too responsible to take one on. Only 6 per cent of cat owners are retired people. They realise far better than younger, more careless owners that a cat is a fifteen-year commitment or more — and that a cat requires stability in its life, becomes devoted to a good owner, and would be devastated by that owner's death, or hospital stay.

So they nobly deprive themselves of a companionship which would be of enormous benefit to both parties. Yet many rescue shelters run OAPP schemes, matching Old Age Pensioner People to Old Age Pensioner Pusses. An older cat wants peace and quiet and companionship, requirements which an older person is more than qualified to provide. Rescue shelters running this scheme will often guarantee to pay veterinary bills and to take the cat back into care if the owner is unable to look after it any

continued opposite

person smell more familiar. An owner who has been out of doors for a time will have lost some of his cat's scent, so the cat renews it. When greeting a returned owner, the cat may be in such a hurry to say 'hello' that it doesn't use any of its scent glands, but simply rubs its side along the owner's legs. By bouncing, the cat can reach higher, and it would probably like its owner to come down to its level so that faces can be rubbed together.

When you are on a cat's level and it sniffs at your face and then rubs against you, sniff back, don't blow. Expelling air in your cat's face is the same as another cat hissing at it, and is seen as a very unfriendly gesture indeed. A cat's sense of smell is much more developed than ours, and one of its uses is to identify other cats. With practice, we can distinguish between different cats by smell alone, too. I have noticed that all the cats in one household develop a scent which is different from that of a group living in another household. And within their own household scent, each cat has its own individual scent. Most cat owners could probably identify their own cat just by sniffing at its nose.

Each *breed* of cat probably has its own scent, and it is possible that each *colour* of cat may smell different. Certain breeds and certain colours of cat appear to get on better than do others; my own belief is that this may be as much to do with their scents as with their temperaments.

When cats greet each other they sniff faces first, then rub along

Cats are wonderful companions for older owners and may even help them live longer

one another's bodies and sniff at the base of the tail. From this, each can tell if the other is a cat they know, if it has been close to unfamiliar cats, where it has been, and what its sexual status is. Often cats from the same household will hiss at a companion on its return from a visit to the vet because of the unfamiliar smell which still attaches to it. And if a human is invited to sniff back at a cat's face — which could be considered an honour — the cat will probably then turn its tail; this is also undoubtedly an invitation to sniff, which most people decide not to accept!

Grooming by licking not only settles the fur neatly and keeps it clean, it also gives it the right smell. As several cats in one household usually eat the same food, their saliva might be expected to smell similar, and this could help mark the fur with a scent familiar to all.

Unfamiliar cats will be shown they are unwelcome by a range of behaviour and language, beginning with the hiss — if the cats have got close enough to sniff faces, this sudden rush of expelled air is off-putting and may be enough for a cat to take flight. From early kittenhood, the sound has become associated with the unpleasant effect of the rush of air, until the sound itself is enough to upset a feline. You may have noticed a cat startling at the sound of air-brakes being applied, or the hiss of a spray can. I also believe this is why cats hate being laughed at: not because the joke is at their expense, but because the sudden outrush of air when we laugh is just as unpleasant to them as a hiss in the face. And when we laugh we bare our teeth, just as a hissing cat does.

Cats will fight only when a fight is inevitable, and they have a range of body postures and noises designed to frighten off an opponent. If a hiss, followed by a short sharp spitting noise, doesn't see the other cat off, the cat will turn sideways to its opponent with its back arched and its tail upright. The hair on the body may fluff out, and so will the tail fur until the tail looks like a bottle brush. This is designed to make the cat look bigger and more threatening; and if it isn't sufficiently frightening, it will execute a sideways skipping dance, stiff-legged in front of its opponent, growling or making a high-pitched yowling sound.

Then the head will quickly duck lower and a paw lash out towards the other cat's head. The second cat will lower its ears against its head to minimise injury, and may spring at its aggressor's shoulder or neck; the weight of its charge will knock it over, or the other cat will quickly twist to roll underneath. The two will roll together, paws around one another's bodies, biting at anything they can reach. Ears will be kept low to the head as they are fragile and vulnerable.

Each cat will continue to duck its head low, not only to protect it, but to help it twist underneath the other cat, because the cat

continued

longer. They may also offer to take the cat back into the shelter for a few weeks each year free of charge to allow the owner a carefree holiday.

With this scheme, they know that an elderly owner need have no worries about the cat's future, and that an otherwise difficult-to-home cat (because of its advanced age) will spend its golden years in front of a loving fireside, instead of in a clinical pen.

Cats make wonderful pets for the elderly because given time and attention they thrive, and this many older owners are more than willing to give. In return, cats provide companionship and an additional interest in life. Studies suggest that pet owners live longer than those without pets, and have a significantly higher survival rate following heart attacks. Physical benefits such as a lowering of blood pressure when a pet is stroked are well documented.

However, elderly owners should take care that they don't trip over their cat, a pet which does tend to get underfoot.

Shaggy cat story

In the 1950s, a Mrs Pounds
from Dorset wrote to her
local newspaper: 'My
daughter has a pure White
Longhaired cat nearly
twenty-two years old. It has
never been ill or sick and
never required spiritual or
other healing, and is perfectly well.

'This cat is most unusual
as it sheds its coat every
year, starting at the tail.
Gradually the whole skin
and fur comes right off and
underneath a beautiful new
fur appears.'

*Checking out the scent and status
of a companion cat*

underneath is in a good fighting position. It can bite and can reach
its opponent's neck and head; it can scratch with four sets of
claws, and rake its opponent's belly. The cat on top has to use at
least three legs to stand on, which means it has only one set of
claws free for the fight. So it will try to twist under the other cat
and the two may find themselves lying side by side, paws outstretched, pushing one another away. At this stage, one may give
up and run off.

All the while the two cats will stare hard at one another, trying
to judge what the other will do; so it is hardly surprising that a
hard stare is considered a threat in the cat world. And if two cats
are weighing up whether to attack each other, you can prevent
them from fighting by placing something in their line of sight: no
longer able to stare, they will amble off or even go to sleep.

A cat which doesn't fancy its chances in combat will not stare
at its protagonist. Rather, it will gaze all around it, looking
everywhere but at the other cat, as if to pretend that the other cat
is not really there. If forced to look at it, it will do so while blinking
rapidly in a desperate attempt to prove it is no threat.

Most cats manage to share limited, and in some cases overlapping, territories without too many battles, and fighting will be
avoided when possible. A cat approaching another's territory and
seeing a cat in residence will usually sit down some distance away.
The two may sit for some time, at an angle to one another,
observing each other's movements from a distance. The usurper
may decide to leave the way it arrived or, if the territory-owner

walks off out of sight, it may continue its journey across the occupied zone.

Fighting will occur over a female in season because her scent will carry over long distances and attract numerous tomcats. Fighting isn't constant, although various scuffles will break out, and often tomcats will sit surprisingly politely and quietly outside the female's home, in neat rows like a theatre audience. It is when

Grooming not only keeps a cat's fur neat and clean, it also transfers the scent of saliva to its fur

they begin to howl and spray that arguments with the neighbours can ensue.

The dominance of wild-living male cats is decided by fighting; the bigger, stronger and younger cat having to win his place in the hierarchy. He doesn't always have to fight to work his way up the ladder, as older or weaker cats may defer peacefully; nor does any one cat have to fight every other cat — in a group where the hierarchy is well established, a cat has only to be dominant to one and inferior to another to have his position known by all. As he matures, a strong young tom may become dominant to one who was dominant to him previously, so working his way up the ladder, and an aging cat will likewise work his way down. In any group of feral cats, the most dominant will be a male. Dominance in wild-living female cats is usually (but not always) linked to the number of litters she has produced; the more litters, the higher she stands in the hierarchy.

In the average group of house-cats, the balance of power may well be different. Sometimes neutering can alter the hierarchy (causing some welfare groups to rethink their policies of neutering feral cats). As many as 90 per cent of house-cats living in the south of England are neutered, and in any household the most dominant cat may be a neutered male *or* female. Where there is a mixture of neutered and entire cats, the most dominant may still be a neuter; it may be the cat which has lived there longest, or perhaps a more assertive young cat.

Cats can make over a hundred different sounds, from the pleasant purr, to a wide variety of miaows, to the fierce growl. They create a range of sounds by passing air over their vocal chords, varying the extent to which the mouth is open, and altering the muscle tension in throat and lips.

Every owner will be able to distinguish between, and understand, various miaows, which will be indistinguishable to another person. House-cats converse much more than feral cats because they have discovered that language is important to us. For example, have you ever fed your cat in complete silence? Probably not. Most of us chat to our cats as we prepare their food, telling them not to be impatient or greedy; if we open a door to let them into the house, we say hello, or complain about their wet feet on the carpet.

In this way, cats associate language with action, and will train us to understand their language. A cat will miaow in a certain way and run to the door, which obviously means 'let me out'. When we go into the kitchen, a cat will give a quite different miaow which means 'I'm hungry'. The owner isn't the only one who can understand; if there are other cats in the home which hear the 'I'm hungry' miaow, they will rush to the kitchen too in the hope of

Domestic cats learn to use their paws to reinforce their demands

Home remedies

Before veterinary surgeons had access to the wide range of drugs now available, cats, like other creatures, had to survive on home remedies. A cat with a digestive upset would be given a whole kipper to eat, so that the bones would scour out any offending material from its insides. A cat with diarrhoea was obliged to swallow crushed clay pipes. Bladder problems were treated with gin, to promote urination. And in the East, a cat with any inexplicable disease was rubbed from nose to tail with a fresh lime.

Opposite:
Every cat has its own particular call which it uses to tell an owner it is hungry

Ears lowered to the sides and lip-licking display anxiety. An anxious cat may also pant

being fed. Their own 'I'm hungry' miaow may sound quite different to the one they have responded to, but they understand it nevertheless, just as we do. We soon learn to distinguish between the different calls if we listen and watch our feline teachers.

In the same way, many domestic cats learn to use their paws more than they would normally if living wild. For example, the cat's only way of stopping an action it dislikes is by grasping with its teeth, but some household cats learn to place their paws on, say, the hand responsible. Others being stroked around the head and face will place a paw, claws carefully sheathed, on their owner's face.

Purring is a sound which owners love to hear, and there is probably nothing more relaxing than having a purring cat on your lap. There are several degrees of purring: the most ecstatic is a rough, loud, rasping purr, which means the cat couldn't be happier. Some cats purr so hard that they overdo it and can start to cough and choke. The rasping purr becomes quieter as the cat becomes sleepy, winding down like a clockwork toy as it falls asleep. A few cats always purr with a loud rasp because they have suffered from feline respiratory disease when younger and it has permanently affected their breathing.

Cats will also purr when they are frightened or in pain. Some cats, severely injured, have purred when taken to the vet for euthanasia. The owners, misunderstanding this as a sign that the cat still wishes to live, have insisted it should be treated and not euthanised, when the latter option would really be kinder. A frightened cat will purr too, and for example may do so when taken to a strange place for the first time. In both cases, purring is probably a comforting displacement activity for the cat, who may associate it with its earliest days when it suckled from a purring mother. It may be the feline equivalent of calling 'Help me, mum' as well as showing it is not a threat.

Cats can also growl as fearsomely as any dog. Growling was thought to be a hereditary trait, but I believe it is learned. When a mother cat returns to the nest with a dead prey animal, she will growl while she eats, demonstrating to her kittens that it is food — and *her* food, not to be eaten by them. All my cats, mostly unrelated, will growl at each other on occasion, especially as a warning not to steal food, and they will growl if they see a stranger walking up the path to the door. New members of the feline household, however, don't appear to know how to growl at first.

Cats do seem able to copy one another's sounds. One of my cats,

Advice for cat-haters (and cat-lovers)

If you don't like cats but cats like you, stare at them. To a cat, a stare is a threat. The reason why cats will always go to people who profess not to like them is that these people will never look at a cat because they're not interested in it. The cat, assuming that the person is no threat to it because there is no threatening stare, will immediately jump onto the person's lap. Cat lovers, on the other hand, will enter a room containing a strange cat and immediately stare at it, or move towards it. The cat feels threatened and runs away. This is what cat-haters should do when they enter a room with a cat in it — but they never do. Secretly, they're rather proud that they've been singled out for attention.

If you want to make friends with a cat, ignore it completely. If you must look at it, look at it obliquely. Don't move towards it; let it come to you. If you are trying to make friends with a very shy or nervous cat, get down to its level. Lie on the floor, without staring at it, so that you don't tower over it. Yawn and blink slowly. Both are indications of friendly intentions. Never make the first move, and don't try to touch a shy cat until it indicates (probably by rubbing against you) that your attentions are welcome.

High ears and a curled-over tail show this cat is feeling happy

167

a young male just reaching puberty and so quiet-voiced that he doesn't even miaow, appears to have copied the 'calling' sound which my females make.

The flehmen response is sometimes mistaken by owners for a growl, although it is soundless, or almost so. The cat possesses the unique Jacobson's organ, which allows it to taste and smell at the same time: the lips roll back in a grimace, allowing the cat to taste and smell the air it inhales as it passes over the roof of the mouth. Flehmen is used when danger threatens, or if a cat is unsure about something, as well as by a tomcat in response to a calling female's scent and her sprayed urine.

A similar expression can be observed on the face of an indoor cat when it is looking at something attractive — for example, a bird outside its reach. The grimace is then accompanied by a yowl or whine and the teeth may chatter. In fact the cat is making the killing bite with its mouth, although it cannot reach the prey animal or bird.

Much can be told about a cat's mood by observing body language. A happy cat will have ears held high and a tall, straight tail; ears lightly swivelled to the side, or a tail held high but bent over at the tip towards its back show that the cat is very happy. A tail carried horizontally means that the cat is feeling so-so; a drooping tail that it is unhappy or unwell; while the tail between the legs denotes a cat which has been routed. A bottle-brush tail means a cat is ready for battle or is very frightened. A mother cat will allow her young kittens to play with her tail, but when she tires of this it will thrash wildly, and teach them to leave it alone. So the thrashing tail indicates that a cat is about to lose its temper (if it hasn't already done so); a slowly wagging tail means alertness.

Fear or anxiousness is also displayed by lip-licking, and possibly purring. Rapid blinking can show anxiety, a sign that a cat has friendly intentions and doesn't pose a threat to another cat. Half-closed eyes or slow blinking display contentment, and many owners believe that blinking at their cat — if the blink is returned — is the feline equivalent of giving and receiving a kiss. Large pupils indicate interest, smaller ones mean the cat is not so alert.

The whiskers drawn forward constitute a sign of pleasurable anticipation, when a cat is about to be fed, or when it catches a prey animal — then they will be almost wrapped around the body. Whiskers are drawn back tightly against the face to emphasise the snarl when two cats confront one another. And in the cat world yawning is not rude behaviour, but a sign of reassurance.

You may be infuriated when your cat refuses to use its cat flap, and instead, calls for you to open the door. However, this too is a valuable survival technique. A cat will not enter or leave a room

Babies and cats

Cats appear to be aware of what babies are — human kittens. As such, they are often protective of them, so cuddling up to a baby in its crib is not just a self-centred desire for warmth. Cats will curl around their own kittens to protect them and keep them warm, and they are possibly a little confused as to why humans don't do the same to their babies. They may be trying to show their owners the proper way to look after them.

A cat will often lick a baby's hair in an attempt to groom it, in the same way that it would groom its kittens. And just as cats are tolerant of their kittens' high spirits, they are remarkably tolerant of babies and toddlers. Most do not object to fur-tugging or tail-pulling from a baby, although they wouldn't tolerate it from an adult.

If play becomes too rough, they simply do what they do when their kittens get out of hand. . . walk away.

unless it can see its way clear, and that no larger predators are lying in wait for it. For this reason, it prefers its people to open doors wide so it has a clear view of what lies ahead. It will wait a moment or two, checking out the territory, before going through the open door. Cat flaps don't allow for this because as soon as a cat begins to go through the flap, it is committed. It cannot turn around and get back in because it will be trapped by the flap. This, and the fact that flaps have to be opened by pushing the head against them, accounts for the reluctance of most cats to use them. And yes, if it is raining at the front door, your cat *will* ask to be let out the back door. Well, it might not be raining at the other side of the house!

Yawning. Not a sign of tiredness in the cat world but a sign of reassurance

FELIX – LATIN FOR LUCKY

How often have people in the cat world heard 'The cat has to go!' from a furious spouse. I was eavesdropping on a conversation and heard about a cat which was to be destroyed the next day. He had been branded as 'dirty' in the house and was annoying the neighbours by climbing in their windows — not surprising, as he was shut out night and day. He had only been kept for so long because of the child who screamed for him, so he had left his farmcat mother too early and endured nearly two years of misery. Mother boasted that her very young daughter threw him downstairs, shut him in drawers and force-fed him, amongst other cruelties.

I interrupted; could he be given a week's reprieve? I would try to have him, but I would have to prepare my father, then nearly ninety years old. He would have risked his life for any animal but was a terrible tease. Would I be taking on trouble?

I said I would pay for a complete veterinary check-up for the cat, and for neutering if he was fit enough, and I would collect him from the veterinary surgery.

This was done, and I brought home a very sad little cat who slept himself better and began to take in his new surroundings. One eye didn't open fully, his hind leg was slightly lame, and he could only eat a very little at a time. He was scared of any noise or sudden movement. For a long time I couldn't put on a coat near him, or bend over him with arms outstretched; the fears of his previous life would catch up with him.

He stayed indoors for some time, and I started to worry about the dangers of living close to a busy main road. However, at the back of my home is a quiet churchyard. I carried him there and put him down — but he bolted back into the main street. I was horrified — my ignorance had nearly caused a tragedy. So I put a small dog harness and leash on him, and to my amazement he walked up the church path at dusk. Then another cat came out of the bushes and Felix (for by now he had a name) went backwards — he came clear of the harness and vanished. I'll never forget the misery of the next two days; endless searching and calling 'Fred' (his previous name) and asking everywhere.

The third evening I was putting out the milk bottles when I heard a little feline voice. He was under a bush at the top of the steps outside my home. I left the door open and retreated — praying that he would eventually have the courage to enter. He did, and I was able to close the door and cuddle him, crying all over him with relief. I'd felt so guilty about his welfare. He ate and slept, and I'll never forget the cleverness and courage he had shown in strange territory.

The experience was a great setback and the right kind of harness made him crawl around the house until he found he could move normally. All fear of the harness gradually went; scratched

BOG AND SHREW

I have two cats, Bog (short for Bogart, a cartoon cat) and Shrew (short for Shrewsbury, where he came from). Bog is pretty boring and doesn't do much other than sleep and eat and he never leaves the garden.

On the other hand, Shrew is the life and soul of the party. He's a character and, I think, quite clever. He can open doors and regularly does so just to check what is going on. He stands on the dustbin and puts all his weight on his front paws on the handle of the back door to open it.

When my wife takes the dogs for a walk it amuses the neighbours because Shrew follows them on every evening outing. He's very popular with everyone and makes long daily visits all around the area to visit his friends. Many neighbours give him a snack and a drop of milk and whilst I don't think this is a very good idea, I don't think I can do much about it.

Before Shrew was neutered he once went missing for eighteen days. We thought we would never see him again. Then, bold as brass, he came back one day as if nothing had happened, to be greeted with much shouting and tears. He always goes into hiding when he hears the dustmen and I can only think that he might have been shut in a shed by the dustmen perhaps.

On one occasion, Shrew halted an enormous lorry. He was lying in the middle of the road sunning himself and the lorry had to stop. After

hands and an anti-tetanus injection later, he began to walk happily in it.

Our territory has changed a lot in the ten years we've been together. The churchyard is still there for walks, but the allotments are gone. I remember the games we had with baby potatoes around the bean sticks and chasing the tufts of long grass.

Felix, still on his leash, would climb the trees until I said 'Don't leave mum,' our code for 'Don't go higher', because I couldn't reach. And in all our years together there has only been one bird casualty; up a tree he put his foot on one! He is a 'take his mum for a walk' sort of chap now; early in the morning before any people are about is our special time.

Even after all these years his poor tum hasn't adjusted to full meals, so he has three small ones and biscuits before bed. It took many years before he would stand to be stroked. Because of his early traumas he hated hands on him, though loved to be kissed and to rub noses. I don't suppose he will ever sit on my lap, only beside me, but now he will at least sleep on my bed — which I rather like! It took years for the vibration of a purr to be heard — but a lot of talking goes on now.

Some people grudgingly admit that cats can understand a few words, but 'It's the tone of voice in which they are said, not the actual words they understand,' they say. I say 'rubbish!' I'm sure many owners understand their cats' 'talk' and, in turn, manage to talk and explain things clearly to their felines, using works and not just tone of voice to communicate.

Obviously, a fierce tone is going to startle an animal to awareness, and a soft accent will encourage receptive listening; but just as a person learns words as sounds before appreciating their meaning, so repetition of words and phrases to your cat in relevant situations brings awareness of a relationship between those sounds and the 'happening'.

I have had a wonderful opportunity over these years to learn to converse with Felix, and a steady stream of conversation and nonsense accompanies our walks. 'Come with mum' is readily understood, as is 'Up you pop' ready to have his harness put on. We have our own phrases to cover most situations, from the routine 'Wait' and 'Steady', to warnings about 'stingers' (wasps and bees) and 'There's a dog', requiring a pick-up if it is a strange dog, or a reassuring 'It's only a good dog' if it is one we know.

Back home, conversation continues and the vocabulary is extensive. Felix knows about 'saucepan on' for his food. The garbage collectors are now 'rubbishy men' (they would be pleased if they knew!) and are no longer the cause of great panic.

Words, words, words — these are only a few of so many that Felix understands. After all he's been through, I even feel privileged when he swears at me in annoyance; he has a beautiful growl, but he never hurts! We both had so much to learn from each other and it's been a wonderful experience. I believe Felix will always be with me in one way or another.

Vivenne Nash

---

several blasts on the horn which he ignored, the driver got down from his cab, picked Shrew up and carried him to our front lawn. When the driver got back in his cab he was not pleased to see that Shrew had returned to his sun spot in the middle of the road. He was obviously a cat lover because he was amused by the incident when I eventually got to the roadside to remove the obstruction.

My daughters used to play badminton in the back garden and when the shuttlecock got stuck in the apple tree Shrew shot up the tree and came back down with it. He continued to do this and would always faithfully return it to the feet of one of the players. For a time after that, whenever either daughter was in the garden, he would go and stand by the tree whether there was a badminton racket in sight or not.

Both cats are fussy eaters and, when I get their dishes out, Bog goes straight to the deep freezer door and looks just like a boxer. I don't know why, but Shrew has a thing about cooked frozen peas. He goes mad when we have some and we always have to save him a few!

Brian Tunbridge

The common complaints

Fat cat

Edward Bear, a black cat from Sydney, Australia, weighed nearly 22kg (48lb). He had been a normal-sized kitten, but his diet of a kilo of rump steak a day plus a carton of cream, a bowl of biscuits and a pint of milk soon piled on the pounds.

The most common complaints of all — and the ones many owners don't like to talk about — concern the problems of indiscriminate urination and spraying: cats which 'soil' or 'dirty' where they shouldn't.

It is a vital chapter in any cat book, for these problems are common and worldwide, and quite understandably upset owners more than any other. I've had so many distressed owners pleading for help 'because if the cat doesn't stop, my spouse is going to get rid of him'. It is a problem which many people simply can't live with, so an understanding of the reasons behind it may help you take steps to prevent an occurrence — even the best behaved cat will probably, at some time, 'make a mess' where it shouldn't.

I'll start with a description of terms. Some owners confuse spraying with urination, others are embarrassed and can't find polite words to describe what their cat is doing, so an understanding of the terms used will not be out of place.

Urination When cats empty their bladders of urine, they squat down to do so, male and female alike, and urinate on a horizontal surface. 'Indiscriminate urination' is a term used to describe urination in a place considered inappropriate by the owner — for example, on carpets or furnishings, not in a litter tray.

Spraying Spraying is another natural function of the cat, using urine, but the method of delivery is slightly different: instead of squatting down, the cat stands upright, backed up to a vertical object. Out-of-doors this may be a tree, bush, shed or car wheel; indoors it may be a wall, door or furniture. The cat raises its tail which becomes stiff and may quiver, while a jet of urine is sprayed backwards onto the vertical object selected. Contrary to popular belief, both males and females spray, although females are less likely to spray than males. Neutered cats will spray too, but are less likely to than entire cats. Again, spraying is usually considered a problem only when it occurs indoors. Outdoor spraying is usually unnoticed or disregarded by most owners.

Defecation Defecation, the emptying of the bowels, worries some owners more than others. No owner wishes to find faeces (droppings or motions) on a bed, for example, but some become upset if a cat shows a preference for defecating in its litter tray indoors, rather than out-of-doors, as they don't wish to clear up afterwards.

All these topics will be discussed at length in the following section, along with other common complaints. If I appear to have given a disproportionate amount of space to soiling in the home, that is because I receive a disproportionate number of enquiries about the subject. And as it causes enormous problems in the home, it is a topic which cannot be overlooked.

I've never had any trouble with my cats until recently. Then one of them climbed into bed with us and sprayed all over my husband's face! Hubby was not amused. Why should my cat have done this?

One of the main reasons for spraying is territorial marking. He could have been marking your husband as his own! Some owners even consider being sprayed on by their cats as a sign of affection. However, most don't. Has your cat's territory been threatened by a new cat moving into the area or by a new cat in the household? Too many cats in one household (in your cat's opinion) can cause spraying, as each one tries to mark its own piece of territory.

Second, cats under stress may spray. This can be set off by a change in routine, a house move, new additions to the family (human or feline), someone leaving the family, owners going on holiday, or an undiagnosed illness in the cat.

Third, is your cat neutered? Neutered cats are less likely to spray than entire cats, so it is important to have your cat neutered at an age before spraying becomes habitual, as it then becomes a difficult habit to break.

Is there an entire female in your neighbourhood? If so, her scent when she comes into season can cause a male cat to spray, even if he is neutered.

The spraying cat was neutered at an early age, but we've recently bought a kitten which means we now have seven cats.

Most cats will tolerate and enjoy one or two other cats living in their household, but it seems that beyond four, spraying often occurs. Of course there are other considerations such as the size of the house, whether or not the cats have access to the outside world, and the temperaments of the cats themselves.

Unfamiliarity with the new kitten may be the reason for the spraying behaviour, in which case it may cease when your cat gets to know it. Or it may be that your cat thinks there are just too many felines in 'his' house, in which case the spraying will continue.

Give him some space of his own, his own territory inside the house — a room of his own to sleep in, or perhaps sharing it with one particular feline friend. Do make sure he knows you still love him and are not punishing him: if he feels secure, he is less likely to spray.

YOU SHOULD introduce new cats or kittens into the household carefully to minimise the possibility of spraying behaviour occurring.

Have your cats neutered at the appropriate age, between four to nine months — and nearer four months if you have a number of cats.

Don't keep more than three or four cats if spraying would upset you.

Give your spraying cat some space of his own, and ensure that he has his own bed and food bowl.

The smells of the other cats in the household can trigger the spraying behaviour, so clean out litter trays several times a day.

If spraying is only an occasional problem and a specific area is used each time, you could place kitchen foil on that area. Cats don't like the noise of urine hitting kitchen foil.

COMMENT Don't punish a spraying cat. He is trying to establish his territory, in the same way humans do when they put a name plate on their homes. Just as you wouldn't understand it if you were slapped for naming your house, a cat simply won't understand punishment — spraying is a natural behaviour which many cats don't indulge in, but those which do are driven to do so. Punishment, whether it be a slap or a shout, will stress your cat further and make him *more* likely to spray.

Many owners learn to live with spraying cats, wiping up after them, and such behaviour doesn't really bother them. Others find it unbearable and get rid of their cats — however, it is difficult enough to rehome an adult cat but practically impossible to rehome an adult cat with a history of spraying. Yet, once suitably rehomed and given time to settle down, many sprayers will cease to spray, especially if they are the only cat in their new home.

OUTCOME This owner decided to rehome her new kitten, and found a home for it easily; she then spent a lot of time with her spraying cat, which seemed to reassure it of its place in the household. Two weeks after the kitten left, the cat sprayed for the last time and settled down again with its five other companions. This owner now realises that her feline family should not increase beyond six, for fear of triggering spraying behaviour again.

I've recently started to breed cats. They live indoors with me as part of the family and I thought I might have problems with my male stud cat spraying once he was mature. However, I didn't suspect that my females would spray when they are calling. Is this normal?

It's perfectly normal, although not all entire females spray. Stud cats will nearly always spray. Urine is a powerful advertisement of a cat's status to another cat. A calling queen advertises that she is in oestrus by rolling on the ground, raising her rump in the air and calling vocally. Spraying also advertises her availability, as a male cat can distinguish hormonal scents in her urine. It acts as a turn-on, too — I have seen males roll in the urine of calling queens.

If a queen is taken to an unfamiliar stud cat, he will often begin his courtship by spraying over her. He is advertising his availability, as well as ensuring that the unfa-

Opposite:
Just as ginger cats are almost always male, tortoiseshell cats are almost always female. The gene which causes the colour is sex-linked

miliar cat he has been presented with smells familiar to him, *ie* he is making her smell like him.

Breeding cats must also feel secure of their territory when ready to mate. Females prefer to mate in familiar surroundings, where they can be sure of safety and food supplies for their kittens. Free-roaming males, although they will leave their territories to mate many miles away, must then fight for the territory on which they find themselves, and will seal their victories by spraying and so marking the territory as theirs, however temporarily.

COMMENT If you keep entire cats you must expect spraying. Many cat breeders minimise this by keeping their stud cats — and some females, too — in outdoor runs where they can spray to their heart's content. However, if you want to breed cats and raise them as part of the family, which has important socialising benefits, spraying has to be accepted. Parts of the house can be converted to the cats' use with washable walls, vinyl flooring and easily washed bedding.

I have an adult male cat who is neutered, yet he sprays. The smell is awful but I don't know how to stop him. My vet says my cat is in good health, he has everything he wants at home, and he is an only cat who gets plenty of love and attention. He's my only companion and nothing has changed in my household in the two years since I got him. Why is he spraying?

If you can rule out all the normal causes of spraying (see p172–3), then you should ask your vet to test your cat's hormone levels.

It does happen that some cats are not 'completely' neutered. If some testicular tissue remains, it continues to produce the male hormone, testosterone, and the cat will behave as if it were an entire tomcat. A further operation can remove the remaining tissue, or hormone levels can be adjusted by a course of drugs.

OUTCOME A course of hormone treatment worked swiftly in this case, and the cat no longer sprays.

COMMENT Some owners are hesitant to approach their vet about this problem, for fear of offending him or her — though any vet realises that this does happen occasionally. Once the operation has been carried out, the cat acquires the behaviour patterns of a neutered cat and spraying ceases.

Remember, if you suspect there is still some testicular tissue, but prefer not to see the vet who neutered your cat, you can choose another vet instead.

My cat has always used his litter tray — until recently. Now he soils on the floor, and sometimes he soils right beside his tray but not in it. Is he doing it to be contrary?

No, he isn't. Many owners think this, or the cat is accused of being spiteful, or lazy, or dirty. Nothing is further from the truth.

Cats are extremely fastidious creatures and if a cat starts soiling where it shouldn't, it is a sign that something is wrong. Your cat may be ill — cats are so stoic that the first symptom of an illness you may notice is the cat urinating or defecating outside its tray. Some illnesses, such as Feline Urological Syndrome, can kill a cat within hours of the owner first noticing something is wrong. *So see your vet immediately if your cat begins to soil outside its tray.*

If illness can be ruled out, the cause may be stress. Just as stress may cause spraying, it can also be responsible for indiscriminate urination and defecation. Has anything in your household changed recently? Additions to the family, whether adult, baby, or pet; someone leaving home; even an owner going on holiday — all

Spraying is used as a territorial marker and cats which pass the same way stop to pick up information

these can cause soiling. The problem may be temporary. For example, a friend's cat always soils the floor once or twice while she is on holiday, but goes back to using its tray as soon as she returns. If the change in the household is permanent, the owner must be patient until the cat becomes used to the change, when the behaviour should cease.

Urine and faeces are also used as territorial markers; this is why many cats will immediately use a litter tray which has just been cleaned, even if they don't really need to urinate. Cats may start to soil around the house if a new cat is brought unannounced into the household; if the two are introduced correctly, however, soiling is less likely to occur. If it does, be patient: the problem should cease when the cat becomes used to its new companion.

Old age or youth may be a reason for soiling. Older cats don't have as much control over their muscles, and often can't get out or get to their trays in time. They find this extremely distressing, just as incontinence distresses a human, so owners must be understanding and helpful. Provide an older cat with at least two trays, one upstairs and one downstairs, or one at each end of an apartment, so that he is never 'caught short'. And litter-trained kittens may soil because they have such small bladders and bowels which require frequent emptying. Always place a tray in any room where a kitten spends a lot of time, tucked out of sight if you wish but easy to reach.

Litter trays should always be provided; even fit, healthy, unstressed cats won't always want to go out-of-doors to relieve themselves if it is wet and cold. And litter trays should be kept clean, as cats won't use dirty trays. I know some

owners who empty their cat's tray only once a week — I don't know how *they* can live with a six-day-old tray, let alone how they persuade their cat to use it.

Yet clean trays can cause a problem, too. Many disinfectants are toxic to cats, and trays disinfected with the wrong products can cause an aversion to their use. Pine disinfectants and any products containing phenols, cresols or related compounds should not be used; if in doubt, assume a disinfectant is unsafe until you learn otherwise. Use only a diluted solution of sodium hypochlorite (ordinary household bleach) to disinfect trays.

Cats also have their preferences about the type of litter used. Some will use one of the clay-based litters but not another; some will use the pelletised wood types but not clay — and so on. Many will not use a litter with litter deodorant added (though if litter is supplied in the correct quantities and the tray is cleaned out frequently, deodorant is not necessary).

Soiling can also be an allergic reaction. It may be caused by something in the diet; manufactured foods may be acceptable to the majority of cats, but a few will react by soiling. Or it may be caused by cleaning chemicals such as a carpet-cleaning solution or even freshly painted woodwork. We must always remember that cats are sensitive creatures which react rapidly to their environment.

YOU SHOULD always take a soiling cat to a vet for a check-up first and immediately.

Minimise the stress caused to your cat by any upheaval at home, and don't be afraid to tell your cat about it — even if he doesn't understand he will appreciate the attention.

If he is marking his territory by soiling, be sympathetic — not a scold. Scolding will increase his stress levels and make the problem worse.

If your cat is old, be sympathetic: it really can't help being incontinent. And give a kitten time: it'll work out the logistics of getting to the tray soon enough.

Always provide at least one litter tray. If you have more than one cat, have more than one litter tray. No-one likes using a toilet someone else has used.

Keep the tray clean and disinfected with a suitable product. Buy the type of litter your cat likes to use. Throw the deodoriser in the dustbin.

Check your cat's diet and environment. Either may hold the cause of the problem.

Ensure that your cat's feeding bowl isn't too close to its litter tray. Preferably, it should be in another room, as cats don't like eating next to their toilet. This can be turned to your advantage: placing your cat's food bowl on a frequently soiled area (after thorough cleaning, of course) may help the soiling problem, as cats won't soil an area where they are expected to eat.

If one area is soiled more frequently than another, can you place a litter tray there? It may be your cat's way of telling you that is where he would like it to be. If it is inconvenient, place it there anyway, and move it slowly over a period of weeks to where you would like it to be.

COMMENT Don't ever punish a soiling cat. Instead, find out why he is soiling and take steps to prevent it.

Always thoroughly clean any area which has been soiled. If you don't, the remaining smell will encourage your cat to use the area again. Wash thoroughly first with warm water. Then, after testing for colour fastness, wash the area again with diluted household bleach, or sprinkle with baking soda (baking soda can also cause colours to run); allow to dry completely, then vacuum up. Both products can bleach or stain some fabrics, so you have been warned.

My cat is clean all day, but when I put paper down at night she goes anywhere but on the paper. What can I do to prevent this?

First of all, we should discuss the use of the word 'clean'. Urination and defecation are not 'dirty', they are natural functions, perhaps considered unpleasant by some owners but ones which have to be coped with. Pet owners must realise that part of having a pet is having to deal with its waste products for some years, and if this is too distasteful to be contemplated, they should reconsider having a pet of any sort.

The next thing to consider is the cat's requirements for relieving itself. This cat is kept indoors at night, which is highly recommended to keep her safe and comfortable. However, sheets of paper are not the natural medium on which any cat would choose to relieve itself. Out-of-doors, a cat will choose soft earth or sand. It will dig a hole, urinate or defecate in it, then will usually cover up what it has done.

Indoors, with only sheets of newspaper to use, it cannot cover up and may look for somewhere else to relieve itself. So always provide a litter tray (called a dirt box or sand box by some) and provide a suitable medium inside it. This cat will really be much happier with a tray; cats don't like to relieve themselves in corners, they do so only when they believe it to be necessary.

YOU SHOULD always provide a litter tray for your cat, even if it has access to outdoors.

Fill it with a litter medium which your cat finds acceptable. Most of the litters on the market are dried clay, others are pelletised softwoods, both of which most cats are happy to use.

If you can't afford to buy litter, you *can* use newspaper — but tear it up into small strips and place it in a litter tray in a *thick* layer (cats hate to get their feet wet when they are relieving themselves). Your cat will use it more readily because she can 'cover up'. You could also use (clean) soil from the garden or small smooth pebbles (which should be washed out regularly).

OUTCOME When the newspaper was taken off the floor, torn up and placed in a litter tray, the cat used it happily. The owner was happy, too: no mess and no expense!

Left: Beanbag beds can cause confusion and many cats use them as litter trays

Right: Outdoor – and indoor-plant pots can be used not only as beds but, less attractively, as toilets. Put a few twigs in the soil to deter cats

I spoil my cat and make sure he is provided with everything he needs. He has a cat climber, a scratching post, a litter tray always kept clean and two beds, one upstairs, one downstairs. It's the downstairs bed which causes a problem: It's a cat beanbag — and he keeps soiling it. Why?

In a word — confusion, if you are sure your cat is not ill or stressed in some way. Beanbags are not totally suitable beds for cats for several reasons. First, when a cat settles down on a beanbag, he scratches around on it to make a hollow to fit his body. And what does it sound like? Right! — just like cat litter. Second, what must a beanbag feel like under a cat's paws? It is filled with polystyrene beads, which are small, hard and roundish. And what must cat litter feel like? Yes! — small, hard and roundish.

Little wonder then that he is confused and this confusion leads to soiling. Given time, most cats learn to distinguish the difference, but it takes a lot of washing beanbags.

If the problem is confined to the beanbag — throw it out.

OUTCOME This owner took my advice, threw out the beanbag, and lived happily ever after with her cat.

My neighbour has a horrible cat which keeps defecating on my flat roof. Why does he do it?

Flat roofs are often covered with small pieces of grit which remind the cat of the natural medium it would use to cover up after defecating: soil and stones. So in fact the cat is being quite logical.

You can discourage it by throwing water over it every time you see it. Or, cover your roof with something sticky which it will hate to get on its paws — honey or treacle are ideal. Or use one of the tricks for keeping cats off gardens — chemical deterrents, holly leaves, or inflated balloons. Or, move house!

My cat keeps soiling on the carpets although I provide a clean litter tray which she uses sometimes. I notice she scratches outside the tray when she uses it. My vet says she's in good health, so what is the problem?

Some cats 'cover up' outside their trays, so when they feel carpeting underneath their paws they can then confuse this with their litter medium. A few cats even squat in their trays with their rear paws inside the tray and their front paws completely outside the tray.

An owner can ensure that confusion doesn't arise in a cat's mind by placing litter trays on a hard surface, such as vinyl, or on sheets of plastic. Cats don't like to scratch smooth, shiny surfaces, so will keep their paws inside the tray. Or place the tray inside a large, cut-down cardboard box; this will also prevent litter scattering over the floor.

Covered litter trays are available which may help, as the cat is unable to scratch outside except through the opening.

YOU SHOULD place litter trays on a smooth surface.

Clean up any accidents thoroughly so that the smell doesn't remind the cat that she once used carpeting.

OUTCOME A sheet of plastic underneath the tray worked in this case.

COMMENT At least one owner has, in desperation, used carpet offcuts to line a cat's litter tray when it refused to use litter. Cut the carpet a little smaller than the tray and place litter around the outside. Each time the carpet is replaced, use a smaller piece and more litter around the outside. After a time you will have more litter than carpet, and your cat should eventually be using litter only.

I provided a litter tray when my cat was a kitten. Now he's older and is allowed out-of-doors, but he still wants to use his tray. How can I stop him?

I don't think you should try. Keen cat keepers scrutinise their cats' trays each time they empty them, as the contents tell them about their cats' state of health. Cats dis-

play few symptoms of ill-health until they are very sick indeed, but signs of illness can often be first spotted in a litter tray.

Faeces which are too hard or too soft, or of an odd colour; diarrhoea; blood-tinged urine; a cat straining to pass urine or faeces but unable to do so; a cat in pain: all are symptoms which require immediate attention. Yet they are signs which two-thirds of British owners will not see at all because their cats urinate and defecate out-of-doors.

Many cats don't like to relieve themselves out-of-doors because they are extremely vulnerable while doing so, obliged to hold themselves immobile long enough to be at the mercy of aggressive cats or dogs. And if your cat relieves himself next door, your neighbours may shout at him or throw things at him.

So reconsider your insistence that your cat relieves himself out-of-doors. It is a simple matter to use a scoop to take any waste matter out of a tray and flush it down the toilet. If you really can't bear to do so, use litter in a shallow layer and throw the whole lot out, daily or twice a day. Place the tray in an out-of-way place (your cat will prefer that anyway), even in an easily accessible cupboard. Or buy a covered litter tray; or cover your existing tray with a cardboard box and you won't have to see the contents until you empty it.

If you really feel your cat must 'go' out-of-doors, place his litter tray a little nearer the door each day. Sprinkle some clean earth on top of the litter to let him know that that is the medium you would like him to use. Eventually, place the tray outside; when he is used to using it there, leave it outside but empty, and he will look elsewhere for a toilet. But do think very long and hard before banishing him outside.

I have always provided a tray for my cats but one of them will not use it. He always waits to be let out-of-doors so that he can 'go' outside. If he is caught short, he urinates in a plant pot. What can I do to persuade him to use the tray?

One of my cats behaves in exactly the same way. She is let outside first thing in the morning, last thing at night, and on demand during the day. If she is ignored, she will spray in the house or defecate on the carpet, despite the provision of five clean trays which she simply won't use.

I've accepted it as the preference of an individual. As she gets older and the outdoors becomes less attractive to her, she may change her mind. In the meantime, I have to keep a particular watch for any other symptoms that she is off-colour as I have no evidence in the litter tray to go by.

Cats eyes

Guide dogs are well known and easily recognised, but mention of guide cats is always thought of as a joke. However, as early as 1946, Mrs Carolyn Swanson of Los Angeles had a seeing-eye cat. Her feline helper, a large White Persian, would accompany her owner on her daily errands while wearing a collar and lead and would warn of intersections by switching his fluffy tail against Mrs Swanson's legs.

Coiled, ready to pounce. Ears are swivelled forward so that no sound escapes them, chin, belly and front legs are close to the ground. Rear legs are raised ready to provide impetus and the tail is laid low

You can at least prevent your cat from urinating on plants by covering the soil in the pot with kitchen foil or wire mesh. Kitchen foil can be crumpled around the plant stem; cut the mesh in a circle, and slit the radius to the centre so as to encircle the stem. Cats love to use pot plants as a toilet, as the soil is soft and loose. They also love to use outdoor planters, so 'plant' a few sticks or twigs in the soil to prevent them squatting on the surface.

I've been buying one type of cat litter but have now discovered one which is more economical. The only problem is, my cat won't use it. How can I persuade her to use it?

Presumably if this is an economical cat litter it is not one with added deodorant. The latter do tend to be more expensive, although many cats won't use them because they object to the smell or may even be intolerant to the deodoriser used.

Most cats, however, will use an acceptable cat litter readily; but if they don't, place a thick layer of their accustomed litter in the litter tray, and sprinkle a little of the new on top. Over the next week or two, increase the amount of new litter and decrease the amount of old, and your cat will eventually be using the litter you want it to use. If this doesn't work, there will be a very good reason and you should go back to using your old litter.

For example, apart from intolerance to additives, some cats will have definite preferences. Longhairs, who have long flowing fur, will be distressed if the litter medium sticks to their fur, and will prefer the expensive litter which doesn't stick, to the cheap one which does. If they express a preference — owners have to respect it.

My kitten is five months old and is a half-Siamese. He is wetting on my bed, but does it in a very peculiar manner. He seems to jump in the air with stiff legs and his tail held high and he urinates backwards, all over the place. Is something wrong with him?

Only hormones. He's growing up. A Foreign-type cat grows up quickly, and at five months of age, a kitten is the equivalent of an eight-year-old child. So it is always a shock to realise that, at that age, a Siamese-type cat can be sexually

mature; they can father litters of kittens while they are still kittens themselves.

Most sexually mature entire male cats spray — and this is what your kitten is doing. Take him to the vet as soon as you possibly can for neutering and your problem should cease.

I provide my cats with litter trays but one of them, my oldest male, leaves his faeces on top of the tray and never covers them up. Consequently, there is quite a lot of smell until the tray is cleaned. Why does he do this?

He is probably the most dominant of your cats. Dominant cats will leave potent scent markers such as uncovered faeces or sprayed urine in their territory. However, it may annoy other cats and many will cover the faeces of other household cats to minimise the scent.

You could provide covered litter trays which will contain the smell to some extent. One type of covered tray has a charcoal filter in the cover which is said to neutralise odours, and you might find that useful.

My Persian cat won't use a tray at all, although my other shorthaired cat does. The Persian almost always defecates on the floor outside the tray. I've taken her to my vet for a thorough physical examination and there is nothing wrong with her. She is not stressed in any way so why does she do this?

She may be concerned about dirtying her long fur. Longhaired cats usually have long fur breeches which they try very hard to keep clean — otherwise they have to lick them clean, a long and unpleasant process.

For two cats, provide two trays, and clean them out often. Your Persian will probably use a clean tray unless she dislikes the type of litter, or the disinfectant used to clean the tray. If she tries to use an already-used tray, she runs the risk of soiling her fur. Try different types of litter; she may prefer one type over another. Many longhairs prefer wood-based litters to clay ones because they don't cling to their fur.

If your longhaired cat is not a show cat, you can help it keep itself clean by *very carefully* trimming short the fur under the tail, as short fur is much less likely to become soiled.

My cat 'goes' out of doors during the day, but although she has a catflap, she soils the landing carpet at night. I think she is just being lazy and can't be bothered going outside at night. I have rubbed her nose in it and told her she is naughty but she still does it.

Cats should never, ever, have their noses 'rubbed in it'. This is an absolutely disgusting action which only makes matters worse, not better, and such owners are simply not taking the time and trouble to understand their cat.

You must work out why your cat is soiling on the landing, and what you can do to improve things.

'Rubbing her nose in it' will worsen the situation because your cat has no idea why *you* are behaving in such a filthy way, and will lose all respect for you. You are adding to whatever stress caused the behaviour in the first place. More stress can lead to more soiling throughout the house.

First, why is your cat soiling on the landing? Are there foxes outside at night, or anything else which could frighten her? Even if your cat *is* 'just being lazy', would *you* go out-of-doors on a wet, windy night, to squat on a patch of mud to relieve yourself?

Second, what can *you* do to improve the situation? If she wants to relieve herself on the landing at night, why not provide her with a litter tray there?

Do please remember that it is always up to you to work out why

---

Electricat

When electrician Iain Murdoch lays wires he doesn't have to take up all the floor boards. He cuts a small hole at each end of the room and sends his cat, Fluffy, under the floorboards with a string attached to his collar. The string is then tied to the wires and simply pulled through. 'Fluffy loves doing the job,' Iain says.

Theatre cat

Many cats live in theatres, where they help keep down the mouse population. One such cat by the name of Moggy, living in a London theatre, had a reputation as a fearsome mouser. Even a broken leg couldn't slow him down. His front leg was protected by a plaster cast after this accident, yet theatre staff were amazed to find there were still dead mice awaiting them when they reached the theatre. So a stagehand kept watch from behind some scenery to see how Moggy was doing it. After a while, Moggy left his box, hobbled over to a mousehole and waited for a mouse to emerge — whereupon he hit it with his plastered leg!

your cat is behaving in the way that it does, and to find some way round the problem which is acceptable to you both.

I don't have a cat — but my neighbours have twelve! They relieve themselves all over my garden, on the lawn and flower beds. The neighbours are not helpful people and I'm not getting any assistance from them. How can I keep their cats out of my garden? I've tried many of the cat deterrents which are on sale, but they don't work.

The first step is always to speak to your neighbours, to see if they are aware of the problem, and can help in any way. If they are unhelpful and won't consider fencing in their garden (which would also keep their cats safe) you might consider fencing in *yours*. Of course this would be very expensive, as a catproof fence would have to be of wire mesh, six feet high with an outward facing wire mesh baffle to prevent them climbing over the top. It should extend all around the garden and be clear of bushes, trees and sheds which would enable cats to gain enough height to jump over.

Catproofing a garden simply isn't an option for most people and, indeed, why should you? They aren't your cats, and you shouldn't have the inconvenience and expense of keeping them out. However, cats are not subject to the law of trespass, so unfortunately you have no legal redress. Nor can you take the law into your own hands by harming the cats in any way.

Most cats prefer to use only soft material to cover up their faeces, so keeping one freshly dug flower bed might encourage them to use that and leave the rest of the garden alone; or try providing a sandbox.

Don't give up on the shop-bought deterrents until you have tried them all. Some are much more effective than others, and new ones are coming onto the market all the

time. Most cats don't like the smell of mothballs, or of citrus fruits, so you could scatter those, or pieces of orange, lemon or grapefruit rind in your garden. The latter will lose their effectiveness in time, as will chemical deterrents.

Holly leaves scattered on the ground will deter most cats. Or you could try balloons, tethered to short sticks in the ground — if a cat lands on one which bangs, it will keep it out of the garden for some time. Or leave a hosepipe coiled in full view on your lawn. Cats don't like snake-like shapes and should keep away from it. And don't forget water as the ultimate deterrent, from bucket or hose.

I worry about the health hazard, because the cats are not well looked after. For instance, I'm sure they're rarely wormed.

A variety of infections can be passed on via cat faeces, including toxoplasmosis, which can have very serious consequences for pregnant women. However, the infection which most parents fear, Visceral Larva Migrans, which can cause blindness in infected children, is not passed on by the larvae of cat worms, only those of the dog, according to K. M. Cahill and M. D. O'Brien in their excellent book, *Pets and Your Health.*

However, if your neighbours' cats are uncared for, they can be reported to your local animal welfare organisation, eg the Royal Society for the Prevention of Cruelty to Animals, who *can* take steps in the event of cruelty or neglect. They will also deal with your complaint in confidence.

TRY reasoning with your neighbours. Reasonable people, once they know there is a problem, may be willing to fence in their garden, or keep their cats indoors for part of the day.

Never encourage cats to visit your garden, for example by speaking in a friendly manner.

Don't feed wild birds in your garden. Visiting birds, as well as bird food, will attract cats.

COMMENT Other people's cats can cause enormous problems and cat owners should be aware of their cats' intrusion. Once, when I appeared on a recorded television programme where I was helping people with their cat problems, a letter was received from a woman who wanted to know how to keep her next-door neighbour's cats out of her garden. When I read the address, I realised it had been written by *my* next-door neighbour!

OUTCOME This questioner attached her children's jointed toy snakes to poles in her garden so that they moved in the wind. She also spent a few hours one morning, out of sight of the cats, and hosed them each time they approached her fence. Now only the bravest comes near so the problem is nearly solved; for a smaller number of cats, such measures should be sufficient.

My cat is only interested in me — no-one else. She sucks my neck all the time. My vet said she would grow out of it but she is two years old now and is still doing it.

A kitten spends the first few months of its life with its mother who is the dominant feline. Good cat owners continue this relationship by looking after their new kitten but, at the same time, making it understand the rules of the household: as such, the human owner becomes the 'mother cat'. And when a kitten goes to its new home, its loyalties transfer from its feline mother to its new human provider (that is, of companionship and affection, not just food).

So it isn't surprising that when a kitten seeks comfort, it turns to its new human 'mum' (who may be male or female). Sucking is a very comforting experience to a kitten who associates it with nourishment, warmth and love, and some

kittens require this comfort more than others. Some are easily weaned from suckling at six to eight weeks, while others want to continue; so neck (or earlobe or arm) suckling doesn't mean that a kitten was weaned or taken from its mother too young. I've known many kittens behave in this way into adulthood, even though they were late-weaned. And if they were suckling their mother until they left for their new home, they may begin to suckle their new owner. The neck is a favourite place as they can tuck their heads in under the chin and feel enveloped and warm; other kittens may suck a hand, arm or earlobe.

Your cat may grow out of it, but not unaided. If you buy a kitten which starts sucking your skin, you should discourage it from doing so — each time it begins to suck, say 'NO' very firmly and remove it. It can take a very long time and a lot of perseverance to break the habit completely, but this will come as no surprise to those of us

who are hooked on eating or smoking. At least neck-sucking isn't hazardous to health!

YOU SHOULD discourage your cat from sucking your skin from kittenhood and discourage it *every time* it sucks or it will soon realise that it is allowed to do so sometimes and will continue.

Try a repellent on frequently sucked areas, vinegar or citrus oils or peppermint oil. There is also a purpose-made spray which vets use to prevent animals from licking injuries, and this can be purchased from any vet. It tastes very unpleasant but is completely harmless and non-toxic.

COMMENT Many owners allow their cats to suck and lick their skin, feeling quite honoured by the attention! It is one of those traits which some owners consider a problem while others don't. If it doesn't bother you, it won't do any harm at all to allow your cat to carry on sucking.

Keeping other peoples' cats out of your garden can take a little feline psychology

Dung deterrant

One person of my acquaintance who has connections with a zoo also suffers from neighbours' cats; he is going to acquire some lion and tiger faeces to spread around his garden! This would undoubtedly be effective, though the raw material might not be easy to to get hold of!

I have just spent a lot of money on buying and installing a cat flap. But my cat won't use it. Why?

Would you go through many doors if you had to bash them open with your head? That's what a cat has to do to open a cat flap. And cat flaps or cat doors are made in many different designs: some require just a few ounces of pressure, others require several pounds.

Many cats try to push the door open with their paws; if they then change their minds and try to withdraw their paws, they find that the flap has trapped them. If you are thinking about buying one, push your finger through the flap then try to withdraw it — if it is trapped, your cat's paw may get trapped, too. Of course, *you* realise that to free a trapped finger you should push it forwards . . . but your cat doesn't. He just keeps on pulling, trapping his paw even tighter. A cat which has had this experience is understandably reluctant ever to use a cat flap again.

Also, a cat will never venture into the unknown; it wants to see what it is letting itself in for. Is there a dog out there? Or an unfriendly cat? It can't tell, before committing itself to a cat flap — once started through, it cannot change its mind because it will be trapped by the flap. So if you insist on your cat using a flap, buy a transparent one.

If he still refuses to use a flap, put him outside — through the door, not the flap — just before dinner time. Allow him enough time to relieve himself and check his territory, then place his food just inside the door and call him. The first time you do this, you can prop the flap up; next time, prop it up a little less; and gradually drop it over a period of days until it is fully closed. If your cat is hungry enough, he will brave the flap for his meal.

COMMENT I don't really like cat flaps. Owners should know whether their cat is indoors or outdoors at any given moment of the day, and this is impossible if a flap is used. Besides which, cats can injure themselves in flaps. All the neighbourhood toms get to know of a cat-flap, and use it to pinch your cat's food and spray all over your house; and burglars adore them — if a flap hasn't been installed far enough away from the lock they can reach through and open the door.

My neighbours have recently bought two kittens for their children. The children treat them as if they were toys, squeezing them, throwing them about and, I'm sure, hurting them. I don't think the kittens are being properly fed, either, and they are left to roam the streets at night. It makes me so angry that I'm thinking of going over there and stealing them.

Whatever you do, don't steal them. Although your motives are of the best, you could find yourself in court on charges of theft. Instead, contact your local branch of the Royal Society for the Prevention of Cruelty to Animals. They will investigate any charges of cruelty or neglect, and will keep the name of the complainant secret, so you needn't worry that your neighbours will find out that it was you who complained.

Many people neglect their animals and are unwittingly cruel to them because they have no understanding of their needs. Sometimes just having a uniformed official appearing on their doorstep is enough to bring them to their senses; and the RSPCA don't just slap wrists — they will always give advice on proper animal care.

An alternative is to ask your neighbours if you can buy the kittens from them. Kittens are often acquired on impulse, and their owners begin to tire of them after a month or two of feeding them and cleaning up messes. You may find that they jump at the chance to offload them.

As an incentive, you could say that the children would be welcome to come over and play with them whenever they wished to. However, if they accept that offer, ensure that there is always an open door through which the kittens can quickly disappear if the children get too rough; this, and your advice, should show the children the proper care of animals, which their parents have failed to teach.

How can I stop my cat catching birds?

Several studies have shown that cats make no significant inroads into the bird population. They most often catch mice — because mice can't fly, and are easier to catch. Those birds which *are* caught by cats are usually old, sick or very young, and may not have survived for long anyway. O.P. Pearson (1964) investigated faeces in a nature reserve in California for a year and discovered that, of 4,771 remains, only eight were from birds.

However, if you don't want your cat to catch birds there are several steps you can take: keep your cat indoors; don't encourage birds to come into your garden; try aversion therapy.

Tie some feathers to a piece of string attached to a pole. Dangle it in front of your cat using birdlike movements and every time it attempts to catch the feathers, squirt it with a water-pistol. As cats hate getting wet, it will soon associate the feathers with a soaking and will eventually cease to chase them. However, I wouldn't do this with my own cats. Owning cats brings with it the realisation that they will occasionally catch a small animal or bird, and that has to be accepted as the natural order of things.

Belling a cat is almost useless. A cat will lie in wait, unmoving, for a long time if necessary before pouncing on a prey animal. A bell on its collar will give no warning to its victim until it is too late.

THE CALICO WAIF

If it wasn't for a certain Calico waif that came to our house fifty years ago, I, my son Harold and my daughter Beth would not be alive to tell this story.

The cat looked so pathetically thin and hungry when she came to us that she stirred my compassion. She was ugly, her irregular and overlapping tricolour patches so bizarre that she might have been patterned after a quilt gone wrong. The children begggged to keep her and I agreed to take her in, at least for the present. Calico cats — tortoiseshell and whites — are reputed to bring good luck.

All during the day she ate and drank in short takes, and washed, purred and slept. By evening, when my husband came home, Waif (I had already named her) was replete, refreshed and clean.

Noting her swollen sides, Hal said 'We can't keep that cat. Don't you see she's going to have kittens?'

As if sensing a crisis in her new home, Waif rubbed against Hal's legs, purred like an outboard motor, rolled over on her back and, with paws extended and eyes on Hal, pleaded to be petted.

'Oh, all right, all right,' he said. 'Let her stay, but we can't keep the kittens.'

With Harold and Beth still toddlers, we were staying in our new beach cottage on the shores of Buzzard's Bay in south-eastern Massachusetts. With such a wonderfully warm September and Hal commuting from his office, we had no reason to return to the city yet.

We were not entirely alone on the beach. Next to us, Mr and Mrs Harding were spending their twenty-fifth season at their cottage. Staying with them were their daughter, son-in-law and their six-month-old grandson. With the easy friendship that accompanies casual beach living, we promised them the pick of Waif's litter for their grandson.

One morning, Waif clumsily disappeared into a tangled wooded patch on the beach near our cottage. We didn't see her again until that evening when she came to the door, hungry and with a flabby stomach. For almost two weeks she was with her family in that jungle of brambles and briars, coming to the house only to be fed.

Impatient to see the kittens, the children were overjoyed one morning when Waif came out of the woods carrying a homely Calico kitten in her mouth. She dropped it into a blanket-lined box I had placed on the front porch, ready for her when she wanted it. The children and I watched and waited while Waif made trip after trip, each time with a kitten in her mouth. After the fifth, as ugly as herself, she jumped lightly into the box and settled down purring, washing each kitten in turn, while they nuzzled and nursed.

I'll never forget that day. Early that morning, something eerie in the quality of the wind had awakened me. Perhaps, I thought, the breeze had sprung up with the incoming tide. Then I went back to sleep and awoke to sunshine, thinking no more about the strange sound.

After Hal left for work, I decided to do a little packing because we would be closing the place in a few days and returning to the city. Soon Mrs Harding came to the door to ask if I wanted anything in town. She and her daughter were going to the city for shopping and lunch, and also to be out of the way while Mr Harding and his son-in-law varnished the downstairs of the cottage. I offered to take care of their grandson, but they said he would stay with the men and would be no trouble as he would sleep most of the time.

My children, Harold and Beth, were happily playing with the kittens on the porch and keeping them out of my way while I packed. But as the morning wore on, I felt unaccountably restless. The sun had gone in, and an oppressive stillness hung over the yellow water. I had never seen it that colour before.

The wind freshened. It activated the incoming tide and stirred whitecaps. By noon it was raining hard, and a real blow had developed. We're in for a real storm, I thought, as I put the children down for their naps. The wind now picked up speed, and it was raining harder.

Then suddenly the sound changed. I heard the same eerie whine I had noted in the early morning, only louder and more threatening now. The waves became angrier as the tide advanced to a point higher on the beach than a full moon tide reached — yet there were more than four hours to go before the peak was due.

I was nervous. I ran over to ask Mr Harding what we were in for.

'This wind and a bit of rain? It's nothing,' he said. 'I've been through a good many of these September storms and they never amount to much. Just batten down your hatches until it blows itself out. But if you're timid alone, bring the children over and ride it out with us.' Then he went back to his varnishing.

continued overleaf

continued

Heading into the storm on my way home across the beach, I found the going tough — in the short time I'd been at the Hardings', it had picked up in force and fury. Wild wind ripped the scarf from my head while angry waves swallowed it. The tide now covered the beach. Several boats, straining at their moorings, broke away, powered by wind and tide.

Down towards the harbour, I could see the spray rise high over the bridge. As I looked, a gigantic wave lifted an ocean-going yacht over the rail and set it down, miraculously on an even keel, on the near side. The wind was fast growing in volume, and its ominous wail was like the shrieking of a hundred banshees.

I fought my way against the wind through water as deep as my porch to get the kittens. Their box was empty.

Then up the hill at the rear of the cottage, I saw Waif. She was dragging a kitten into an empty house, its door blown open by the storm. I knew the other kittens must be safely there.

Inside our cottage, I had to barricade the front door with furniture. Then I watched out of the window. Visibility over the water was poor, yet I could see the shape of boats bumping each other as they rushed past. The wind blew harder, its howl louder and more shrill. The rain beat in horizontal sheets with tremendous force. What trees were left standing were being torn up by the roots and crashing.

By now I was really frightened. How could Mr Harding be so sure this was just another September storm? Then I knew. The thing that nobody would believe could ever happen in New England was actually here. The coast was being battered and devastated by a freak tropical hurricane.

Just then a huge wave hit the cottage. The walls shivered and trembled. Vases toppled from the mantel and broke. Water poured under the door and around the windows where I stood.

Oh God, tell me what to do! Should I take the children and go the the Hardings' for shelter? There was still time, I thought, to make it by the back way.

Suddenly I remembered Waif. Just why had she brought her kittens up from the woods that morning? Why had she moved them again to higher ground? What extra sense guides an animal when all human reason proves inadequate?

I made the most important decision of my life. I would follow Waif.

I woke the children and dressed them quickly. I took the key off the hook and stepped out on the back porch into water above my ankles. I locked the door. In my nervous haste I dropped the key in the water.

The children were not afraid; rather, they were happily excited to see the ocean all over the land. I lifted a child to each shoulder and told them to hold on tight. Carefully feeling for each step down, I reached the ground in water above my knees.

Please God, don't let me panic now. I clutched the children in a frantic hold while they buried their faces in the hollow of my shoulders for protection against wind and rain. Great masses of seaweed and loose boards were churning in the wild tide.

I measured progress more by the height of the water on my thighs than by the number of steps I took. A broken oar banged against my leg. I tottered and almost fell.

When at last the water was below my knees, I braced my back to the wind in order not to fall forward, and was literally blown the last forty feet to Waif's refuge.

The children scrambled over to a sofa in a sheltered corner of the porch where mother cat and kittens were snug and safe. I slid the bolt on the door. Even though windows rattled and banged and the floor was awash with wind-driven rain, I knew we were safe from the tide. But now that our danger was over, I began to feel concern for my neighbours. The water had risen up to the roof of our cottage and it covered most of the first storey of the Harding house.

At this moment I heard a car come down the road and stop on the hill, blocked by wreckage in its path. It was Mrs Harding and her daughter. They had driven as far as they could, then they sat anxiously looking towards their house. Mr Harding, on the first floor, waved a flashlight to show they were all right, his son and grandson standing next to him.

Suddenly, a vicious fifty-foot wave shook itself free from the rest and raced shoreward. This was no ordinary comber. It was a giant cable of water power, twisting and writhing, snarling as if in frustration.

It struck the Harding house and mine, booming its pent-up fury. When the wave receded, my cottage went with it. The Harding house, larger and sturdier, was still standing — but only for a second. Before our horrified eyes the entire building shuddered and collapsed. Mother and daughter in the car looked on in powerless terror as the three people dearest in all the world to them were swept away.

Had I not heeded the protective maternal in-

stinct of a poor stray cat, my two children and I would have perished too.

Now, a half century later, many families like ours have cleared the rubble and rebuilt their cottages. They have resumed their peaceful and tranquil way of life at the shore, showing no visible signs or indications of the horrors of that day.

In our house, however, there was Waif to keep us always thankful for whatever strange quirk of fate prompted a scrawny and very pregnant cat to seek sanctuary with us.

Starr King

RECOMMENDED READING

Allan, Eric, Bonning, Lynda, & Blogg, J. Rowan. *Everycat* (Peter Lowe)

Angel, Jeremy. *Cats Kingdom* (Souvenir Press)

Cahill, K.M. & O'Brien, M.D. *Pets and Your Health* (Kingswood Press)

Edney, A.T.B. (Ed) *Dog & Cat Nutrition* (Pergamon Press)

Hunter, Francis. *Before the Vet Calls* (Thorsons)

Leyhausen, Paul. *Cat Behavior* (Garland STPM Press)

Mc Hattie, Grace. *Supercat* (Mandarin)

Mc Hattie, Grace. *The Cat Lover's Dictionary* (H.F. & G. Witherby)

Nieburg, H.A. & Fischer, A. *Pet Loss* (Harper and Row)

Tabor, Roger. *The Wildlife of the Domestic Cat* (Arrow)

Pond, Grace & Raleigh, Ivor. *A Standard Guide to Cat Breeds* (Macmillan)

Turner, Dennis C. & Bateson, Patrick (Ed). *The Domestic Cat: the biology of its behaviour* (Cambridge University Press)

West, Geoffrey. *All About Your Cat's Health* (Pelham)

REFERENCES

Baines, F.M. (1981). Milk substitutes and the hand rearing of orphaned puppies and kittens. *Journal of Small Animal Practice,* 22, 555–578.

Braastad, B.O. & Heggelund, P. (1984). Eye-opening in kittens: effects of light and some biological factors. *Developmental Psychobiology,* 17, 675–81.

Kuo, Zing-Yang (1976). *The Dynamics of Behavioural Development* Plenum Press 3, 66–69.

Leyhausen, Paul (1979). *Cat Behavior* Garland STPM Press 24,286

Meier, G.W. (1961). Infantile handling and development in Siamese kittens. *Journal of Comparative Physiology and Psychology* 54, 284–6.

Mitchell, John & Rickard, R.J.M. (1982). *Living Wonders* Thames and Hudson.

Pearson, O.P. (1964). Carnivore-mouse predations; an example of its intensity and bioenergetics. *Journal of Mammology* 45, 177–88.

Thorn, F., Gollender, M. & Erickson, P. (1976). The development of the kitten's visual optics. *Vision Research* 16, 1145–9.

Villablanca, J.R. & Olmstead, C.E. (1979). Neurological development in kittens. *Developmental Psychobiology* 12, 101–27.

USEFUL ADDRESSES

CHARITIES AND CAT WELFARE ORGANISATIONS

Adopt-a-Cat, P.O. Box 1112,
Shoreham by Sea, West Sussex N43 6SD.
*Send an S.A.E. for lists of cat rescue
shelters throughout the UK and details of
the Adopt-a-Cat free behavioural
problem clinic.*

Cats Protection League, 17 King's Road,
Horsham, West Sussex RH13 5PP.

National Petwatch, P.O. Box 16, Brighouse,
West Yorkshire.

People's Dispensary for Sick Animals,
PDSA House, Whitechapel Way, Priorslee,
Telford, Shropshire.

Royal Society for the Prevention of Cruelty
to Animals, The Causeway,
Horsham, West Sussex RH12 1HQ.

MAGAZINES

CATS, 5 James Leigh Street,
Manchester M1 6EX.
Cat Fancy, P.O. Box 6050,
Mission Viejo, California 92690, USA.

REGISTRATION ORGANISATIONS

Cat Association, Mill House,
Letcombe Regis, Oxon OX12 9JD.
Telephone: 02357 66543

The Governing Council of the Cat Fancy,
4-6 Penel Orlieu, Bridgwater, Somerset TA6
3PG. Telephone: 0278 427575.

*Both hold cat shows and can give informa-
tion about cat clubs.*

SEEDSMEN

Thompson and Morgan, London Road,
Ipswich, Suffolk,
For the purchase of catnip seeds.

ACKNOWLEDGEMENTS

The author would like to thank the many people who assisted with the production of this book; in particular, Kenneth Bryson MRCVS, Julian Clegg, Mark Evans B Vet Med, MRCVS, Jill Jackson, Hilife Pet Foods, Pet Plan Insurance, all those who contributed their own cat's tales, the photographers, those whose cats were photographed, the cats who allowed themselves to be photographed, and even those which ran away.

Photographs are by: **Tony Cox** (83, 143, 155 upper); **Mary Cregan** (90); **Graham Hart** (66 upper, 122 lower); **A. J. Kelsey** (13, 45, 50 lower, 53, 54, 56, 61, 65, 84, 86 lower, 89, 93, 100, 101, 104, 109, 110, 119, 121, 124, 127 upper, 134, 140, 145, 149, 153, 156, 164, 169, 176, 187); **D. E. Lennon** (8, 9, 22, 23 upper, 24, 25, 34, 42 lower, 69, 85, 105, 129, 154, 157 upper); **Dorothy Mc Conkey** (2, 6, 11, 12, 14, 18, 19, 21, 23 lower, 26, 30, 31, 35, 39, 47, 51, 55, 58, 59, 66 lower, 67, 70, 75, 76, 77, 78, 79, 80, 81, 86 upper, 87, 88, 91, 95, 106–7, 114, 122 upper, 127 lower, 131 lower, 133, 135, 138, 139, 141, 146, 155 lower, 157 lower, 158, 159, 160, 162, 163, 165, 166, 167, 171, 175, 178, 179, 180, 183); **Gordon Mc Hattie** (98); **Grace Mc Hattie** (15, 38, 42 upper, 43, 50 upper, 63, 71, 99, 102, 103, 111, 118, 123, 131 upper, 147, 151)

Index